"Hemda Arad weaves together a rich tap
thought, brain research, trauma theory, and attachment theory to illumi-nate how integrating Eye Movement Desensitization and Reprocessing (EMDR) into a relational-psychoanalytically informed clinical practice can be invaluable in working with patients to help release the affective and embodied experience that lie beyond the reach of words. In clear and often movingly poetic language, she synthesizes research and scholarship with vivid clinical examples that bring to life the ways in which the human mind operates to shield itself from painful experience. She offers clinically relevant and experience-near illustrations of how EMDR can serve as a valuable addition to psychoanalytic treatment and, conversely, of how processing material arising from EMDR sessions psychoanalytically can enhance its clinical effectiveness. This book will be invaluable to clinicians seeking a better understanding of how to help patients for whom the 'talking cure' is not enough."—**Karen E. Starr, PsyD**, editor, *Relational Psychoanalysis and Psychotherapy Integration* (2015); author, *A Psychotherapy for the People* (2013) and *Repair of the Soul* (2008)

"Hemda Arad's book translates solid EMDR function to poetic analytic introspection in an extensive, comprehensive manner, including research, deep exploration of both techniques, and case histories that interweave them."—**Robin Shapiro, LICSW**, editor of *EMDR Solutions, Pathways to Healing; EMDR Solutions II: Trauma Treatment Handbook;* and author of *Easy Ego State Interventions* (Norton, 2016)

"This is a ground-breaking book which brings together two apparently disparate approaches to treatment—relational psychoanalysis and EMDR. Arad makes a distinction between analytic goals and therapeutic goals, arguing that at certain moments of emotional impasse, when words are not available to facilitate the process, EMDR can offer a different, bodily, avenue of approach. She observes that 'The actual travel into thought, feeling, or pain during EMDR sets is dynamic in nature, and resembles a deep primary process in analysis.' She finds this dual approach seems particularly useful for patients with dissociated self-states, in that, 'EMDR helps ground [the patient] in a feeling state that otherwise is prohibited from entering her consciousness.' Couples therapy might benefit especially from this integration, because Arad

discovers that self-states can frequently shift between partners at times of conflict, creating an opening for EMDR strategies. In these ways Arad imaginatively challenges her readers to expand their therapeutic repertoires by bridging two approaches that at first glance might seem antithetical. This is a courageous and much needed text."—**Robert Winer, MD**, an editor of *Who's Behind the Couch?: The Heart and Mind of the Psychoanalyst* (2017) and the author of the book *Close Encounters: A Relational View of the Therapeutic Process*. Co-founder and co-chair of the program, New Directions: Writing with a Psychoanalytic Edge at the Washington Center for Psychoanalysis, member of the editorial advisory board of Psychiatry: Interpersonal and Biological Processes

Integrating Relational Psychoanalysis and EMDR

Integrating Relational Psychoanalysis and EMDR: Embodied Experience and Clinical Practice provides contemporary theoretical and clinical links between Relational Psychoanalysis, attachment theory, neuroscience, and Eye Movement Desensitization and Reprocessing, all of which bring both the patient's and analyst's embodied experience into the forefront of clinical thinking and practice. The author grounds an in-depth view on the ways psychoanalysis and EMDR can be effectively integrated to complement each other through a presentation of fundamental concepts and an abundance of insightful and moving clinical vignettes.

Hemda Arad outlines the theoretical and clinical concepts that allow the integration of Relational Psychoanalysis with EMDR's unique contributions, specifically appreciating the neurological and embodied experience in an individual's development in relation to the classic talking cure's approach to dealing with "big *T*" trauma and with "small *t*" everyday attachment-related trauma. Arad describes a view of a modified EMDR approach capable of reaching many patients, beyond the trauma work for which it originally became known, in order to lend its more embodied approach to the advancement of the relational endeavor. Vivid clinical illustrations, chosen to elucidate theoretical concepts, make the complex theoretical ideas more accessible. The clinical portions illustrate a range of ways that EMDR and relational work, which may at first seem incompatible, may be integrated to help therapists navigate the two methods.

Integrating Relational Psychoanalysis and EMDR: Embodied Experience and Clinical Practice will appeal to psychoanalysts, psychoanalytic psychotherapists, and psychodynamic therapists who wish to learn about the relational tradition in theory and practice or are seeking a way to integrate their work with other versatile approaches such as EMDR, as well as advanced students studying across these areas and EMDR clinicians who would like to broaden the scope of their skills.

Hemda Arad, PhD, is a psychoanalyst, consultant, and Washington State Approved Supervisor. She is also an EMDRIA Certified Eye Movement Desensitization and Reprocessing therapist. She has served on the faculties of the Northwest Center for Psychoanalysis and the Washington Center for Psychoanalysis program New Directions: Writing with a Psychoanalytic Edge. She works in private practice in Seattle with individuals, couples, and groups.

RELATIONAL PERSPECTIVES BOOK SERIES

The Relational Perspectives Book Series (RPBS) publishes books that grow out of or contribute to the relational tradition in contemporary psychoanalysis. The term *relational psychoanalysis* was first used by Greenberg and Mitchell[1] to bridge the traditions of interpersonal relations, as developed within interpersonal psychoanalysis and object relations, as developed within contemporary British theory. But, under the seminal work of the late Stephen A. Mitchell, the term *relational psychoanalysis* grew and began to accrue to itself many other influences and developments. Various tributaries—interpersonal psychoanalysis, object relations theory, self psychology, empirical infancy research, and elements of contemporary Freudian and Kleinian thought—flow into this tradition, which understands relational configurations between self and others, both real and fantasied, as the primary subject of psychoanalytic investigation.

We refer to the relational tradition, rather than to a relational school, to highlight that we are identifying a trend, a tendency within contemporary psychoanalysis, not a more formally organized or coherent school or system of beliefs. Our use of the term *relational* signifies a dimension of theory and practice that has become salient across the wide spectrum of contemporary psychoanalysis. Now under the editorial supervision of Lewis Aron and Adrienne Harris, with the assistance of Associate Editors Steven Kuchuck and Eyal Rozmarin, the Relational Perspectives Book Series originated in 1990 under the editorial eye of the late Stephen A. Mitchell. Mitchell was the most prolific and influential of the originators of the relational tradition. Committed to dialogue among psychoanalysts, he abhorred the authoritarianism that dictated adherence to a rigid set of beliefs or technical restrictions. He championed open discussion, comparative and integrative approaches, and promoted new voices across the generations.

Included in the Relational Perspectives Book Series are authors and works that come from within the relational tradition, extend and develop that tradition, as well as works that critique relational approaches or compare and contrast it with alternative points of view. The series includes our most distinguished senior psychoanalysts, along with younger contributors who bring fresh vision. A full list of titles in this series is available at https://www.routledge.com/series/LEARPBS.

Note

1 Greenberg, J. & Mitchell, S. (1983). *Object relations in psychoanalytic theory.* Cambridge, MA: Harvard University Press.

Integrating Relational Psychoanalysis and EMDR

Embodied Experience and Clinical Practice

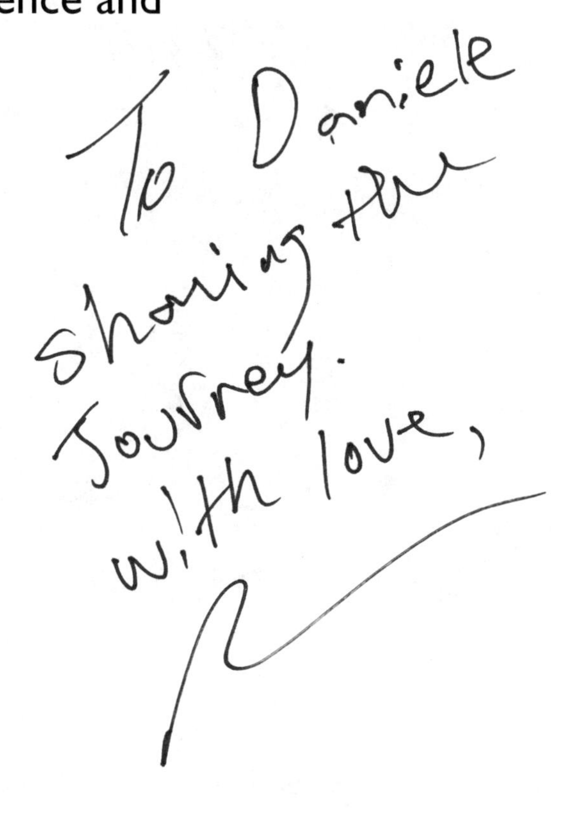

Hemda Arad

LONDON AND NEW YORK

First published 2018
by Routledge
2 Park Square, Milton Park, Abingdon, Oxon OX14 4RN

and by Routledge
711 Third Avenue, New York, NY 10017

Routledge is an imprint of the Taylor & Francis Group, an informa business

British Library Cataloguing-in-Publication Data
A catalogue record for this book is available from the British Library

Library of Congress Cataloging-in-Publication Data
Names: Arad, Hemda, author.
Title: Integrating relational psychoanalysis and EMDR [electronic resource] : embodied experience and clinical practice / Hemda Arad.
Description: Abingdon, Oxon ; New York, NY : Routledge, 2018. | Series: Relational perspectives book series ; 93 | Includes bibliographical references and index.
Identifiers: LCCN 2017019710 (print) | LCCN 2017021109 (ebook) | ISBN 9781315159775 (Master) | ISBN 9781351660556 (Web PDF) | ISBN 9781351660549 (ePub) | ISBN 9781351660532 (Mobipocket/Kindle) | ISBN 9781138065345 (hardback : alk. paper) | ISBN 9781138065369 (pbk. : alk. paper) | ISBN 9781315159775 (ebk)
Subjects: | MESH: Eye Movement Desensitization Reprocessing—methods | Psychotherapy—methods
Classification: LCC RC506 (ebook) | LCC RC506 (print) | NLM WM 425.5.D4 | DDC 616.89/17—dc23
LC record available at https://lccn.loc.gov/2017019710

ISBN: 978-1-138-06534-5 (hbk)
ISBN: 978-1-138-06536-9 (pbk)
ISBN: 978-1-315-15977-5 (ebk)

Typeset in Times New Roman
by Swales & Willis Ltd, Exeter, Devon, UK

To my beloved Yuval, Daniele, Orren and Matan

And in loving memory of my mother
Gila Arad

Contents

Preface

Following the 9/11 and Hurricane Katrina crises, many in the psychoanalytic community felt the urge to help amidst the chaos and great need of so many people affected by these disasters and their aftermath. Those of us who had helpful tools, including Eye Movement Desensitization and Reprocessing (EMDR), that could be of potential help in reducing stress for those affected by events like these in a relatively short time span, were envied for the ability to intervene effectively when the need was so great. Typically, psychoanalytic therapy takes time. It relies on creating intricate intersubjective matrices and careful examination of the relational, transferential, and countertransferential fields. Yet as a psychoanalyst, it is not surprising that I felt a need to include EMDR in my professional tool kit. I had read and heard from colleagues about the virtues of this method, and eventually took the time to train and become an EMDR therapist. Never a purist in my practice, I kept elements of different treatment methods at attention to help navigate difficult moments with patients, although they were smoothly integrated into my analytic practice. That said, I thought of EMDR as a distinct method to be used as a whole without introducing new elements to it in the form of other therapeutic methods, let alone those from the psychoanalytic realm.

The idea of blending EMDR with my relational psychoanalytic practice did not occur to me until I encountered a situation in which I felt that I could not help a patient engage affectively, no matter how we tried. Just as I began to doubt my ability to help this person's process along, the patient showed me the way. Unwittingly, she engaged in a motion that for the first time brought about genuine emotional engagement, after months of work. Not only were we both moved by what transpired, it also made me realize that EMDR was a tool I could use for productive exploration in conjunction with relational psychoanalysis. My thought was that

EMDR can offer important opportunities for the patient to subsequently engage in the relational psychoanalytic process. I presented my initial theoretical formulations and case material to colleagues in professional meetings, and was met with curiosity. Many were versed in both methods, yet, like me, considered them mutually exclusive until I described my experience of integrating them in this case. Some made the suggestion that I should publish not only this case, but a book that would include my ideas about the integration of psychoanalysis and EMDR and its merits, with additional case material to help the psychoanalytic clinician navigate through potential pitfalls, and to specifically direct my effort toward psychoanalytically informed clinicians to help them combine their work with EMDR to benefit their patients' growth. This book aims to spell out my considerations and findings along this path, with the hope that it will help others in the field find a way to consider some variation of this combined method, once they feel proficient in each method individually.

Acknowledgments

The long process of developing the ideas and writing this book involved many conversations with colleagues, friends, and family members over many years, all of whom undoubtedly contributed to my understanding of concepts and clinical implications of integrating relational psychoanalysis and EMDR. Though it will be impossible to name every one, I wish to mention here persons who were especially present along the way.

Adrienne Harris, my teacher and mentor, who has seen me through thick and thin over the better part of two decades, stood by me with direction and guidance for the entire length of this book. As always, she was at my side with her infinite intellectual depth, wisdom, patience, and generosity. Her thoughtful critique challenged me to make this work the best it can be.

Stephen Daniel, from the International University for Graduate Studies, recognized from our earliest conversations the relevancy and potential of this book and saw that I had enough energy to carry me through this long project. For his sensitive reading of early drafts, I am immensely thankful.

Robin Shapiro listened to my EMDR modifications and thinking early on in this project. I am grateful for her knowledge and support, and for reading a segment of the book.

My friend, Yavin Shaham, reviewed the chapters involving brain research. His expertise in the field of neuroscience made his comments invaluable.

Joy Crawford assisted me throughout this project with research, while encouraging me to think and rethink the English of my sentences, doing so with much grace and consistency. Her help allowed me to lose myself in the writing process when I was ready to do so.

My deep gratitude to Sigrid Asmus, the most wonderful copyeditor I could have ever hoped for. Her thorough knowledge of psychoanalysis and close reading of the manuscript were combined with professional expertise and invaluable advice.

The Washington Center for Psychoanalysis New Directions: Writing with a Psychoanalytic Edge program is a wonderful home that fosters the writing spirit in our field with much skill and compassion. I am blessed to be part of it, having the opportunity to study, teach, and write with such a talented group of friends, students, and colleagues. A special thank you goes to Robert Winer, co-founder of New Directions, who read a segment of the book, to Anne Adelman for her insightful feedback, to Sharon Alperovitz, co-founder of New Directions, for her encouragement, and to Kerry Malawista for always being there for me.

I thank Karen Starr for reading the manuscript, and feel a special kinship to her as a scholar and clinician who deeply appreciates and writes about integrating relational psychoanalysis with other psychotherapy methods.

To Sylvia Flescher for inviting me to present at the New Jersey Psychoanalytic Society, and to Alitta Kullman for inviting me to talk at the Newport Center for Psychoanalytic Studies and the Newport Psychoanalytic Institute. These early opportunities to discuss my thoughts and experiences regarding the integration of relational psychoanalysis and EMDR in my practice were invaluable and made it apparent that there is a great interest in this work, and for introducing me to Deborah Lodge.

I would be remiss not to mention the unique contribution of the Relational Perspectives Book Series and its co-editors Lewis Aron and Adrienne Harris, who created a natural home for this book and so many other books in our field.

My gratitude goes to Kate Hawes, Charles Bath, Abigail Stanley and the many others at Routledge, as well as Laura Christopher at Swales & Willis who so ably and patiently saw me through the editing and publishing process.

To my patients, who taught me so much about how to become a better partner in our work together, who trusted, doubted and challenged, I am privileged, and forever grateful for the opportunity to work with you.

I am indebted to Yuval Neeman for reading drafts of this work and for his willingness to ask me frequently what I am about to write. I thank him for setting the stepping stones along the way to help me see my way back home, to the core and purpose of this project. Together we saw the beauty in a staircase on a hike in the Cascade Mountains. The image Yuval took appears on the front cover of this book. My gratitude goes to Daniele Arad-Neeman who steadfastly supported my writing, and provided ideas on setting and keeping realistic goals. I am thankful to Orren Arad-Neeman for her valuable critique and editorial comments, and to Raanan Naftalovich for providing just the right technical tool for the long hours in front of the screen. Containment seems to appear in many unexpected ways, and in Matan Arad-Neeman's violin lessons with Margaret Pressley I wrote some of my favorite pieces of this manuscript. To my family, for always encouraging me to sit and write, and for their love and keeping me busy and distracted as needed.

To the best of my ability, all biographical details were altered to protect patients' privacy so that only they will be able to recognize who they are.

This book describes complex psychotherapy approaches and their application in my practice. To gain proficiency in each approach requires formal training, including supervision of the clinical work. Its suggestions should not be employed unless you are a licensed mental health clinician and you have completed an EMDR approved training through EMDRIA or the EMDR Institute. In addition, psychoanalysis, psychotherapy, and EMDR should only be used to the level of your expertise, as work with certain persons facing a high level of mental challenges requires advance training and supervised clinical work.

Permissions

Every effort has been made to contact the copyright holders for their permission to reprint selections of their work this book. The publishers would be grateful to hear from any copyright holder who is not here acknowledged and we will undertake to rectify any errors or omissions in future editions of this book.

The image on the front cover was taken by Yuval Neeman and is used with permission.

The quote at the beginning of the Introduction from Ariane Mnouchkine is courtesy of Guardian News & Media Ltd.

The epigraph for Chapter 1 includes song lyrics by Yaacov Rotblit. Both the Hebrew lyrics and their English translation are printed by permission: © All rights in the song "Roim Rahok Roim Shakuf" are reserved to the author Yaacov Rotblit and ACUM.

The EMDR Psychotherapy Flow Chart © 2016 in Figure 1.1 is from Natalie S. Robinson, MSW, LICSW, EMDRIA Approved Consultant, Boston, MA. USA. Used with permission.

The epigraph for Chapter 2 is an excerpt from *Glottal Stop: 101 Poems*, by Paul Celan © 2000 by Nikolai Popov and Heather McHugh. Published by Wesleyan University Press. Used with permission.

The epigraph for Chapter 3 is from an untitled poem by Israel Eliraz, from *How Much Time Is Left Is Not a Question but a Door* Helicon-Modan (2013) © All rights in the poem "Kama Zman Od Nishar" are reserved to Israel Eliraz and ACUM. The reprinting of this excerpt and its English translation are used with permission from Israel Eliraz and Helicon-Modan.

The epigraph for Chapter 4 is republished with permission of Routledge, a Taylor & Francis Group, from *Meetings: Autobiographical Fragments*, by Martin Buber, edited and introduced by Maurice Friedman, 3rd edition, © 2002; permission conveyed through Copyright Clearance Center, Inc.

The lines of poetry in the epigraph for Chapter 5 are excerpted from "The Woman Who Could Not Live with Her Faulty Heart," from *Selected Poems II: Poems Selected and New, 1976–1986* by Margaret Atwood, © 1987 by Margaret Atwood. Reprinted by permission of Houghton Mifflin Harcourt Publishing Company. All rights reserved. The poem also appeared in Margaret Atwood, *Selected Poems 1966–1984*, © 1990 Oxford University Press Canada. Reprinted by permission of the publisher. The lines of poetry are also reproduced with permission of Curtis Brown Group Ltd., London, on behalf of Margaret Atwood. Copyright © Margaret Atwood 1978.

The line of poetry in the epigraph for Chapter 7 is from "Metai/My dead," a poem by Rachel Bluwstein written in 1931, public domain per ACUM (Association of Composers, Authors and Publishers of Music in Israel).

The poem "Meeting Wolf" included in chapter 7 is from *Evidence*, by Mary Oliver, published by Beacon Press Boston. Copyright © 2009 by Mary Oliver. Reprinted by permission of The Charlotte Sheedy Literary Agency Inc.

In Chapter 8 the epigraph is a quote from *Every Man Dies Alone* by Hans Fallada, courtesy of Melville House Publishing, Brooklyn, NY.

The epigraph for Chapter 9 is an excerpt from *Musica Humana*, copyright © 2002 Ilya Kaminsky. Used with permission of the poet and Chapiteau Press.

Introduction

> "It's a ceremony, a ritual—You should go out of the theatre more human than you went in."
>
> —Ariane Mnouchkine, *The Guardian*, 10 August 2012

Ariane Mnouchkine's unintended paraphrase of Harry Stack Sullivan's assertion that "we are all much more simply human than otherwise, be we happy and successful, contented and detached, miserable and mentally disordered, or whatever" (Sullivan, 1953, p. 16) nonetheless captures an important reality. Our patients are often drawn into our offices feeling that in some important way they are lacking as members of the human community. At times, patients are holding the secret of being mistreated; they may feel they possess some inherent vulnerability that predisposes them to their unfavorable destinies, or that they are ill-equipped to deal with the hardships of their situation. The living theater of the psychoanalytic relationship, both emotionally evocative and real, yet simultaneously futureless in actual terms, is nevertheless the place from which both partners emerge as more richly human than they went in.

As analysts, we try to engage with the person to help them get to the bottom of what they feel and find what stands in the way of expanding the range of possibilities, so that they can live a fuller life. Over the past few decades, the idea that the person of the analyst participates in a meeting of minds with the patient, in an asymmetrical but equal dialogue, has been elaborated upon in relational psychoanalytical literature (Aron, 1996; Aron and Starr, 2013; Kuchuck, 2014) following earlier attempts to hone the theoretical and clinical usefulness of mutuality (Aron and Harris, 1993;

Ferenczi, 1988). A new understanding of such concepts as enactment, and of the relevance of both partners' subjectivities (Benjamin, 1995) to the therapeutic action, guided us away from being a neutral bystander and toward seeing our role as more participatory, changing the way we work with patients. For example, we use countertransference diagnostically not only to understand the patient's dynamic processes, but also, as therapists, to help ourselves recognize the ways in which we participate in the re-creation of certain psychodynamics. Countertransference became an important tool that raised further questions about the therapeutic action, such as the usefulness and challenges of self-disclosure (Aron, 1996; Kuchuck, 2014).

From a binary perspective of "do" and "don't do," the questions turned to defining what would offer a greater optic-resolution of the clinical action. Psychoanalysts began to notice that they were self-disclosing much about themselves even when they did not share a word of personal information. Patients felt and read their therapist's responses and reactions from their words and nonverbal ways of being, as well as unintended and intended self-disclosures. Patients are attuned to their therapists as closely as infants are attuned to the state of mind of their primary caregiver, and therapists as closely as the mother is attuned to her infant's shifting emotionality. The importance of misattunement became a focus that was different from the traditional psychoanalytic theories, in which the clinician was focused on the patient's reaction to the therapist solely as a form of acting out, stemming from a set of defenses or projections meant to avoid intrapsychic conflict originating in early childhood frustrated or forbidden wishes for drive-based gratification. As an alternative, relational psychoanalysts began to take into consideration their own participation in the co-construction of the analytic situation in which both partners participated and contributed to its creation (Aron, 1996; Mitchell, 1997; Slochower, 2013).

From early on, relational psychoanalysts, and historically some clinicians in earlier generations (Heimann, 1950; Sullivan, 1953), recognized the influence of real-life experiences on the mind, necessitating a Bonsai-like pruning and training of development to deal with external and internal forces. These forces started at home, but were also defined by gender, ethnic and racial affiliation, sexual orientation, and socioeconomic status. Most importantly, relational psychoanalysts, as did the emergence of feminist critiques, shifted the decades-long misperception of childhood sexual abuse from one of perceiving it as a fantasy to accepting the reality that it is an actuality in their patients' lives (Benjamin, 1995; Davies and Frawley, 1994; Ferenczi, 1988; Grand and Alpert, 1993).

Once the reality of these occurrences took hold in the field of psychotherapy, room became available for working with the consequences of such traumas on the psyche, and for considering the relational price paid. In addition, recognizing aspects of dissociation also opened the possibility that through both relational and other forms of work the effects of trauma could be engaged and changed over time. One central purpose of this book is to study the ways now available to clinically leverage the growing knowledge from the fields of brain research, attachment studies, contemporary theories of the mind, and various clinical methods in order to more effectively engage our patients who suffer from trauma.

This may be an important meeting point in which relational psychoanalysts are open to learning from different fields, including the field of trauma studies. Due largely to the shift in the understanding of what motivates individuals to behave in certain ways, relational psychoanalysis became a primary collaborator with various points of view on the development of the human mind and the acceptance of working from an interdisciplinary perspective (Bresler and Starr, 2015).

Eye Movement Desensitization and Reprocessing (EMDR), from its inception, was a comprehensive theory that made use of a synthetic approach to traditional therapies (Shapiro, 2001, 2002). Shapiro has written that, over time, EMDR procedures and protocols became more complex and integrative (Shapiro, 2002, p. 27). Behavioral, cognitive, and dynamic learning are represented in the EMDR protocols. These target etiological events, with their related disturbing affect and compartmentalized perceptions, are at times unmetabolized or unexamined. They also address early stimuli and perceptions that stay remarkably unchanged from the time of their creation by the original experience, and contribute to patients' disturbing feelings and inability to function effectively.

Through EMDR processing and reexperiencing of the target events, memory retrieval takes place and environmental and proprioceptive triggers become clearer, more accessible, and less affecting (Shapiro, 2002). The cognitive approach is further represented in the understanding that beliefs impact behaviors, and that a change in belief may lead to changes in behavior. Shapiro has clarified that in EMDR the cognitive process is largely used diagnostically to interpret the stored affect, and less frequently to identify the cause for it or to serve as a change agent (p. 29).

EMDR uses psychodynamic understanding through listening to the patient's self–other constructs, and by using negative and positive cognitions (which I describe in Chapter 1). In addition, EMDR makes use of the information-processing perspective to determine the patient's self-interpretive belief about the self as a verbalization of stored sensory experience arising from the original disturbing event (Shapiro, 2001). EMDR targets the affect associated with fixed beliefs of this kind.

Traditionally, the talking cure focused on verbal communication and strived to evoke affective responses triggered by a word that symbolized or signified a deeper emotional connection relevant to the person's history. The goal was for the patient to recognize hidden or split-off, unresolved conflict. Different theories of the mind gave slightly or significantly different explanations for the operating mechanisms of the mind, and out of this theoretical understanding a therapeutic approach evolved.

Because language can be used defensively to keep an emotion split from awareness, some patients never arrive at the ability to articulate their emotions early enough to have an effect on their psychic and real life. It is useful to think of EMDR, above and beyond its other virtues, as a method that prioritizes embodied experience, as for example in prioritizing bodily sensations over verbal expression. Some of the chapters in this book represent a psychodynamic approach that helps patients listen to their verbal and nonverbal communication in various intersubjective contexts. Other chapters tap into both relational and EMDR approaches. In both cases, I keep the possibility of potential integration in mind. This includes the contributions of brain research to our understanding of human interaction and behavior, and making the case for introducing approaches that involve the body's response, while discussing the limitation of using EMDR without a psychodynamic interpretive context and vice versa.

Currently, the theory supporting the psychoanalytic approach to clinical work argues that each analytic pair creates a unique way of working together, just as different analysts vary in their clinical work. However, many psychoanalysts see themselves as purists when it comes to affiliating with additional clinical methods, while EMDR practitioners adhere to its protocol and method alone.

In my clinical work, I resort to hints suggesting extra-psychoanalytic work when I feel the patient is unable to move consistently enough through painful experiences without blocking out a certain amount of affect. Since change is already taking place in an affective interaction with important others, the question is, How can I help a patient achieve and stay longer with the emotion of the transferential, potentially transformative, experience? Using my countertransference, I can feel when fleeting moments of connection come and go. At times they stay with me, as I am the conduit of the affective work, without ever touching the patient, who continues to report painful and, at times, horrendous experiences as if they had happened to an inanimate other, rather than themselves. I notice that the dissociative process is also split off into somatic expressions, such as halting the breath, tension or pain in various parts of the body, and the patient's stifling of speech. Calling attention to these phenomena helps to lift some of the anxiety and set affect in motion, while at other times this same intervention ushers in greater anxiety with accompanying symptoms of dissociation, such as cognitive impairment, mental fog, and forgetfulness, to mention only a few examples.

By chance, a patient who previously could not express any feelings one day approached a figurine in a sand tray in my office. Holding it gently, she began to talk, in a primary process voice, to the glass woman. She continued to stroke the figurine while tears came down her face. The touch, the cadence of her stroking motion, brought about intense emotions she wished to stay with for a while. Although I had used the sand tray at times with children and adults to tell an unspoken or at times unspeakable story, and to create a nonverbal narrative, I was not prepared for this woman's raw emotional engagement. Mirroring her emotional state, with not much of a context, I saw an opening into a great deal of pain I wished for her to access. In subsequent meetings, the patient looked at the object as if it were someone who was loved and dangerous, to be avoided. The experience was profound, yet foreign and feared. Wondering what might help reengage her with her feelings while helping her develop better tolerance of the ensuing anxiety, I offered, not without a sense of some trepidation, that we might use EMDR. I realized that EMDR could be used in conjunction with a relational psychoanalytic approach, not only to deal with trauma itself as suggested by Francine Shapiro (2002), but also to help patients engage in and emerge from emotionally deadened moments that had turned habitual and defensive over time.

Seeing EMDR and psychoanalysis as discrete in nature, it had never occurred to me to try to more formally introduce the two seemingly foreign methods together in a treatment until this opportunity presented itself.

Parnell (2013) has written that her work with EMDR is based on working in a client-centered way, trusting the inherent wisdom in the client, and following the process with minimal intervention (pp. 18–19). She has also written about the division among practitioners, in which some adhere rigidly to the EMDR protocol while others adapt the protocol to meet the needs of the client (pp. 12–14). Further, Parnell has suggested that most EMDR research has been done on simple cases, at times for example a study of a single case of PTSD in one patient, while studies of complex cases, where relational trauma created difficulties, were avoided. In addition, she has described the introduction of significantly modified EMDR in a study of children. Her formulation has suggested that some current EMDR practitioners may be open to incorporating a more dynamic approach to working with their clients.

Outline of the book

This book has two parts. Part I, Literature and theory, is dedicated to the professional literature in the fields of relational psychoanalysis and EMDR. Both approaches make significant use of available research, primarily in the fields of neuroscience and attachment theory. Though these are not mutually exclusive, I have chosen to separate them here as they each emphasize segments of the human experience from a slightly different angle. Brain research looks inward to examine the expression of cell and neurological change, and to describe how these internal changes due to internal and external environmental influences are then projected back onto the environment, including through interaction with others. Attachment theory and research look primarily at the interactional fields in which a mother's and infant's shared subjectivities are developed in the unique ways of their interaction, and the effect of these interactions on both parties' relationship-forming capabilities. Attachment theory is chiefly interested in the early development of human bonds, and the influence of these early bonds on forming and maneuvering in later relationships.

In Part I, I chose to open with the chapters that deal with the EMDR protocol and brain research because they both contain concepts that I use in all the following chapters, and I believe this organization will contribute to the understanding of the work I describe there. In my practice as a relational psychoanalyst, I embed a modified EMDR protocol to support the psychoanalytic work. Because EMDR concepts are interwoven into the book's psychoanalytic chapters and are not universally known to segments of the psychodynamic community, I decided to begin by introducing these areas here, as I see them as welcome, perhaps even essential, companions rather than representing the foreground of my clinical work. Part I then offers a literature review and the theoretical underpinning of the relational tradition and attachment theory and research.

Part II, Case studies using both relational psychoanalysis and EMDR, contains four clinical chapters that describe and demonstrate some modifications of EMDR that I developed in my practice to meet the complex needs of individual patients. Although the variations possible in incorporating these clinical methods are potentially vast, I chose to present examples that may give the interested clinician, who may be trained both in psychoanalysis and EMDR but who has not yet tried to interweave the two approaches simultaneously, a chance to imagine some possible ways of working to benefit their own patients. The personal information is disguised and biographical details have been changed throughout the book to maintain privacy, and to ensure that only the persons represented in these chapters will be able to recognize themselves. Yet the themes depicted in these clinical chapters illustrate dynamic moments that, in keeping with the confidentiality principle, are fair representations of clinical intersubjective moments.

Following are summaries of each chapter in Parts I and II of the book.

In Chapter 1, EMDR—history, method, protocol, and modifications for integration with relational psychoanalysis, I describe the history, theoretical underpinning, and pragmatic aspects of EMDR. Beyond this history and overview, the chapter makes the case that EMDR and psychodynamic psychotherapy are productively integratable. I expand the understanding of the potential uses of EMDR's highly structured protocol, which was originally established to treat big *T* trauma cases. I then describe how EMDR originated, as well as some of the existing variations in the use of this therapeutic method. In this chapter, I also delineate the spectrum of current trends in EMDR's thought and practice, and emphasize views that appreciate psychodynamics as part of a whole approach to treatment.

In addition to describing the underlying brain function related to EMDR and how its intervention can assist in the service of engaging blocked emotions, I present some of my ideas about the reasons EMDR might be effective, beyond what we know from published research.

With infant and adult attachment research in mind, I suggest that EMDR might provide interactions analogous to and essential in basic mother–infant interactions, as well as those between intimate partners or partners in therapy, in establishing patterns of interrelatedness, presenting some patterns that are anxiety provoking and others that are more organizing. I argue that EMDR may offer the missing link often sensed in this work between the semblances of bodily connection and organizing yet desire-restricting speech.

In Chapter 2, The influence of big *T* and small *t* trauma on the brain, I offer an overview of relevant brain research that suggests changes in the process of normal brain development to which the human brain resorts as a compromise in its efforts to survive traumatic events. I draw on research in the fields of neuroscience, EMDR, and Relational psychoanalysis to describe the process of developing and maintaining affect regulation under different circumstances, including the stress that arises in everyday life as well as that resulting from outstanding trauma. This chapter emphasizes, through recent research and vignettes, both developmentally and clinically, the development of neuro-networks and the unfolding of outcome following the impact of trauma, be it a big *T* trauma or relational small *t* trauma. In this second chapter, I present EMDR as a theoretical bridge between the two modalities of our artificially dichotomized self-perception of mind and body, interweaving it with a relational psychoanalytic sensibility in order to incorporate what new research has brought to our understanding about the brain's function. I feel this extension of both fields is important for the purpose of using the clinical environment to more fully engage with both our patients' and our own embodied experience in the consulting room.

Chapter 3, The relational perspective within the psychoanalytic tradition, describes the evolution of the relational approach in the psychoanalytic context. I highlight its centrality as a stepping stone that invites further consideration of an interdisciplinary approach, first theoretically and then in everyday clinical work. I delineate the influences of early theories of the mind and those that followed in order to bring out the roots of contemporary relational thinking and practices. I also explore the relevance of two-person versus one-person psychoanalysis, describing the emphasis relational thought places on subjectivity, transference, and countertransference.

In Chapter 4, Attachment: Companionship in action, I make a case for the ways in which relational psychoanalysis, EMDR, and attachment theory may be valuable in dialogue. My goal here is to outline the importance of attention given to minimal cues, failures of attunement, the effects of big *T* and small *t* trauma, and their potential use in therapy. As many psychotherapists draw on attachment theory to conduct therapy with their patients, I explore how understanding and attention given to minute changes in self-states may be a cue for the therapist to shift from verbal to nonverbal intervention. A growing body of relational thinking involves the reviving and exploration of the analyst's use of her subjectivity, including both verbal and nonverbal intersubjective relatedness. Although EMDR's understanding and method do include elements of psychodynamic sensibility, as for example those incorporated in the negative and positive cognition of the EMDR protocol (Shapiro, 2002), I describe the more recent explicit use of a focus on attachment and understanding in technique, as offered by EMDR clinicians (Parnell, 2013).

Chapter 5, In the trenches: Digging for lost passions—The use of EMDR in psychoanalytic work, opens Part II of the book. This chapter describes my analytic work with a woman during which several specific characteristics of the work led to my decision to use a modified rendition of treatment based on EMDR technique to enhance our analytic work. Here, EMDR was used as an adjunct to analytic work to help bridge the patient's splitting and fragmentation. This alteration felt necessary, as the experience of being in the room with this patient was quite palpable; the dissociation could not be mediated simply by verbal exchange. My attempts to engage this patient affectively led me to think that we were trapped, and that I might ultimately be unable to help her engage intersubjectively with me, and indeed, with important others in her life. Her particular circumstances created a sense of urgency, on which I elaborate in this chapter. These circumstances led me to the unorthodox decision to interweave EMDR into the analytic work. Following my observation that the use of EMDR did benefit this patient, that realization led me to try variations of integrating EMDR and relational psychoanalysis with other patients as well.

In Chapter 6, Working in tandem, I focus on my work with couples who were lost in old unspoken relational trauma(s). After my recognition of how being mired in their respective old pain was reenacted in their relationships, I introduced them to activities they could mutually perform outside of the session. In particular, this chapter describes the mutual activities that served as a natural individual bilateral stimulation (BLS), releasing emotions that had been frozen in their bodies. I describe here how this highly modified BLS allowed a renewed intimacy and a more spontaneous exchange. I then describe how the relational psychodynamic approach set the tone for attention to containing the emotional whole, thus increasing the attachment bond in the couple. This renewed bond provided a ground for each person to support his or her partner's early needs and space for the beginning of trauma recovery.

In the formulation, I suggest that working with couples oftentimes resembles the work done with a person who suffers from dissociative identity disorder, as self-states shift between partners as a way of sharing unbearable emotional stress. Consideration is given to the idea that EMDR sessions done individually, as well as while each partner is present in his or her partner's processing, can increase both empathy and support in the observing partner. Familiarity with this observing participation can help in the couple's relationship outside of the consulting room.

Chapter 7, I-dentity: Is trusted love ever an option?, illustrates my work with a woman who came in after experiencing frightening events in which she felt out of control with rage, anxiety, and underlying depression. I discuss the use of EMDR to access current events alongside early experiences and explicit memories from various developmental points in her life, as well as preverbal visceral and deeply embedded experiences that had been haunting her for much of her life, relationally depleting her to the extent that she had minimal personal and meaningful relationships. In addition, I discuss some modifications I made to the EMDR protocol, while keeping a psychoanalytic approach in mind, for the sake of blending the two methods without diminishing the benefits of either approach. I show how the use of EMDR, in accessing and clearing embodied relational trauma, can help establish the beginning of a mobilized mourning process, which in turn reveals attachment to that which is lost as a form of I-dentity, especially in the presence of limited actual relationships. I also discuss the difficulty of launching a more open life in the wake of early identification with the hollowness of real and meaningful human connection. Through the use of EMDR and the strong transferential-countertransferational bond that formed in this treatment, some mental representations of loved objects as subjects formed, and a transient intersubjectivity gradually began to emerge.

Chapter 8, EMDR in absentia—The power of "No", raises the question of how far the tool of EMDR can be modified and still be considered a modification rather than a new technique. Through illustrating the clinical process, I explore the use of tools that the patient and analyst co-conceived during the patient's tenuous and extended effort to conceive a baby and see it through to fruition. While the patient was reluctant to use a formal EMDR technique, following our conversations regarding incorporating this option into the psychodynamic work she reported that she found herself in a state of reverie when she spontaneously engaged in completing a puzzle. This process allowed her to see the value of unwittingly occupying the thinking brain to allow for the emergence of affective content, in a way similar to that of EMDR. This led to a conversation about other forms of bilateral stimulation she could use in the session and continue to feel safe, while also remaining in the service of affect emergence and process, both through the EMDR protocol and relational exploration of emotional material that was otherwise bracketed.

Chapter 9, Conclusions: Reintegrating the music with the lyrics, following the earlier clinical examples, returns to the book's main ideas and suggests potential directions for future interdisciplinary exploration of the way elements of EMDR may be embedded into relational psychoanalysis, and highlights the mutual benefit of at times allowing collaboration between analyst and patient to help the therapeutic process evolve. In this chapter, I ponder the usefulness of interweaving of this kind as offering a benefit to certain patients at certain stages of their treatment. I conclude with my belief that helping patients feel formerly frightening feelings with the help of both authentic analytic holding and EMDR's ability to usher in greater tolerance of their relational trauma anxieties, while also working to reduce their power in patients' lives, opens new potentials that are well worth exploring further.

Note

The quote by Ariane Mnouchine in the epigraph is from Andrew Dickson's article, "Ariane Mnouchkine and the Théâtre du Soleil: A life in theatre" (*The Guardian*, August 10, 2012; see www.theguardian.com/culture/2012/aug/10/ariane-mnouchkine-life-in-theatre, accessed 8-17-16).

References

Aron, L. (1996). *A Meeting of Minds: Mutuality in Psychoanalysis*. Vol. 4. Hillsdale, NJ: The Analytic Press.

Aron, L., and A. Harris. (1993). *The Legacy of Sándor Ferenczi*. New York: Routledge.

Aron, L., and K. Starr, editors. (2013). *A Psychotherapy for the People: Toward a Progressive Psychoanalysis*. New York: Routledge.

Benjamin, J. (1995). *Like Subjects, Love Objects*. New Haven, CT: Yale University Press.

Bresler, J., and K. Starr, editors. (2015). *Relational Psychoanalysis and Psychotherapy Integration: An Evolving Synergy*. New York: Routledge.

Davies, J., and M. Frawley. (1994). *Treating the Adult Survivor of Childhood Sexual Abuse: A Psychoanalytic Perspective*. New York: Basic Books.

Ferenczi, S. (1988). Confusion of tongues between adults and the child. *Contemporary Psychoanalysis* 24(2): 196–206.

Grand, S., and Alpert, J. (1993). The core trauma of incest: An object relations view. *Professional Psychology: Research and Practice* 24(3): 330–334.

Heimann, P. (1950). On countertransference. *International Journal of Psychoanalysis* 31: 81–84.

Kuchuck, S. (2014). Guess who's going to dinner? On the arrival of the uninvited third. In S. Kuchuck, editor, *Clinical Implications of the Psychoanalyst's Life Experience*, 135–145. New York: Routledge.

Mitchell, S. (1997). *Influence and Autonomy in Psychoanalysis.* Hillsdale, NJ: The Analytic Press.

Parnell, L. (2013). *Attachment-focused EMDR: Healing Relational Trauma*. New York: Norton.

Shapiro, F. (2001). *Eye Movement Desensitization and Reprocessing: Basic Principles, Protocols, and Procedures*. 2nd ed. New York: Guilford.

Shapiro, F. (2002). EMDR treatment: Overview and integration. In F. Shapiro, editor, *EMDR as an Integrative Psychotherapy Approach: Experts of Diverse Orientations Explore the Paradigm Prism*, 27–56. Washington, DC: American Psychological Association.

Slochower, J. (2013). Analytic enclaves and analytic outcome: A clinical mystery. *Psychoanalytic Dialogues* 23: 243–258.

Sullivan, H. S. (1953). *Conceptions of Modern Psychiatry*. New York: Norton.

Part I

Literature and theory

Chapter 1

EMDR—History, method, protocol, and modifications for integration with relational psychoanalysis

צר היה כל כך
הייתי אז מוכרח
לפרוש כנפיים ולעוף
אל מקום שבו
אולי כמו הר נבו
רואים רחוק רואים שקוף

בן אדם כעץ שתול על מים
שורש מבקש
בן אדם כסנה מול השמיים
בו בוערת אש
— יעקב רוטבליט

So sad and narrow it was
I had to
spread my wings and fly
to a place perhaps like
Mount Nebo
from which to see far, to see transparently

A human, like a sapling planted over water,
seeks a root
A human, like the burning bush against the skies,
within a fire burns
— Yaakov Rotblit

At times, patients find themselves in dire straits. In wanting to help, we, their companions on the path of seeing more clearly, look and listen through what they tell us, while trying all the tools in our toolbox. At other times, we may feel as if our patients' pain and sense of urgency to reduce their pain is mirrored in our mired responses to their wish. We may feel frustrated and helpless. Remembering peoples' basic needs and acquiring a bird's-eye perspective may then help us seek out and look into unexpected places for help, while holding in mind the potential of bridging over the abyss even while standing there with them.

This chapter describes the history, theoretical underpinning, and pragmatic aspects of Eye Movement Desensitization and Reprocessing (EMDR). Beyond the history of this technique and an overview of the stages and conditions of its use described below, this chapter makes the case that EMDR and psychodynamic psychotherapy are productively integratable. In presenting this option, I hope to expand the understanding of the potential uses of EMDR's highly structured protocol, one that was originally established to treat trauma cases. I describe the origin of EMDR and some of the current major variations in the use of this therapeutic method. I also delineate here the spectrum of current trends in the thought and practice of EMDR, and emphasize views that appreciate psychodynamics as a valuable part of a whole approach to treatment.

In addition to describing the underlying functions of the brain that are related to the successful introduction of EMDR, and a discussion of how it may be used to intervene in the service of engaging blocked emotions, I present some ideas about additional reasons supporting EMDR's potential effectiveness, beyond what we know from research. I suggest, based on the literature of infant and adult attachment, that EMDR might provide interactions that are analogous to those essential in mother–infant interactions, as well as to those between intimate partners or partners in therapy, in establishing patterns of interrelatedness, including some patterns that are anxiety provoking and others more organizing. I argue that EMDR may offer the missing link between the emergence of bodily connection in the session, and the use of organizing yet desire-restricting speech.

The journey

Moving into the clinical realm, some decades ago I had already begun to observe the impact of embodiment on psychic life. Until then, talk therapy, especially the psychodynamic, psychoanalytic approach, seemed to demand going the extra distance to listen out fully, taking as long as needed to observe shifts in moods and states of mind. The quiet space created was not unlike the mother–infant environment in which attunement is a key factor in the ebb and flow of the baby's emotional regulation. However, since adults walk into our offices with complex attachment experiences, very frequently it happens that reaching a point in which attunement is attained can take a relatively long time through talk therapy alone. In contrast, I at first observed the effectiveness of the less verbal and more embodied method of psychodrama, which carries the patient more rapidly into her affected experience. In psychodrama, attention is given to breathing patterns, to sounds, to body contours, to dissociation, to new discoveries that emerge wordlessly along with a narrative to create an embodied experience that closely matches known mimetic repetitive word experiences, yet deconstructs and reconstructs their interpretation. Observing this allowed me to consider how closely these new versions still fit the old paradigmatic existence.

Further, in the consulting room, I noticed that when a person feels "stuck" in a space without emotion, the option of promoting the patient's own movement, either through a simple motion that had already been initiated, such as hand clenching, or gross motor movement, as in walking with or without talking, can move the person toward feeling. Invariably, emotions emerge in the patient.[1] It is hard to dissociate in motion. The connection of the feet with a ground surface, the movement away from thought and control, and even breathing bring the patient back to life. Here, encouraging the patient to imagine a situation that preoccupies their mind serves as a mitigating factor. From a psychodynamic perspective, we know that what is close to the surface is not necessarily a defining founding experience, yet it may serve as a screen memory that represents a dynamic form that is experienced over and over again.

In following these movements, I was fascinated by the way, within a short period of time, hours or days, a person could move from a frozen emotion to a full expression of it that was rich in affective detail. I will not discuss here the merits and limitations of psychodrama, except to say that although all efforts are made to integrate the newly founded emotional material and anchor it within a reality check and mentalization of available attachment objects both within and without the group, much was left to be desired in the form of integration of the material in the following days and weeks of affective exposure. It felt to me that the ideal situation would be an affective exposure that was closely followed by a sustainable psychodynamic, indeed psychoanalytic integration, grounded again in the transference-countertransference matrix in which exploration could blossom and affect regulation be enhanced, so as to prevent the reoccurrence of the original trauma of overwhelming exposure with no foreseeable containment.

In a less dramatic form, the EMDR process targets early remembered experiences that are similar to the new situation at hand (F. Shapiro, 2001). With the embodiment of current images and experiences through EMDR, the mind tracks earlier experiences that feel the same, or that hold the bodily memory of a traumatic experience. Again, attention is given to minimal cues in breathing patterns, eye activity, body posture, and changes in general bodily representation of affective shifts. Here they are contained by the EMDR practitioner with the smallest sound or comment or perhaps with witnessing alone during the bilateral stimulation (BLS; also known as dual attention stimulus [DAS]) segments of the EMDR protocol. At an alternate time, the observation is then shared with the patient when the BLS sequence is at a break, in order to elicit a direction to follow. The patient's affective responses can vary from minimal to expressive, and the intervention consists in following the change in the emotional or narrative path, assuming that neural pathways are opening up as the signifier[2] neurologically recognizes the signified.

EMDR operates on the premise that traumatic events often cause a person to develop harmful beliefs and behaviors, and that EMDR processing opens patients to fresh understanding and insights that allow them to cast off these destructive tendencies (Parnell, 1997; F. Shapiro, 2001; R. Shapiro, 2005, 2009). Parnell (1997) has asserted that EMDR can be successful in relief of childhood trauma symptoms ranging from "physical and/or sexual abuse, grief and loss, medical procedure trauma, accidents, or witnessing violence" in work with patients where other forms of therapy have yielded limited results (p. 113). According to Parnell, EMDR processing of trauma takes the patient to a deeper level. But what is this deeper level? Both EMDR and psychodrama engage the mental sphere through their relatively rapid access to emotions through embodied experience. In psychodrama, patients are both setting and observing the scene, as it is played out by others, who take the roles of the original perpetrator and the patient's self as they are currently stored in the patient's memory, increasing the chance of approaching the original neural pathways and activating the shared circuitry by proxy. In both EMDR and psychodrama, what follows is the processing of elements of traumatic events and the resultant anxieties, in a process in which a repaired scenario is played out. In EMDR, the emotion is played out with a vision of a desired situation and reaction. In psychodrama, it is the played-out situation that triggers the mind to seek alternatives to an unwanted situation, whether traumatic or developmental.

Self-defense classes for women frequently use the playing out of a dreaded scenario, often with a male volunteer who takes the part of an attacker to help trigger anxieties based both on self-talk and in working through these anxieties with movement and action. The idea in psychodrama, as in EMDR, is to activate the debilitating anxiety and to allow the mind to consider alternatives that the mind and body together come to find can be activated in a stressful situation. As Sapolsky (2004) pointed out, most of our anxieties have nothing to do with actual fear of survival. However, a situation of actual fear in our past can trigger repeated anxiety that is debilitating and that continues to have severe consequences on our well-being. Stress can enhance emotional memories that are stored in the amygdala (Sapolsky, 2004). What EMDR does is to activate the sympathetic nervous system slightly, so that symptoms of anxiety are activated with some moderation, because the patient knows that they are in a relatively safe environment in which unsafe images can be played out and processed to a level of desensitization at which the sympathetic nervous system is no longer triggered (F. Shapiro, 2001). This process is then mediated as new factors are introduced, as for example in the integration of imagined positive cognition into the original dreaded situation. With the original situation in mind, its playing out, with a newly projected outcome, typically activates the sympathetic nervous system as the parasympathetic nervous system recedes to the background. It is important to mention that the completion of this action will be activated with a calming element only at the point when the entire pathway is cleared in which the parasympathetic nervous system has come to the fore and the sympathetic nervous system has receded into the background.

For example, if the processed material had to do with a recent event, as if a patient is terrified of waiting for her mammogram results because her sister just died of breast cancer, then clearing the reaction to her association with her too being at risk of being diagnosed, treated, and dying of cancer may be in order. In this example, another pathway of anxiety may be activated, that of loss and the fear of being completely alone and without protection as family members pass from this earth, leaving her alive but having to fend for herself. It is important to recognize the full complexity of the anxiety, not only the presenting anxiety. EMDR practitioners are trained to search for what is called the *target*, the source of the original anxiety that triggers all the others on this path (F. Shapiro, 2001). The process must be flexible, as what may seem to be a bedrock target may be the tip of an anxiety iceberg.

What I realized with psychodrama first, and then with EMDR, was that even with effective integration of the processed trauma or anxiety-provoking situation, there was much residue to be processed in the days that followed. This is a prime time during which the mind happens upon new realizations regarding other aspects of life. Although these could be processed through another psychodrama or EMDR session, there are problems which, at that stage of the work, are better addressed with an analytic process. For example, psychodrama sessions are usually done in groups, and in intervals where there may be months between sessions, which does not allow for immediate processing. Similarly, EMDR discourages expanded discussion into the presenting issue. Yet both are activating the nervous system, mind, and amygdala through motion, and once these pathways are open psychoanalysis can allow analytic deepening while the attachment element hovers over the deliberation.

Another approach I have used over the years with both adult and child patients is sand play. Observing children as they occupy their hands and engage in quiet play in a sand tray in the presence of a therapist can often bring out similar reactions.

I have often thought that mixing therapy with play in a fashion similar to the way both D. W. Winnicott (1971) and Margaret Mead (2001) describe it, can bring about a real-world experience that defies cerebral rationalization, breaking earlier barriers established to block traumatic awareness in the service of an internal sense of psychological cohesion. It is important to emphasize the centrality of the perceived benevolence in this process. Play can occur only in situations of relative psychological safety when there is an observer or inner activation of observer representation, as when the mother is in close proximity, or the child feels protected when sensing that the therapist is keeping an eye out and has given the patient permission to play or play out (Winnicott, 1971). Similarly, EMDR attempts to explain the reason why a motion or emotion like those triggered by BLS can evoke a psychodynamic response in the mind and body, and how this embodiment can open the door to modification in the response to the traumatic experience. In theorizing about the way EMDR works, one can look back on the psycho-dramatic movement that lies at the base of the actual dramatization of a scenario and see how it primes the patient emotionally. EMDR uses a similar but less dramatic system of movement in which an external motion is applied to the patient to occupy the thinking mind and release the feeling mind-body, essentially allowing the patient to bypass the apparatus set in place to help avoid frightening or sad thoughts.

In the everyday to and fro, we find ourselves in situations that spontaneously call upon procedural knowledge to help us in potentially stressful situations. Consider an example from outside the consulting room that is mildly stressful.

When playing table tennis competitively, confronted by a capable opponent, the space to think strategically disappears into a motion that feels slowed down tremendously; the racket becomes an extension of my hand, the world disappears, and all I can hear is the syncopated skip of the ball and my own breathing. No thinking interferes, yet I am more alive than in any other engaged conversation. I become my breathing, my movement, my thoughtless aliveness. How did that happen? More importantly, how might I recreate this synchronized, satisfying sensation in other realms of my life?

Having traditional psychodynamic and cognitive training, and although grateful for words in exploring and analyzing states of mind, sentiments, and behaviors, I can also feel the limitation of words. I have noticed that more embodied approaches, such as psychodrama and sand play, offer quick ways to help a reserved patient get to emotions, a movement that then allows some verbal processing. However, what I found was missing for me was the continued observation and processing of all that unfolded from the emotional experience. Early on, I felt that combining a psycho-dramatic approach to embodiment should be interfaced with a psychoanalytic approach in which intense emotions can be transferred to the analyst and explored via verbal exploration of visceral and emotional experiences. But at that time, about two decades ago, mixing any method with the psychoanalytical could often be regarded as only an externalization of the transference experience, rather than a way of opening up emotional viability in order for the transference to flourish in the analytic realm.

We know that without affective engagement there is no transformative and lasting therapeutic effect, and yet to wait for an emotional engagement in analysis can take years in persons with significant traumatic experiences. In response, I have developed a gentle integrative practice in which elements from EMDR and other approaches such as psychodrama and sand play that favor embodiment over narrative are used. Attention is paid to minimal cues, such as changes in breathing pattern, changes in the body (such as posture, holding, stretching, scratching, and blinking), and these are reflected upon. At times I may ask the patient to exaggerate the action to increase an awareness of its relationship with the body, which often induces the emergence of a related, held-back emotion. Words then follow the emotional embodied experience, first as a narrative and later as transference-laden text followed by reflection.

I have found this combination of ways of working freeing, because if there was an element of the structure of psychoanalysis that I struggled with it was the Puritan approach that I felt limited the analyst's access to being helpful when things do not move along. I have become acutely aware of this limitation when the consequence of holding back and waiting for a patient to metabolize transference interpretations in the absence of affective engagement threatened actual real-life relationships, and the waiting was impacting families and careers. At times, as I elaborate in Chapter 5, an imminent sense of expiring time can be detrimental, and further waiting will only result in growing agony.

Theory

EMDR was launched because of Francine Shapiro's (2001) chance observation as she walked in a park, and its development and continued refinement have been the result of ongoing clinical observation. Theories that explain why EMDR works have arisen after the fact and for the most part have not yet been confirmed (Parnell, 1997; F. Shapiro, 2001).

It was observation of the effects of EMDR treatment that led to the adaptive information-processing model. According to Francine Shapiro (2001), the human mind is designed to have a physiologically based information-processing system that takes in and processes experiences and then stores memories in a relatively accessible way. Various memories are linked in networks that contain related thoughts, images, emotions, and sensations. For learning to take place, associations and links are made with information that is stored in memory.

With the onset of trauma, interference with this process occurs, with the result that links are made based on the traumatic process rather than that of associative learning (F. Shapiro, 2001). Part of the reason for this change is that overwhelming emotions, images, or sensations often result in traumatic dissociation that hinders learning through information processing. As a result, adaptive information in other memory networks cannot be successfully accessed. Consider the following example.

A war veteran is haunted by images of his command car buddy dying next to him in a bombing. He feels that, as the driver, he should have anticipated the attack and saved his pal's life. He is aware of the impossibility of this scenario, but senses that he should have known. Here, the associative connection is severed between the rational knowing and the partially processed sensory knowing. The unprocessed information is stored in a nonadaptive form. As a result, triggers in the environment that resemble a piece of the traumatic event will call up the bodily and affective responses, images, and partially processed thoughts of the original trauma. A trauma survivor will experience the trigger as if it were the original traumatic event. This repetitive process then reinforces the belief in the validity of a nonadaptive thought process.

EMDR attempts to set adaptive association links in motion by processing trauma target material to reduce its disturbing interference in current psychic and relational life, hence increasing appropriate learning and allowing new experiences to be processed with newly acquired links to nontraumatic memory.

The information-processing model has proven useful both as a therapeutic road map and as a unifying concept that integrates the salient aspects of most of the major psychological modalities (Schore, 2003a, 2003b; F. Shapiro, 2001; Solms and Turnbull, 2002). In physiological terms, the model incorporates the physiological aspects of network activation and the assimilation of emotionally corrective information, which are then accommodated within comprehensive adaptive networks. This means that the stored memory of an event is brought to consciousness, relevant information needed to experience and remember it in a healthy manner becomes incorporated within it, the person learns from it, and the memory can then take its place as a functional part of the client's overall life history. It is no longer an isolated trauma with ongoing negative effects; it becomes one of many past experiences that appropriately inform and guide.

Protocol

An interesting aspect of EMDR's use of bilateral stimulation (BLS) is its activation of both sides of the brain (F. Shapiro, 2001). In EMDR literature, bilateral stimulation is considered to help occupy the frontal cortex as a way to allow the release of amygdala-embedded memories that lie more in the realm of primary process rather than thinking. Yet from brain research we learn that both sides of the brain do indeed have a role in both primary and cognitive rational processes (Damasio, 1999). The importance of activating both sides of the brain simultaneously is that both sides of the brain that may be responsible for the surfacing of affect-laden activity are prompted.

Along the same line of body and mind, it may be helpful to think of EMDR with the following sequence in mind: EMDR eye movement (material) leads to brain activity (material), leads to desensitization, and reduced anxiety (immaterial), leads to a sense (immaterial) of safety in both the external (material and immaterial) and internal environment (immaterial).

To get a sense of how EMDR might work in a given session, I present here the EMDR Psychotherapy Case Flow description (Figure 1.1).[3] It is adopted from Natalie Robinson's (2016) chart with my additions for clarification. It is my experience that most EMDR sessions vary from the chart below, based on the patient's readiness and time constraints, due to the emergence of new material, the reaction during processing, and the use of various methods integrated into the session. It is also important to emphasize that EMDR is a whole method of which the following chart is only a part, and that the desensitization phase may take multiple sessions before final closure is reached. Hence the following chart represents a "perfect day" scenario for illustration purposes only. However, having the eight-stage diagram in a chart form may offer a bird's-eye view of a segment of the Eye Movement Desensitization and Reprocessing modality. Please note that only practitioners who have completed their EMDRIA or EMDR Institute approved training should use this chart or attempt doing EMDR in clinical work or otherwise. For more on Lightstream,[4] mentioned in Phase 2 of the figure, see the endnote.

Phase 1: Client History and Treatment Planning

Presenting Problem, Risk/Crisis Assessment, Client History, Goals, Strengths, Internal and External Support Systems, Diagnostic Evaluation, Dissociative Evaluation.

- **Stable** (but with limited access to emotions): Unexamined life due to lack of meaningful emotional connection, or environmental and multigenerational trauma that is not perceived as personal. (For example: awareness of incest of sibling, or loss of abusive grandfather before patient's birth.) **Proceed.**
- **Sufficient Stability:** Sufficient affect tolerance, trust, and self-regulation and good enough support system and resources. **Proceed.**

- **Relatively Stable:** (But with limited affect tolerance and limited self-regulation—often history of significant childhood trauma.) Add resources to strengthen, soothe, ground. Teach how to manage affect. Strengthen alliance. If appropriate, initiate Dissociative Disorders procedures.
- **Unstable—High Risk:** Stabilize, hospitalize/medical evaluation, contract for safety, crisis intervention. Important to bring the patient to relative stability before attempting EMDR.

Phase 2: Preparation

Explain EMDR Psychotherapy, Theory and Model. Introduce basic resources. Create Safe/Calm Space (Some practitioners prefer a rest space, especially with patients who find it hard to fathom the idea of a safe space). Address fears of, for example, the unknown EMDR process, being overwhelmed with emotions, or being unable to control the outpour of emotions, and return to functioning following EMDR session.

Are client and therapist ready for EMDR Trauma Reprocessing?

- **No—Client not ready:** Safe space does not go well. Consent unsure or fearful. Continue resource and crisis work: Lightstream, Container, Build trust, Psycho-ed, Explore fears, Prepare until client is ready.
- **Yes:** Clinical rapport good. Safe space goes well. Informed consent given (for new patients). **Proceed.**

Phase 3: Assessment

Choose target(s) issue/memory using 3-Pronged Plan (past/present/future):

Choose specific image/picture:

- **Negative Cognition (NC):** Answer the question: "When you think about this image, what negative belief about yourself comes up for you now?"
- **Positive Cognition (PC):** Answer the question: "When you think about this image, what positive thoughts do you wish you could have about yourself now?"
- **Validity of Cognition (VOC) on PC:** Ranging from 1–7 with 1 representing disbelief in its validity and 7 representing a complete syntonic match for PC on image/incident, emotions/feelings. ("How much do I believe that I possess the positive trait I have attached to the image?")
- **Focus on target image. Check emotion and Subjective Units of Distress (SUDs):** Ranging from 0–10 in which 0 represents no distress, and 10 represents most distress on NC and image/incident; locate bodily sensations.

Phase 4: Desensitization

Use Bilateral Stimulation (BLS) on target: Link target image/incident with NC, emotion, and bodily sensations, "GO WITH THAT."

Ask "What comes up?" Does new material emerge?

- **NO:** Material doesn't move or change; is negative, overwhelming, looping, or blocked. (Change modality or direction. Do longer BLS sets. Focus on sensations. Use Cognitive Interweaves. Identify and reprocess Blocking Beliefs, Feeder Memories, and/or Blocking Ego States. Install more resources. Reprocess smaller bits with BLS.)
- **YES:** Clear each channel, keep reprocessing with more sets of BLS.

Figure 1.1 (continued)

(continued)

End of channel: No change for 2 sets, return to target.

Check SUD: Reprocess until SUD = 0 or ecological 1.

Phase 5: Installation

Is PC still relevant?

- **NO:** Get relevant PC.
- **YES:** Link original image with PC. Check VOC. Reprocess with BLS.

Does VOC increase?

- **NO:** Ask "What prevents PC from being a 7?" If not ecological, work through blocks or another target if necessary. (Accept if ecological "6".)

Does VOC = 7 (or ecological 6)?

- **NO:** Continue BLS to 7 (or ecological 6).
- **YES:** Strengthen with slow BLS sets.

Phase 6: Body Scan

Link image and PC.

Check for bodily disturbance. "Is body clear of disturbances?"

- **NO:** Body Scan not clear, disturbance exists. Use BLS sets on negative bodily sensations until body is clear.
- **YES: Proceed.** Strengthen positives with slow BLS sets.

NOTE: Most EMDR sessions end before completion of protocol. Leave time near the end of session for sufficient closure (Phase 7).

Phase 7: Closure

Close down safely. Debrief—"What was achieved?"

Contain, calm, and orient to present.

Read closure statement about intersessions.

Discuss supports, resources.

Homework—notice, log.

Phase 8: Reevaluation at Follow-up Session

"What came up?" Check log. Re-look at SUD of original incident.

Continue work if unfinished, if SUD about 0 or ecological 1, VOC below 7 or move to new target of 3-Pronged Plan (past/present/future).

Figure 1.1 EMDR Psychotherapy Case Flow

Controlled clinical outcome studies of EMDR in the treatment of PTSD

EMDR's pioneer, Francine Shapiro, introduced the first controlled study of EMDR in 1989 (F. Shapiro, 1989a, 1989b). Because of the small number of subjects used, and other factors, the study was a preliminary one and in need of confirmation by independent replication and careful clinical observation. In the years since Francine Shapiro's initial reports, much research investigating the effectiveness of EMDR for treating PTSD has been done (Bisson and Andrew, 2007; Carlson, Chemtob, Rusnak, Hedlund, and Muraoka, 1998; Silver, Rogers, and Russell, 2008; van der Kolk, Spinazzola, Blaustein, Hopper, Hopper, Korn, and Simpson, 2007). Overall, these studies point to EMDR's effectiveness in treating trauma-related disorders.

For example, in a systematic review of published trials of various psychological treatment approaches for PTSD, Bisson and Andrew (2007) found that Trauma Focused Cognitive Behavioral Therapy (TFCBT), Stress Management, and EMDR were effective in treating the symptoms of PTSD. Although the authors say that the small number of studies, sample size, and heterogeneity observed should suggest the use of caution when interpreting this data, they further found that of those three approaches, only TFCBT and EMDR were effective when the treatment was measured after two to five months.

In a large study, van der Kolk et al. (2007) conducted a randomized clinical trial with 88 patients with PTSD, comparing the efficacy of EMDR with flouxetine (a selective serotonin reuptake inhibitor or SSRI) and a placebo pill. They found EMDR to be an effective treatment with lasting benefit after six months but with a marked difference between adult-onset trauma with a 75 percent remission rate versus a child-onset trauma remission rate of 33 percent. Neither the drug nor the placebo had any long-lasting effect.

Although these studies indicated the effectiveness of EMDR for the treatment of PTSD, there are some that point to a more cautious optimism for treating combat-related PTSD effectively with EMDR (Carlson et al., 1998; Verstrael, van der Wurff, and Vermetten, 2013). For instance, a more recent meta-analysis study by Verstrael et al. (2013) surveyed research on the use of EMDR to treat patients with combat-related PTSD, emphasizing that such patients tend to exhibit more acute symptoms due to prolonged and repeated exposure to traumatic events. They found that in contrast to a meta-analysis on EMDR used for the general population, which showed substantial and significant efficacy (Bisson and Andrew, 2007), the result of their meta-analysis for combat-related trauma could only show a nonsignificant medium effect (Verstrael et al., 2013). In trying to reconcile this difference they noted that only seven articles met their inclusion criteria, and that these had included a total of 60 patients. Significantly, only one of the included studies had a full set of 12 EMDR sessions administered. Verstrael and colleagues speculated that combat-related PTSD can be more severe and that it is often associated with chronic diseases, which could make it more difficult to treat effectively. Another speculation was that trauma of this kind is often associated with feelings of guilt and shame, which might make such patients reluctant to respond to interventions. They also highlighted the paucity of research articles published after the year 2000 on the use of EMDR for a military population; all the papers they reviewed were published between 1994 and 1999. However, when looking at the one study that insisted on the full set of twelve EMDR sessions for patients with combat-related PTSD done by Carlson et al. (1998), the findings demonstrated a 77 percent remission of PTSD and no dropouts during the treatment. The effects were maintained at nine months follow-up.

In a more recent study, Silver et al. (2008) presented two case studies that illustrated the efficacy of EMDR in treating combat veterans with persistent PTSD and related social and physical symptoms. In their survey of previous research, they noted that when comparing twelve sessions of EMDR to Exposure Therapy and CPT (Cognitive Processing Therapy), EMDR therapy had a remission rate of PTSD diagnosis of 77 percent with a dropout rate of zero compared to a remission rate of PTSD diagnosis of 40 percent for both Exposure Therapy and CPT with a 42 percent and 34 percent dropout rate for the two therapies respectively.

The cases Silver and colleagues (2008) presented were of two combat veterans with severe PTSD symptoms. The first was a young Iraq veteran who was discharged after attempting suicide and who was subsequently hospitalized twice following further suicide attempts. In his case, the treatment was completed in two weeks while he was still hospitalized. A follow-up after three months showed lasting impact, with the patient reporting he was doing well with no disturbances. The second case was a

73-year-old Vietnam veteran who had suffered from physical symptoms alongside PTSD. Since 1968 he had had "twitches" in his upper body more than 50 to 60 times per day. He became alcohol dependent and lost his family. Following the treatment, the twitching disappeared, and the mental issues were in check. Follow-ups after one month and six months showed all symptoms in remission.

Silver and colleagues (2008) suggested a number of factors that make EMDR particularly effective with veterans. First, veterans tend to have suffered multiple traumatic experiences. EMDR is well-suited to treat such multiple, often linked experiences that frequently lead to different emotions and physical sensations. Combat veterans tend to avoid discussing the details of traumatic experiences. The EMDR protocol does not require the specific details of the trauma, which helps veterans engage more readily in the EMDR process, and then proceed to describe the entire event. Further, they found that veterans, reflecting their military training, tend to be action-oriented and expect change in their condition to happen relatively quickly, an expectation that, if not met, as with psychotherapy, can lead to frustration and cessation of treatment. In addition, Silver et al. (2008) noted that EMDR sessions can be administered on consecutive days (no patient "homework" was needed), which helps accelerate outcomes. Importantly, these authors suggested that EMDR integrated well with other forms of therapy such as group therapy. They noted that such combination of treatment can help break down isolation, provide skill training, and offer a safe environment for testing of new behaviors as patients are released from the yoke of PTSD symptoms.

Summary

In summary, this chapter describes the history, theoretical underpinning, and pragmatic aspects of EMDR, and makes the case that EMDR and psychodynamic psychotherapy are productively integratable. It expands the understanding of the potential uses of EMDR's highly structured protocol, which was originally established to treat trauma cases. In addition, it describes the origin of EMDR and the existing variations of the use of this therapeutic method. The chapter offers a spectrum of relevant current trends in EMDR's thought and practice, and emphasizes views that appreciate psychodynamics as part of a whole approach to treatment.

In addition, both the underlying brain functions related to EMDR and the use of this method in intervention in the service of engaging blocked emotions are described. Here, I explore some initial ideas on what might promote EMDR's efficacy. I suggest that EMDR might provide interactions analogous to those that are essential in mother–infant interactions, as well as between intimate partners or partners in therapy, in establishing patterns of interrelatedness, with some patterns that are anxiety provoking and others more organizing. I argue that EMDR may offer the missing link between the semblances of bodily connection and the organizing, yet desire restricting language.

This chapter introduces EMDR concepts and terms that are used throughout this book to help guide the reader, and to provide references to EMDR's conceptual and technical terms. Additionally, I have described some modifications I made to the protocol to better suit relational psychoanalytic work. An EMDR protocol chart is also presented in Figure 1.1, in which I combine a more traditional EMDR process with modifications to allow for a better integration with a relational psychoanalytic approach within a given session, and across the course of treatment. To conclude the chapter, I highlight some important current research and discuss its efficacy as it relates to using EMDR in a clinical setting with relational thinking in mind.

Notes

The passage by Yaakov Rotblit in the epigraph is from a book of songs titled *Meabed Tamlilim* (Israel: Kineret, Zmora-Bitan, Dvir Publishers, 1996).

1 In this text, I use the terms *patient* and *client* interchangeably. The psychoanalytic literature often uses the former while EMDR scholars prefer the latter.

2 In simplistic terms, Saussure's concepts of the signifier and signified stem from the field of semiotics. The *sign* is the whole that results from the association of the signifier with the signified (Saussure, 1986). The relationship between the signifier and the signified is referred to as *signification*. To take a linguistic example, the word *open* (when it is invested with meaning by someone who encounters it on a shop doorway) is a sign consisting of a signifier (the word *open*), and a signified concept: that the shop is open for business. Many think of this relationship as referring to mental constructs, though clearly it can also refer to things in the world.

We can compare Freud's *conscious* with Saussure's *signified* and *unconscious* to the *signifier*. However, Lacan (1977) turns the formulation on its head so that the signifier represents the signified that is buried, where the unconscious sexuality and fantasy can be pictured as the signifier over the signified. The unconscious is constituted in the same way as our intrinsic ability to speak. Desire is left always unsatisfied and is either displaced from signifier to signifier or is substituted for—one signifier for another—and the whole process makes up a "chain of signifiers" that remains unconscious but which, like the unconscious, leaves traces of itself, traces which may be read. See http://courses.nus.edu.sg/course/elljwp/lacan.htm (accessed 4-21-16).

3 Natalie Robinson, EMDR Psychotherapy Case Flow Chart (Trauma Recovery EMDR Humanitarian Assistance Programs, 2016), n.p.; with author modifications. It is important to note that this chart is for illustration purposes only, and should only be used by clinicians who completed a professional EMDR training by the EMDR Institute or EMDR International Association's approved trainers. See Figure 1.1.

4 For the reference to the Lightstream Grounding Technique in Phase 2 of Figure 1.1, *Lightstream* is used in EMDR as a grounding technique to decrease aversive affect. If the patient reports upsetting bodily sensations, the clinician asks about the potential shape, size, color, temperature, texture, sound, and their quality. Then the clinician directs the patient to imagine light coming through the body from the head down having a favorite color and temperature of its own, finding the shape and surrounding it. Once the image of the body flooded is achieved, the clinician asks what changes are noticed in the shape and other qualities of the bodily sensation as the body resonates with the flooding light. This process repeats until the shape dissolves or loses its power, and the flood of light is directed at the body in its entirety (F. Shapiro, 2001).

References

Bisson, J., and M. Andrew. (2007). Psychological treatment of post-traumatic stress disorder (PTSD). *Cochrane Database System Review* 18(3): 1–22.

Carlson, J. G., C. M. Chemtob, K. Rusnak, N. L. Hedlund, and M. Y. Muraoka. (1998). Eye movement desensitization and reprocessing (EMDR): Treatment for combat-related post-traumatic stress disorder. *Journal of Traumatic Stress* 11: 3–24.

Damasio, A. (1999). *The Feeling of What Happens: Body and Emotion in the Making of Consciousness*. Orlando, FL: Harcourt.

Lacan, J. (1977). *Ecrits: A Selection.* Translated by Alan Sheridan. London: Tavistock Publications.

Lacan, J. Lacan and Language. http://courses.nus.edu.sg/course/elljwp/lacan.htm (accessed 4-21-16).

Mead, M. (2001). *Growing Up in New Guinea: A Comparative Study of Primitive Education.* New York: Harper Collins. Perennial Modern Classics.

Parnell, L. (1997). *Transforming Trauma: EMDR.* New York: Norton.

Robinson, N. (2016). EMDR Psychotherapy Case Flow Chart. Hamden, CT: Trauma Recovery EMDR Humanitarian Assistance Programs.

Sapolsky, R. (2004). *Why Zebras Don't Get Ulcers: The Acclaimed Guide to Stress, Stress-Related Diseases, and Coping*. 3rd ed. New York: St. Martin's Griffin.

Saussure, F. de (1986). *Course in General Linguistics*, translated by R. Harris. 3rd ed. Chicago: Open Court Publishing Company. [Original work published in French in 1916.]

Schore, A. (2003a). *Affect Regulation and the Repair of the Self.* New York: Norton.

Schore, A. (2003b). *Affect Dysregulation and Disorders of the Self.* New York: Norton.

Shapiro, F. (1989a). Efficacy of the eye movement desensitization procedure in the treatment of traumatic memories. *Journal of Traumatic Stress Studies* 2: 199–223.

Shapiro, F. (1989b). Eye movement desensitization: A new treatment for post-traumatic stress disorder. *Journal of Behavior Therapy and Experimental Psychiatry* 20: 211–217.

Shapiro, F. (2001). *Eye Movement Desensitization and Reprocessing: Basic Principles, Protocols, and Procedures*. 2nd ed. New York: Guilford.

Shapiro, R. (2005). Introduction. In R. Shapiro, editor, *EMDR Solutions: Pathways to Healing*, 1–7. New York: Norton.

Shapiro, R., editor. (2009). *EMDR Solutions II: For Depression, Eating Disorders, Performance, and More*. New York: Norton.

Solms, M., and O. Turnbull. (2002). *The Brain and the Inner World: An Introduction to the Neuroscience of Subjective Experience*. New York: Other Press.

Silver, S. M., S. Rogers, and M. Russell. (2008). Eye movement desensitization and reprocessing (EMDR) in the treatment of war veterans. *Journal of Clinical Psychology* 64(8): 947–957.

van der Kolk, B., J. Spinazzola, M. E. Blaustein, J. W. Hopper, E. K. Hopper, D. L. Korn, and W. B. Simpson. (2007). A randomized clinical trial of eye movement desensitization and reprocessing (EMDR), fluoxetine, and pill placebo in the treatment of posttraumatic stress disorder: Treatment effects and long-term maintenance. *Journal of Clinical Psychiatry* 68: 37–46.

Verstrael, S., P. van der Wurff, and E. Vermetten. (2013). Eye movement desensitization and reprocessing (EMDR) as treatment for combat-related PTSD: A meta-analysis. *Military Behavioral Health* 1: 68–73.

Winnicott, D. W. (1971). *Playing and Reality*. London: Tavistock.

Chapter 2

The influence of big *T* and small *t* trauma on the brain

rush of pine scent (once upon a time),
the unlicensed conviction
there ought to be another way
of saying
this.
— Paul Celan

In this chapter, I offer an overview of relevant neuroscience research that suggests that a state of normal brain development exists to which the human mind resorts as a compromise in its effort to survive traumatic events. I then describe the process of developing and maintaining the regulation of affect under different circumstances, including stress stemming from everyday life or as a result of major trauma. This chapter emphasizes, through recent research and vignettes, both developmentally and clinically, the development of neuro-networks and the unfolding of outcomes due to trauma, be it a big *T* trauma (such as rape, loss through violent death, or severe neglect) or relational small *t* trauma (such as a momentary feeling of being unattended to by a loved one, an encounter by a stranger, or a scuffle with a sibling).

In this context, an Eye Movement Desensitization and Reprocessing (EMDR) approach serves as a theoretical bridge between the two modalities of our artificially dichotomized self-perception of mind and body, one that can be interwoven with relational psychoanalytic sensibilities to incorporate the understanding that new research is offering about the brain's function. This interweaving is helpful for the purpose of using the clinical environment to more fully engage with our patients' and our own embodied experience in the consulting room. The relevance of this basic information to an understanding of the triggering of traumatic content, as well as the importance of engaging these experiences both in holding and restructuring the environment, is crucial to our discussion of EMDR.[1]

Clinical vignettes illustrating small *t* and big *T* trauma

Frankie darted past me into the office. When I greeted her in the waiting room, she seemed different than the day before. Her gaze was on me, yet distant, as if she were focusing someplace past me. On the couch she sat, but did not recline as she typically did. She was speaking in a fast, pressured manner. If she cared about my presence in the room, it was to affirm her assertion that a menace had tried to harm her, intentionally. Watching her, I felt that she was going through a sequence of cinematic experiences, with no reflection or rewind available to her in these moments. Frankie was in the throes of a trigger event stemming from a daily interaction. Her reaction was one that resembled many well-known interactions in her early upbringing in which she felt invisible as a person with needs. Instead she felt used as an auxiliary to her parents' wishes.

When triggered today, her reaction was to return to the old assertion that she does not exist—surely her needs are overlooked. She felt abandoned again, and her otherwise bright mind was one-tracked: I am important to no one, I feel dropped, and I am destroyed. Suddenly, there was a wasteland of pain and rage that Frankie could not overcome. In a parallel form, Frankie brought her sense of nonexistence into the room as an unconscious way for me to feel unseen for who I was for her. No words could sway her out of this mode. I had to sit with her convicted by the facts as she saw them, but also with her assertion that her world was a permanently dangerous one that would never change. If cognitive reframing could be a tool at times with her, here Frankie's conviction was unshakable.

What causes that transformation in an otherwise rational person who can follow her behavior and reflect on her irrational thoughts? It is not that Frankie suddenly became a different person. Instead, her natural tendencies took a severe turn into a place where she had no reflective capacity. Her body and mind were locked into a life-threatening scenario accompanied by a life-preserving behavior. She flew through an automatic neuropathway. It was an express highway with no apparent exits.

Yet, the next day, after Frankie realized that her facts were misguided, she reassessed her convictions. She now had to deal with embarrassment over her reaction, but also seize the opportunity to examine what was at the base of it that was still worth exploring.

This chapter attempts to use this and other examples to elucidate some of the complex processes patients experience that make them temporarily feel out of their minds. Sometimes, as in the case of Frankie, an everyday relational trauma will translate into a perfect storm of resemblance that will trigger a reaction, as if the past is now the present.

We sometimes call such an occurrence small *t* trauma to denote its similarity to and difference from big *T* trauma, in which an extraordinary, horrifying event transcends the daily routine and throws a person into extreme physical and mental imbalance. Clinjically, both relational small *t* trauma and big *T* trauma may set a person on a familiar neuropathway that requires treatment to reduce its effects on the patient.

As an example of a big *T* trauma, consider the following incident I experienced growing up in Israel. A man and a 10-year-old child board a bus. The man, proceeding to the middle of the bus, his head ducked, is stretching his arms as if aiming a gun at his fellow riders. He is yelling. Like a child he makes shooting sounds. His shirt is splattered with blood. He doesn't seem injured but he clearly seems psychotic. This man was terrorized minutes earlier by a group of terrorists who kidnapped the bus he was on, killing many of its riders. The man saw his wife shot and was convinced she had died. For long moments he occupied the terrorist's space as he was shooting at the riders. He then shifted to become the good, responsible, and functioning father to his son, and then went back to the shooting. He was not psychotic, nor sane. He lived in several places at once, with some success. Was it just the automatic pilot reflex that got him and his son out of the situation? When he responded to a touch and comforting sounds, although not to words, this man began occupying another state of mind; the space of the horrible realization about the possible loss of the rest of his family. He started to cry.

These two examples illustrate the difference between small *t* and big *T* traumas. The case of Frankie is an example of small *t* trauma. She went down a neurological pathway leading to an old but uninterrupted scenario that seemed hyper-focused on internal conviction, simulating the early relationship with her parents. However, when reality presented itself in the form of evidence to the contrary she restored her balanced view of the experience, where she was able to reflect on the situation and her reaction to it.

In the second example, when an extraordinary experience took place (big *T* trauma), the father was clearly in the grip of physical and psychological trauma where fear of death for him and his family was real. His reaction was psychotic-like, and no words could help him out then. He was dissociated. Shifting between being terrorized, replaying the overwhelming events, and being the compassionate father to his traumatized son, he then, with the calming touch from another person, felt some compassion for himself. It became possible to feel safe despite the horrifying events.

Contemporary research views the mind as containing an introspective element that allows us to subjectively interpret our being, an internal mirror of sorts that often assists psychoanalysts in their inquiry into the minds of patients. Relational psychoanalysts often explore their own subjective physical and mental responses at any given moment in the analytic situation to help guide them to where the patient might be (Cooper, 2014). The mind also consists of the brain, which may be seen as the embodiment of our "objective" perspective, namely the mind as an object, the way it may be perceived from outside our self.

Let us take a relational moment: a mother is cooing at her infant. She waits and is animated, her brows rise, her smile anticipating. She waits patiently. After what seems to be a long pause, the baby shapes her lips to mirror the mother's. She repeats her interpretation of the mother's full expression. Mother–infant waiting is a most rewarding interaction. In our clinical experience, oftentimes words are left unsaid, yet the intervention that is not made can be reflected in a surprising outcome. Something other than words is mimicked, something that is inherent to the person's inner world, representations that are otherwise lost in translation. Yet the translation of the analyst through interpretation can sometimes take away the important sense of being held without words. An important part of the EMDR protocol is the space it offers in between reflective breaks. Something is experienced in the presence of another, who has the patience to wait for an emotionally rich experience to emerge, beyond words.

Changes in *implicit relational knowledge*, a term coined by Stern and his colleagues (1998), and at times referred to as *procedural relational knowledge*, are relevant to our discussion of EMDR's understanding of how experiences, notably traumatic experiences, become embedded in our mind. Since patients develop implicit relational knowledge through embodied and often nonverbal experiences, these experiences can in turn change their perception and responses to stimuli by focusing on their current embodied experience. For example, the human scream is distinguished from normal speech in that it activates a fear response in the amygdala rather than just the auditory center in the brain (Arnal, Flinker, Kleinschmidt, Giraud, and Poeppel, 2015). Future research may venture to explore whether patients who find ways to notice and listen to the internal scream of their original traumatic experience may be able to tone down the soundtrack that runs parallel to all other activities with the help of newly witnessed embodied experience.

Both EMDR therapists and relational psychoanalysts rely on this understanding to help their patients alter the course of their reactions to situations that trigger neural reactions to a new relational situation. Research shows that changes in nonverbal implicit (procedural) relational knowledge are at the core of therapeutic change (Schore, 2003, 2011). Schore (2003) wrote, "Towards that end, affectively-focused interpretations are directed towards a deeper understanding of the patient's emotion-enhancing and emotion-distancing coping mechanisms, and at the conflicts and tensions between autoregulation (autonomy) and interactive regulation (interconnectedness)" (p. 146).

Unlike the notion advanced by traditional psychoanalysis, in which the early dynamic occurrences that took place shaped the patient's mind, relational analytic work emphasizes the search for the inner workings of the patient's self-regulation, and interactive regulation. Here we can see the connection to relational perspectives in which the here and now of the transference-countertransference matrix is triggered by the here and now of the patient's state of mind.

In EMDR, the search for coping strategies is explored to reveal the patient's representational, nonverbal, and relational knowledge through a rerun of familiar, anxiety-provoking scenarios that are then exchanged through modification to enhance the representations. Schore (2001, 2003, 2011) has argued that what therapeutic—and primarily psychoanalytic—engagement offers is a nonverbal relational knowledge that can curb the sense of lack of attachment or of a betrayed attachment process.

Clinical vignette: The internal landscape and its influence

June opens the session enlivened, unlike her disposition on the previous day. She says, "I avoided telling you what was bothering me yesterday. My friend Jake is on my mind again. We were friends for so many years. I am done with him. . . . I am so tired of his critical view of me. . . . But I can't get him out of my mind. He behaves as if he is superior to me. It used to be so different." I ask June if she always felt this way with Jake. "Absolutely not," she says. "We used to share so much. There was a sense of respect. This is gone." I wonder, "When did it stop?" June continues, "Just as I came back from Connecticut. Suddenly it all changed for the worst." "How did you separate from Jake?" I ask. "Oh, I didn't," June replies, waving her hand in dismissal, "I was overwhelmed with the job transfer and didn't say goodbye." In fact June disappeared for several years from Jake's life. When she returned, she was surprised to find a friend who was reluctant to play as if she had never left and had cut the ties. In June's mind, Jake was just like her father, who repeatedly pushed her and her love for him away.

In the past, we focused on June's sense of worthlessness, but today we recognized that June had incorporated her parents' reaction to her for being worthless, and similarly denied her importance in Jake's life, so that she dumped him as if there were nothing of importance between them. June never considered the possibility that her strategy of dealing with her sense of being rejected translated into her rejecting loved ones in her life, believing they didn't care and wouldn't miss her. When Jake behaved with anger toward her, she again felt rejected and attributed his behavior not to his disappointment in her abandonment of the relationship, but as a continuation of past rejection. Yes, it was painful, but it felt like home. Today, June sits with the sadness and the feeling that her inconsideration to herself translated into lack of consideration of her best friend's feelings for her. The self-regulation was June's lack of recognition of this and instead living as if there were no friendship. The interconnected regulation happened upon June's return when, as in the past, she searched for care, or at least respect, in a relationship that no longer felt secure for either partner.

EMDR and psychoanalytic work emphasize different aspects of the clinician's role in promoting the patient's well-being. EMDR capitalizes on the notion that the therapeutic environment can be both an emotion-enhancing and an emotion-inhibiting process. However, along with the encouragement of primarily nonverbal relational dynamics, there is a minimal emphasis on the transference as an important part of the therapeutic interaction. Stern and colleagues' (1998) idea of implicit relational knowledge is helpful here as a way to represent the integration of relational psychoanalysis with EMDR, rather than adhering to the goal of the unmodified EMDR protocol.

Attachment, in the form of witnessing the patient by the EMDR practitioner as the patient processes his or her trauma along the etched neural pathways, resembles a permission to consider different ways of being. At the level of the brain, it is the witnessing that is essential to enable early attachment to build affect regulation from the outside in. For example, in Rhesus Macaque monkeys, when a mother from a lower-ranking troupe recognizes a fight between other members of a higher-ranking troupe, and sees her infant become curious about the fight, she is unable to rescue her infant from trouble because of her lower social standing in the group (Suomi, 1994). Instead, she will distract the infant's attention from the fight by quickly picking a flower and getting her infant's attention, while maintaining a close and constant gaze with her offspring until the danger dissipates. Not only does she save the moment and the child, but she also turns the provision of safety into an attachment opportunity for her baby's relationships with others in the future, including her infant's own offspring when she becomes a mother in a few years.

Inhibition: Precondition to thinking

The brain's inhibitory prefrontal lobes are arguably part of our unique human tapestry. Their effect is to prevent action, both primitive and patterned, that is urged by our genetic and collective memory. The ability to think and the choice to do or not to do something makes us different from other closely related primates, although this idea is currently challenged by researchers of Rhesus Macaque monkeys (Ferrari, Paukner, Ionic, and Suomi, 2009). Whether this behavior is unique to humans or is shared with other close relatives in the animal world, the capability of inhibition is fostered by experience, both by parental modeling and parental verbal cues (Solms and Turnbull, 2002).

For example, when Libby was a little girl she loved climbing on the jungle gym. Her mother, who could not contain her own fear of her child's potential harm, looked up, stressed, and shouted repeatedly to Libby: "Get off! You will fall down!" Libby can vividly remember how a chilling fear expanded in her veins, along with anger at her mother's interruption of her pride at her capabilities and the thrill of seeing the world upside-down. That external warning translated over time to aborted beginnings in opening her world's desired oysters. Creative and capable, she often initiated new projects, while at the same time having a sense that imminent failure awaited her behind every corner. Libby's mother's prophecy operated in two different directions: in avoiding projects that could bring "too much pleasure," and in overriding her own inhibitory signals to act without regard to potential danger, as she knew her mother was overemphasizing the danger. She was there up high to know it was fun. In this example we can see the inhibitory mechanism embedded in the mother's reaction of certainty that turned Libby's trajectory of play into a disaster. Libby learned from her mother that what she has to take into consideration is her mother's cautionary tale, even when she is engrossed in the moment of pleasure. The registration of that information, supported by words, is mirrored through the mother's stress, conveyed in her facial expression and tone of voice, and is perceived through Libby's perception of her mother's affective response, no doubt based on many previous experiences between mother and daughter. Though Libby does not fall, from now on she runs scenarios of potential pitfalls that are accompanied by that tingling sensation in her body.

The human brain responds to such environmental influences, and is particularly malleable to change in the first two decades of life, though later experiences can intervene with these early learning experiences as well.

Such inhibitory thinking is akin to a dry run or imagined action, a step that allows us to make a choice to act or not to act, and by itself it is an action that replaces the urged motoric action (Solms and Turnbull, 2002). It allows for deliberation rather than impulsive action. The inhibition is a precondition to thinking as well as a tool of expression, while the combination of our inherited inhibitory mechanism and our learned inhibitory abilities is determined by early experiences.

Getting back to Libby, as she was walking home from class one day she saw a group of men approaching her on the sidewalk. She remembered noticing an alarm going off in her head, yet she was dismissing it, ridiculing herself for profiling the men as potential assailants. She did not cross the street to avoid contact despite the initial warning signals. She was mugged. Looking back, Libby realizes that she consistently aborts thought processes that can save her from further trauma. Her inner talk originates from her mother in the form of an internalized prohibition. This process then interferes with her own natural inhibition, which at times becomes compromised.

As a result of trauma, the thought processes that control motor action can be compromised (Solms and Turnbull, 2002). We can observe a reaction to a trigger in the environment or to internal memory in the form of a flashback without the ability to control the *re-action* of the original trigger. Heightened urges or lack of inhibitions are two simple examples of possible disruptions. Each person, of course, responds to their environmental pressures and internal wishes differently, creating a host of solutions, some of which are more adaptive than others. For example, Frankie responded to her current situation as if it was an ongoing experience of her past. Back then, when her parent was unresponsive to her needs, she felt that her actual person was being dropped. Now in her current relationships, while she is often considered sincerely and with care, with only the occasional misattunement in her environment, her reaction originates in the embodied sense of being completely dropped, as if then were now.

The development of our complex personality is shaped around the consequences of its constrictions throughout life. We learn the language of living within this limitation, and use it to create the widest range of opportunity.

Let's look at an everyday small *t* trauma that captures a moment in the bank of experiences that contributes to the development of the complex personality. Grant remembers being a toddler, lying in his bed at night, and feeling that his father is about to leave the room for the night. In a surge of willpower, he jumps out of bed, running toward the door. His father's strong hand stops him. Grant realizes that though his deep wish is to delay the frightening separation, he cannot fight his gentle but firm father, who explains that Grant must stay in his bed for the night. Grant recognizes that he has no choice but to accept the request. Though sometimes Grant rebels, cries, or tries to negotiate, this time he melts into his father's arms instead.

How real is an invisible phenomenon?

Another question that is relevant to our discussion of EMDR is this: How real is an invisible phenomenon? If we do not see it, how come it exists and has an effect on our actions? We do know that a feeling can lead to action. Science cannot ignore the influence of the immaterial on the material. Yet the real is not necessarily material. Much of the EMDR outcome research at its early stages was based on observations in which the material was seen to affect the immaterial. For example, an eye movement changed patients' reactions to their external and internal realities (Shapiro, 2001).

Solms and Turnbull (2002) have claimed that current brain research has yet to achieve a satisfactory explanation of the *self* or the *talking cure* (p. 273). However, there are some intriguing clues that hint at a direction for future research. Furthermore, brain researchers believe that as they approach an understanding of the inner world, they need to rely on psychoanalytic inquiry to move further in their search. And we, analysts, who attempt to comprehend our patients' minds, should strive not only to find a "cure," but also to grasp how our patients may be able to approach an understanding that is blocked due to brain activity related to small *t* traumas and big *T* traumas. This experience is closely related to the early development of our brain's prefrontal cortex and its inhibitory capacity. Champagne and Mashoodh (2009) reported finding that environmental conditions at critical developmental phases may change gene structure, and that these had an impact on attachment quality and behaviors not only in lab rats who suffered a lack of attachment due to neglect and abuse, but, in an almost Lamarkian fashion, changed genes throughout generations. Although Champagne and Mashoodh (2009) were reporting on their rat research, similar behavioral impacts have been observed in primate ethology research (Ferrari, Paukner, Ionic, and Suomi, 2009). These findings are important additions to our discussion of the lasting change on neural pathways that both EMDR and psychoanalysis may have after trauma. If indeed, as research suggests, neural pathways can be altered based on treatment that addresses trauma, perhaps intervention that activates the brain in a nontraumatic way, and in which attachment to others and with the self is established, can launch new neural pathways that will minimize the effect of trauma on a person's relationships.

Brain: The interconnection of sensory inputs, thinking, and action

So how does it all work? How does stress from internal or external sources activate a reaction? We know that the brain is an organ, and that it is connected to other organs in our body. It is also connected to the internal and external worlds and serves as a bridge and mediator between these worlds. The brain mediates between the internal demands of our body and the changing world around us. Conflicting internal and external demands can lead to confused reactions and doubt about the self.

Clinical vignette: Negotiating internal and external demands

Stephanie's father handed her a large bag of her favorite fruit taffy before her second-grade field trip that he chaperoned. All she could think of as she boarded the bus was how lucky she was to have enough to share with her classmates. As her friends approached her she felt a sense of abundance and warmth. Finally, she was able to share her riches with others, a rare occurrence in her childhood of limited means. After the first round of sharing, still in the green, in balance, her father scooped his hand around her ear and whispered: "Don't be a fool Steph. They will cheat you out of candy and will leave you empty-handed. They only care about the candy. They are not your friends. Once the candy is gone, they too will be gone." Stephanie, looking down at her still rather full bag of candy, felt betrayed by her father. He could not see the exchange as part of a larger social scheme of sharing. Her cheeks burning, Stephanie said with vehemence "That's not true." The fun of having enough to share left her. She did not know why her father betrayed her. Why did he give her so much, to share with none of her friends? Why couldn't he see that the very act of sharing was the fulfilling part for her? A lump in her throat, she held the bag in her hand, unable to give or take, her hand numb, as if it had became a foreign object that did not belong to her anymore. Though Stephanie knew how she felt about this event, from that moment on, she oscillated between her wish to give and hearing her father's warning, then ridiculing voice. Over time she wondered if she even knew which voice belonged to her. Which advice, her own, or her father's would keep her standing in this world?

LeDoux (2002) and others, including Damasio (1999), Solms and Turnbull (2002), and Edelman (1988, 1989), have elaborated on the relationship between stress and the emotional (physical and mental) responses to it. They have emphasized triggers that originate in the environment as well as triggers that originate in the mind and body of the person. To our discussion about "what happens" and how we experience it, I will discuss briefly the cycle of stress.

As LeDoux (2002) pointed out, "stress impairs explicit memory by altering the functioning of the hippocampus" (p. 223), a finding supported by Sapolsky (2004) and others (Kim and Yoon [1998], McEwen [2000], Pavlides, Nivon, and McEwen [2002], Shors and Dryver [1992]). The explanation is that under extreme stress the adrenal cortex in the brain releases the stress hormone cortisol into the bloodstream (LeDoux, 2002). LeDoux has further suggested that threatening stimuli activate the amygdala and that the cortisol it releases "travels to the brain and binds to receptors in the hippocampus," interfering with hippocampal activity and compromising the ability of the temporal lobe's memory system to form explicit memories (p. 223).

Edelman (1988) wrote about the importance of the processes of development to the genes, stating that "DNA and the findings of molecular biology are not alone 'the answer to life' – there is another side to biology, that of epigenesis" (p. 210). Edelman developed the concept of topobiology as a theoretical effort to explain how a single cell develops into a complex organism, and how cells read their environment and adjust in the development of the organism. Edelman's goal in part is to investigate and determine how cellular and molecular processes are at the base of our consciousness. It may be helpful to consider Edelman's (1988) theoretical ideas to help understand patients' psychic pain and its consequences.

It is possible that somehow, like the cells that learn in the embryo in utero, our conscious mind similarly responds to its environment at times when the stress is too great to contain, and adjusts, or often over-adjusts, with response to the environment, after being activated by hints of possible resemblance to the traumatic environment.

This argument is essential to our discussion, as we have to consider the meaning of that place-dependent development as a part of the way stress influences the human mind by affecting the gene, the cell, the ability to learn, and recovery from trauma (Bangasser and Shors, 2008; Champagne and Mashoodh, 2009).

Memory modalities

Memory cannot be identified only by the short- and long-term changes in synaptic efficacy that together provide its basis (Edelman, 1989). It is also not a replicative store that uses external information as it receives it, like a clean and simple carbon copy. Edelman (1989) has suggested that memory is the specific enhancement of a previously established ability to categorize. As he wrote,

> This ability is procedural, and it emerges from the continual dynamic changes in synaptic populations and global mappings that allowed a particular categorization to occur in the first place. Memory thus arises from alterations of synaptic efficacies in global mapping as a result of the facilitation of particular categorizations or of motor patterns. (pp. 109–110)

In an analysis of a visual cue in the environment, as for example in an advertisement, our brain is compelled to complete a story. We tend to associate a gold band on a person's finger as meaning that person is married, following a social convention that is universally accepted in western societies. Edelman's neuroscientific assertion directs us to the understanding that our memories are also established in context. So although the person in the advertisement may not be married at all, the depiction was categorized as an image of a married person, and when this image is recalled the image is enmeshed with the perceived knowledge of the categorization at the time of its recording. In essence, we are creating a story triggered by a sensual cue that melds with our existing implicit knowledge.

Damasio (1999) proposed that "wordless storytelling is natural" (p. 188). As he suggested, that may be the reason we ended up creating dramas, books, and motion pictures (p. 188). EMDR uses that idea, both implicitly, by inviting an image of a situation to be played out in the patient's mind, and explicitly, through following the protocol to seek several repetitions of a scenario with the patient's emotion, position, or cognition altered, based on a desired outcome to increase positive cognition, or what a relational analyst would consider to be an expansion of the mental possibilities to allow for the development of a more complete life narrative.

In a more recent contribution, Fosshage (2011) contemplated the question of how do we "know" what we know, and more important to our discussion, how do we change what we know? He has drawn on cognitive science and neuroscience to help us understand our thinking paradigm. He asked, how do we make the connection between the implicit nondeclarative learning and memory system and the explicit declarative domain? How is information encoded in each system and how does this format of encoding and formative learning affect the higher-order reflective conscious accessibility of implicit processing? The responses to these questions are important in order to delineate a theory of multiple pathways for therapeutic action.

Fosshage refers to the distinction in neuroscience between a core, primary consciousness (conscious awareness) and an extended and higher-order consciousness (complex reflective awareness). This *reflective consciousness*, as Fosshage (2011) termed it, is an important agent for change (pp. 56–57). To be more specific, attitudes learned explicitly can vary in their access to reflective awareness even though they are conscious, and therefore susceptible to perception as reality, precisely because they have little access to higher-order reflective awareness. He added that in a history of emotional traumatic learning, the frequency of repetition, the age of learning dissociation, and the current analytic intersubjective context determine accessibility to reflective awareness of both explicit and implicit learning (p. 57). He further suggested that the ability to maintain attachment and self-object ties is also relevant to the degree that both explicit reflective explorations can be done as well as new implicit and explicit relational experience obtained (p. 59). This is particularly important as relational psychoanalysis has shifted toward exploring *implicit* and *explicit relational knowing* (p. 57).

The convergence of the cognitive science concepts of implicit processing and implicit mental models with the neuroscience concept of neural memory networks is also relevant to our discussion of EMDR and its intersection with relational theory. Implicit memory patterns parallel psychoanalytic terms such as internal working models, principles of organization, pathogenic beliefs, mental representations, expectancies, and implicit relational knowing (Fosshage, 2011, p. 59). This conceptual convergence allows us to "explain that continuity and intractability of organizing patterns is related cognitively/affectively to their long-term or permanent implicit and explicit memory status, neurologically to the establishment of primary neural memory networks, and psychologically to their past and current adaptive value" (p. 59). With imagistic symbolic encoding at birth, and later the cognitive symbolic systems of toddlerhood on, the sensorial is followed by perceptions, mental images, and, later, verbal systems.[2]

Both systems are involved in thinking. This may be the place to remind the reader that although "imagistic thinking is more prevalent in emotionally based, right-brain functioning and verbal processing dominates analytic left-brain functioning . . . each cerebral hemisphere shows some capacity in the nondominant encoding format" (Fosshage, 2011, p. 62). Hence, "each hemisphere recognizes the other hemisphere's dominant form of processing more intricately connecting imagistic and verbal processing" (p. 63). As Fosshage mentions, Damasio (1999) believed that at the base of any thought process the image is primary, and indeed fundamental to all thinking, suggesting that the encoding and processing of the image are similar for the implicit and explicit systems (Fosshage, 2011, p. 63).

The Boston Change Process Study Group (2005, 2008) proposed that the implicit and explicit systems use a distinct form of encoding with parallel paths having little interconnection, and that change occurs in the relational field and is less language-based. Specifically, they argued that, primarily, *enactive representations* (a nonsymbolic format) are used throughout life by the implicit system (Fosshage, 2011, p. 63).

Clinical vignette: Increasing implicit and explicit systems connections

Keep in mind the following clinical vignette when reading further on the EMDR components and their potential efficacy. In this vignette, Kelly wants to play a little more in her life. She got a coloring book, but reports that she only looks at it, thinking of picking it up to color. She never does. She wants to do it in company. The next session she hauls in a bag with an intricately patterned coloring book. She puts it on her lap and goes on to retrieve a beautiful set of colored pencils.

The story, though, is more about Kelly's trouble with her new puppy. Today it is about the puppy pulling her in the park. I ask Kelly to tell me how she manages. In response, she demonstrates with a meek voice, saying "no," feeling a bit guilty for having the dog being stuck with her rather than with a playful buddy.

We use an EMDR BLS tapper device under her knees while she sits and colors in her book. In this session she feels freer than before to describe her feelings of the previous week. I realize she is not using her breath to speak up firmly. We talk about the ways in which she learned to doubt her power and how it is reflected in her voice. Doing a simple voice exercise, following her feelings, recognizing tension and its release, Kelly practices saying "no" to her dog, and other important persons in her life. It takes a while for the word to feel congruent with what she feels. She comes back the next week reporting improvement in being heard using her full voice. Toward the end of this session, Kelly bemoans the end of the hour and the dread of a long week before we meet again. She recently cut back her sessions for financial reasons, and though we talked about accommodations, her fear for the future won. I ask, "May I be a bit obnoxious?" wishing to state the obvious. "No!" she says. Her voice clear, not loud, but commanding.

Elements of EMDR and the brain

In this section,[3] let us now look at the elements that make up EMDR, and put them in the context of current research, both conceptual and empirical. It must first be noted that at this time we do not have a complete understanding of how the EMDR protocol affects the brain. Fortunately, we have clinical experience and empirical research showing its efficacy, so we can use it without fully understanding the mechanisms that achieve this change. Many of the elements of the EMDR protocol are used in other psychotherapy approaches and have thus been studied and researched in those contexts.

Activation of the information-processing system is one way to think about the effect of EMDR. "Target events remained unprocessed because the immediate biochemical responses to the trauma have left it isolated in a neurobiological stasis" (Shapiro, 2001, p. 338). By tracking a moving finger or attending to another dual-stimuli tool, "active information processing is initiated to attend to the present stimulus" (p. 338). The dual attention to the traumatic memory and to the stimulus invites the active information processing to link to and process the target event and the current stimulus, eventually configuring, physiologically, the information to a more adaptive resolution (p. 338).

In its simplest form, the EMDR protocol can be broken down into three key phases: (1) retrieving and reliving the traumatic memory, (2) stimulating the brain's memory storage mechanism, and (3) re-recording the memory in a "normal" form (Shapiro, 2001). We will look at the effect of EMDR on the brain via its procedural elements as separated into these three phases. The following subsections discuss these phases of EMDR, while highlighting segments of EMDR's utilization of therapeutic methods and brain processes that are particularly relevant to integrating EMDR with relational psychoanalysis.

Retrieving and reliving the traumatic memory

Almost all therapeutic approaches for working with trauma or PTSD involve retrieving and, to a degree, reliving the traumatic experience. In particular, desensitization therapy uses repeated prolonged exposure to the traumatic memory as its core element. Empirical research has shown that desensitization therapy has a positive impact on the reduction of PTSD symptoms. For example, Marks, Lovell, Noshirvani, Livanou, and Thrasher (1998) reported that the use of ten sessions of imaginal and in-vivo exposure, together with 112 prescribed hours of homework, resulted in the elimination of 75 of the PTSD diagnoses.

In contrast to most other approaches that emphasize prolonged exposure, EMDR employs short, interrupted exposures to disturbing material, which demonstrates to the patient through her own experience that palpable sensation can recede as well as intensify. This is the primary method used in behavioral treatment of trauma, because it allows a shifting between overwhelming anxiety to cognitive awareness of the physical sensation that accompanies fear. The idea that feelings and sensations can come yet also go instills self-awareness and a sense of self-efficacy. This process of short exposure interspersed with interactions, and with reassurance by the therapist providing a holding, safe space, may increase awareness of the safety of the clinical context and may foster counterconditioning.

Attention to physical sensation happens by focusing on the effect of traumatic imagery on the body for short periods (Shapiro, 2001). The patient is assisted in identifying and separating the sensory effect of the trauma from the cognitive affective interpretations of these sensations.

The patient can then see that they are more than the sum of their trauma-related anxieties. For example, the patient may say that they feel tightening of their shoulders when they are afraid. Shapiro (2001) suggested that this identification of physical sensation was effective due to the patient's recognition that their sensations were changeable. She suggested that this may give rise to counterconditioning similar to exposure therapy.

Cognitive reframing guides the patient in identifying "negative self-assessment stemming from the trauma," and helps the patient recognize the irrational basis of these ideas, in addition to seeing the trauma as the source of such ideation (p. 320). Restructuring and reframing those ideas by formulating positive cognition facilitates the therapeutic process and at times improves information processing through the process of trying on associations "with more adaptive information that contradicts the negative experience" (Shapiro, 2001, p. 321).

The (re)alignment of memory components helps attach the negative image and cognition to the physical sensation so the patient is able to access the skewed information. As Shapiro (2001) suggested, "This state-specific information is subsequently linked to emotionally corrective information through the positive cognition" (p. 321). This is "consistent with the BASK (behavior, affect, sensation, knowledge) levels" within a time-continuum model of dissociation as suggested by Braun (1988) (Shapiro, 2001, p. 321). The process of reconnection of the traumatic material helps the patient with recording the new understanding in narrative memory, as opposed to traumatic material that is assumed to have been stored in fragments in multiple locations (van der Kolk, 1994). Hence, Shapiro (2001) suggested that EMDR may facilitate the bringing together of traumatic fragments through the creation of connections among various bits of traumatic material, and in doing so "facilitate the storage of information in narrative (or explicit) memory" (p. 321).

Research (Ehlers, Mayou, and Bryant, 1998) has determined that negative reactions to intrusive symptoms increase the severity of the symptoms and potentially interfere with information processing. In between BLS segments, patients are encouraged to use free association to notice their thoughts and the sensations that arise in response to traumatic images. They are asked, "What do you get now?" (p. 321). This is an invitation to free associate, and typically new information will surface. Shapiro (2001) believed that "this sequential targeting may be a much more effective way to access the most relevant distressing material than the procedure (used in systematic desensitization or direct therapeutic exposure) of returning repeatedly to the initial traumatic image" (pp. 321–322). She added that free association ensures that the most important "aspects of the entire memory network are accessed and processed" (p. 322). "Let whatever happens, happen," and to "just notice the trauma" and related disturbance are two examples of instructions given to the patient (p. 322). They permit the patient to maintain a sense of safety and allow "the internal processes to function without interference" (p. 322). In addition, Shapiro (2001) has speculated that they may also interfere positively with the patient's "tendency to be afraid of the fear" (p. 322).

Stimulating the brain's memory storage mechanism

Shapiro (2001) wrote that in order to resolve a traumatic memory, activation of the dysfunctional memories is necessary, as this leads to the activation of a chain of events dissimilar to those activated in a normal recall of the traumatic material (p. 327). It is assumed that eye movements are shifting

> the state of the brain into one that facilitates the healthy reprocessing of these memories, allowing the brain to identify and strengthen new associations to the traumatic memories and eventually to weaken the hold of the familiar, stereotypical associations and emotions that had blocked the adaptive resolution of the traumatic memories. (Shapiro, 2001, p. 327)

There is some evidence that repetitive redirecting of attention via eye movement in EMDR-induced changes in regional brain activation and neuromodulation is similar to changes produced during REM sleep (Stickgold, 2002). A speculation made by Stickgold (2002) suggested that the effectiveness of EMDR was due to the patient's need to constantly shift her attention across the body's midline, as this stimulated a REM-like neurobiological mechanism that activated integration of the traumatic event into cortical semantic memory. Stickgold's (2002; Stickgold, Scott, Rittenhouse, and Hobson, 1999) theory received some support from Christman and Garvey (2000), as they found that alternating between left and right eye movement produced beneficial effects for episodic but not semantic retrieval memory tasks. It is possible that the BLS device or eye movement locate the patient in a place where she can experience the memory in a space slightly apart from the disturbing material, and in doing so can lead the patient into a state of *mindful experiencing* of the traumatic memory (Shapiro, 2001). A point worth making is that the best processing effects appear to be achieved when the client is not allowed to associate too intensely in response to the internal experience, and simultaneously is not allowed to become disrupted by external circumstances (Shapiro, 2001).

Shapiro (2001) posited that eye movements may also induce a relaxation response "by way of the reticular formation," which "causes muscular inhibition in the REM state," or in "other mechanisms that activate the parasympathetic nervous system" (pp. 333–334). The latter "would inhibit the sympathetic nervous system, which is associated with the 'fight-or-flight' fear responses" provoked by trauma (p. 334). The inhibitory effect was studied by Hedstrom (1991) and Stickgold (2002). In addition, Shapiro (2001, p. 334) cited a study by Wilson, Silver, Covi, and Foster (1996) which, through employing biofeedback equipment, supported the idea that eye movements seem to "cause a compelled relaxation response."

Although most EMDR-related research was done using the eye-movement method to dual-attention stimuli,[4] the assumption is made, based on clinical experience, that other dual-attention stimuli such as bilateral tapping or sound will produce similar physiological effects with good therapeutic results (Shapiro, 1991, 1994). Shapiro (2001) suggested that "these may contribute to EMDR's therapeutic effect by maintaining the client's simultaneous external awareness during a period of internal distress or by activating brain functions inherent in the movements or in the attention paid to two simultaneously present stimuli" (p. 323).

Re-recording the memory in a "normal" form

Shapiro (2001) has described the shift from dysfunctional to functional as taking place when, given a target, memory, affect, and feelings are identified, and are also accompanied by a negative cognition. "The information stored regarding this memory is encapsulated in a neural network highly constrained by the high level of dysfunctional affect" (p. 329).

This network contains "information with the most self-destructive affect and self-assessment," whereas another network is "associated with the most appropriate affect and assessment" of the self (pp. 329–330). It is assumed that different neural networks store the two distinct assessments of the self. "It is hypothesized that the highly negative valence of the target network . . . precludes its linking up with more adaptive information, which is stored in other networks with neural to positive valences" (Shapiro, 2001, p. 330).

The thinking is that when the processing system is catalyzed by EMDR, two critical events take place (2001, p. 330). The association between the target memory (negative) and the negative affects is weakened, and, at the same time,

> by shifting the brain state to be biased toward weaker associations, EMDR makes it possible for the brain to form and strengthen associations with affect networks that are progressively less negative and then more positive in their valences, and thus to incorporate the more adaptive information that is stored there. (Shapiro, 2001, p. 331)

For example, "when EMDR is used to target the dream image, a high level . . . of terror is evoked. As a sufficient amount of information is processed, the affect shifts" toward a more positive realm (Shapiro, 2001, p. 331). "The more positive valence allows the appropriate cognitive connections to be made by the linking of different neural networks" (p. 331). The movement from symbolic representation to cognitive reconstruction will shift with the changing affect. It is assumed that this shift allows for the removal of the disturbing image, so that the patient can then "perceive the present with no distortion" (p. 331).

Shapiro (2001) has reminded us that there is little doubt that trauma causes information processing to be blocked. "This blockage keeps the original incident in its anxiety-producing form" (p. 334). She cited the Pavlovian idea that "the essence of psychotherapeutic treatment is the restoration of a neurological balance" (p. 334).

Summary

From the research results presented in this chapter, we can conclude that thus far there is no conclusive evidence to show precisely what the specific mechanisms are that render EMDR effective. However, based on currently available brain research, we can both see directions for future research, and at the same time infer, or in some cases speculate, that EMDR seems to have an effect on the processing of memory, and especially on processing traumatic memories, that surpasses that achieved by other therapeutic methods. As such, it may be a useful tool to support psychodynamic work with patients whose symptoms seem resistant to treatment. In my experience in treating patients' relational trauma, the use of EMDR opens the door for relational psychoanalytic treatment that was blocked or limited prior to the use of EMDR. Even with many of the studies done to directly assess the effects of EMDR and its outcome, as well as those pursued indirectly through current neuroscience research, we still assume that our theoretical formulations of how EMDR works are speculative. However, I feel that the use of EMDR in treatment should be considered while studies are amassed, as clinical experience is showing us that important pathways are opened to rich relational analytic work that otherwise would be considered unattainable due to patients' high level of uncontrolled anxiety with exposure to in-depth clinical material. In the following chapters, examples of this important connection are explored.

Notes

The passage by Paul Celan in the epigraph is from his book *Glottal Stop: 101 Poems* (Middletown, CT: Wesleyan University Press, 2000).

1 A comprehensive review of the background and method of EMDR can be found in Chapter 1.
2 Fosshage (2011) has clarified that *imagistic symbolic encoding and processing* refers to thinking in images based on any of our sensory modalities, as well as motoric and visceral information, while the term *somatic memories* refers to memories that are primarily comprised of bodily sensations and experience (p. 62).
3 This section is based on the work and writing of Francine Shapiro, the inventor of EMDR who researched it and developed the original clinical EMDR method described in this book, which I use as a base to develop necessary modifications to be integrated with relational psychoanalysis. Much of the brain research and many of the outcome studies described in this section were originally compiled by Shapiro in her book *Eye Movement Desensitization and Reprocessing: Basic Principles, Protocols, and Procedures* (2001). In addition, I have found her later book, *EMDR as an Integrative Psychotherapy Approach: Experts of Diverse Orientations Explore the Paradigm Prism* (2002), to be helpful in delineating some of the rationale for integrating EMDR with other therapy methods. For a full appreciation of Francine Shapiro's opus, I would suggest reading these works.
4 Current EMDR literature prefers the term *bilateral stimuli*, which is the term used in this book.

References

Arnal, L. H., A. Flinker, A. Kleinschmidt, A. Giraud, and D. Poeppel. (2015). Human screams occupy a privileged niche in the communication soundscape. *Current Biology* 25: 1–6.

Bangasser, D. A., and T. J. Shors. (2008). The bed nucleus of the stria terminalis modulates learning after stress in masculinized but not cycling females. *Journal of Neuroscience* 28(25): 6383–6387.

Boston Change Process Study Group. (2005). The "something more" than interpretation revisited: Sloppiness and co-creativity in the psychoanalytic encounter. *Journal of the American Psychoanalytic Association* 53(3): 693–729.

Boston Change Process Study Group. (2008). Forms of relational meaning: Issues in the relations between the implicit and reflective-verbal domains. *Psychoanalytic Dialogues* 18: 125–148.

Braun, B. G. (1988). The BASK model of dissociation. *Dissociation* 1: 4–23.

Champagne, F., and R. Mashoodh. (2009). Genes in context: Gene-environment interplay and the origins of individual differences in behavior. *Current Directions in Psychological Science* 18(3): 127–131.

Christman, S. D., and K. Garvey. (2000). Episodic Versus Semantic Memory: Eye Movements and Cortical Activation. Paper presented at the 41st Annual Meeting of the Psychonomic Society, New Orleans, LA, November 16–19.

Cooper, S. H. (2014). The things we carry: Finding/creating the object and the analyst's self-reflective participation. *Psychoanalytic Dialogues* 24(6): 621–636.

Damasio, A. (1999). *The Feeling of What Happens: Body and Emotion in the Making of Consciousness*. Orlando, FL: Harcourt.

Edelman, G. (1988). *Topobiology: An Introduction to Molecular Embryology*. New York: Basic Books.

Edelman, G. (1989). *The Remembered Present: A Biological Theory of Consciousness*. New York: Basic Books.

Ehlers, A., R. A. Mayou, and B. Bryant. (1998). Psychological predictors of chronic post-raumatic stress disorder after motor vehicle accidents. *Journal of Abnormal Psychology* 107: 508–519.

Ferrari, P. F., A. Paukner, C. Ionic, and S. J. Suomi. (2009). Reciprocal face-to-face communication between Rhesus Macque mothers and their newborn infants. *Current Biology* 19: 1768–1772.

Fosshage, J. L. (2011). How do we "know" what we "know"? And change what we "know"? *Psychoanalytic Dialogues* 21: 55–74.

Hedstrom, J. (1991). A note on eye movements and relaxation. *Journal of Behavior Therapy and Experimental Psychiatry* 22: 37–38.

Kim, J. J., and K. S. Yoon. (1998). Stress: Metaplastic effects in the hippocampus. *Trends in Neuroscience* 21: 505–509.

LeDoux, J. (2002). *Synaptic Self: How Our Brains Become Who We Are*. New York: Penguin.

Marks, I. M., K. Lovell, H. Noshirvani, M. Livanou, and S. Thrasher. (1998). Treatment of posttraumatic stress disorder by exposure and/or cognitive restructuring: A controlled study. *Archives of General Psychiatry* 55: 317–325.

McEwen, B. (2000). Effects of adverse experiences for brain structure and function. *Biological Psychiatry* 48(8): 721–731.

Pavlides, C., L. L. Nivon, and B. McEwen. (2002). Effects of chronic stress on hippocampal long-term potentiation. *Hippocampus* 12(2): 245–257.

Sapolsky, R. (2004). *Why Zebras Don't Get Ulcers: The Acclaimed Guide to Stress, Stress-related Diseases, and Coping*. 3rd ed. New York: St. Martin's Griffin.

Schore, A. (2001). Effects of a secure attachment relationship on right brain development, affect regulation, and infant mental health. *Infant Mental Health Journal* 22(1–2): 7–66.

Schore, A. (2003). *Affect Regulation and the Repair of the Self*. New York: Norton.

Schore, A. (2011). The right brain implicit self lies at the core of psychoanalysis. *Psychoanalytic Dialogues* 21: 75–100.

Shapiro, F. (1991). Eye movement desensitization and reprocessing procedure: From EMD to EMDR: A new treatment model for anxiety and related traumata. *Behavior Therapist* 14: 133–135.

Shapiro, F. (1994). Alternative stimuli in the use of EMD(R). *Journal of Behavior Therapy and Experimental Psychiatry* 25: 89.

Shapiro, F. (2001). *Eye Movement Desensitization and Reprocessing: Basic Principles, Protocols, and Procedures*. 2nd ed. New York: Guilford.

Shapiro, F. (2002). *EMDR as an Integrative Psychotherapy Approach: Experts of Diverse Orientations Explore the Paradigm Prism*. Washington, DC: American Psychological Association.

Shors, T. J., and E. Dryver. (1992). Stress impedes exploration and the acquisition of spatial information in the eight-arm radial maze. *Psychobiology* 20: 247–253.

Solms, M., and O. Turnbull. (2002). *The Brain and the Inner World*. New York: Other Press.

Stern, D. N., N. Bruschweiler-Stern, A. Harrison, K. Lyons-Ruth, A. Morgan, J. Nahum, L. Sander, and E. Tronick. (1998). The process of therapeutic change involving implicit knowledge: Some implications of developmental observations for adult psychotherapy. *Infant Mental Health Journal* 19(3): 300–308.

Stickgold, R. (2002). EMDR: A putative neurobiological mechanism of action. *Journal of Clinical Psychology* 58: 61–75.

Stickgold, R., L. Scott, C. Rittenhouse, and J. Hobson. (1999). Sleep-induced changes in associative memory. *Journal of Cognitive Neuroscience* 11: 182–193.

Suomi, S. (1994). Risk, resilience, and gene X environment interactions in Rhesus monkeys. *Annals of the New York Academy of Sciences* 1094: 52–62.

van der Kolk, B. (1994). The body keeps the score: Memory and the evolving psychobiology of posttraumatic stress. *Harvard Review of Psychiatry* 1: 253–265.

Wilson, D., S. M. Silver, W. Covi, and S. Foster. (1996). Eye movement desensitization and reprocessing: Effectiveness and autonomic correlates. *Journal of Behavior Therapy and Experimental Psychiatry* 27: 219–229.

Chapter 3

The relational perspective within the psychoanalytic tradition

כמה זמן עוד נשאר איננה שאלה אלא דלת
— ישראל אלירז
How much time is left is not a question but a door
— Israel Eliraz

This chapter describes the evolution of the relational approach in the larger psychoanalytic context. I highlight its centrality as a stepping stone that invites an interdisciplinary approach, first theoretically and then in everyday clinical work. I delineate the influences of early theories of the mind and those that followed in order to highlight the roots of contemporary relational thinking and practices. The relevance of two-person versus one-person psychoanalysis is explored and described to provide some background, with the emphasis on subjectivity, transference, and countertransference, all from a relational perspective.

In pursuing understanding of how relational psychoanalysis and psychotherapy can be integratable with EMDR, I discuss the importance of each participant in the analytic dyad, as well as how the roots of the relational perspective are intimately based not only on knowledge and clinical experience per se, but also and importantly on the emotional experience of each analyst with each patient (Grossmark, 2012; Slochower, 1992, 1994). I then visit the concept that relational thinkers, with the idea of *minds in interaction*, and following various other ideas such as the intersubjective, object relations, and self perspectives, create an environment that shares certain ideas that are psychoanalytic, while yet differing from them both in their understanding of the human emotional experience and their approach to clinical engagement with enough variation to make this theory particularly permeable to ideas from various other disciplines (Aron and Lechich, 2012; Mitchell, 1999). My focus here is to introduce the general principles of a relational perspective as well as to present concepts that are particularly relevant to understanding the potential of its embedded integration with the practice of EMDR.[1]

Additionally, I elaborate here on the importance of understanding multiplicity, both as a normal human phenomenon and as a response to extreme stress, and I describe how relational psychoanalysts approach shifts in self-states, a point particularly relevant to the integrative practice of EMDR and relational therapy. Issues of traditional "must dos" and "do nots" will be explored, among other issues that are important to the relational discourse. Together, all these matters lead to the idea that the relational approach to psychotherapy is one that offers a perspective most amicable to its integrative use in a therapeutic context in conjunction with another modality such as EMDR.

Roots of the relational approach

Over the past several decades, many efforts were made to move psychoanalytic theories and practice toward more deeply illuminating the worlds of emotional experience, both as these evolved in development and in the psychoanalytic situation, and to the organization of emotional experience in a relational or an intersubjective context (Stolorow, 2012a, 2012b; Stolorow, Atwood, and Orange, 2002).

These efforts were made with the hope that they might alter the uncomfortable attempts to shoehorn patients into a relatively narrow developmental model and a therapy that originated in a theory of the mind into which patients were meant to fit and to which writers tried to adhere. In a plea for a renewal of humanism in psychoanalytic therapy, Stolorow (2012a) and others (Orange, Atwood, and Stolorow, 1997) have suggested that such a contemporary therapy is now characterized by the impact of existential philosophy, or what they described as *post-Cartesian psychoanalysis*, a psychoanalytic perspective they characterize as *phenomenological contextualism*. As Stolorow (2012a) explained the term that he and his colleagues (Orange et al., 1997) developed, it refers to the investigation and illumination of "organizations or worlds of emotional experience," and an understanding that such organizations of emotional experience take form both in human development and in the psychoanalytic situation (Stolorow, 2012a, p. 442).

Similarly, Stephen Mitchell, who is widely recognized as one of the relational tradition's contemporary originators, along with Jay Greenberg (Greenberg and Mitchell, 1983; Mitchell, 1999), offered a dialectical turn from classical intrapsychic theorists and de-emphasized the internal world and the intrapsychic structure. Greenberg and Mitchell (1983) presented the term *relational model* to the field of psychoanalysis as an alternative to classical drive theory, not as an addition to it (Mitchell, 1999). In his preface to the first volume of the *Relational Perspectives Book Series*, Mitchell (1999) resurrected Harry Stack Sullivan, Eric Fromm, and Clara Thompson's ideas and influence during the 1930s and '40s on contemporary psychoanalytic theory in the United States. He also mentioned Guntrip's popularization in the 1970s of Fairbairn[2] and Winnicott from the British object relations Middle Group. Both were more concerned with human relationships than with human drive, with Fairbairn (1952) proposing, for example, that the libido was more object-seeking than pleasure-seeking, a distinction that separated their views from Kleinian and Freudian ideas. In the late 1970s, Kohut's work on narcissism branched off from American ego psychology, and later broadened into self-psychology proper, which not only became a distinct school with a theoretical and clinical framework but also offered a general sensibility that influenced clinicians practicing various other methods. Along that same time period and in the early 1980s, feminism entered the psychoanalytic discourse with its emphasis on contextual gender development and the impact of linguistics on the mind, along with feminist activism (Mitchell, 1999). For Greenberg and Mitchell (1983), *relational* meant a way of working that bridged interpersonal and object relations theory. From the mid-1990s, the relational tradition emerged in American psychoanalysis with a distinctive set of concerns, concepts, approaches, and sensibilities.

Stolorow and colleagues, following Aristotle, distinguished between *Techne* and *Phronesis* in relation to analytic practice, where Techne is a method as well as the body of knowledge required for the production of things such as the traditional standardized rules of uniform psychoanalytic technique, as these are claimed by all patients and all analysts, all analytic couples and all relational situations (Stolorow, 2012b, p. 471; Orange et al., 1997, p. 21). They suggested that psychoanalysis should instead be grounded in Phronesis, or the practiced wisdom that is always oriented to the practitioner, to the uniqueness of the individual, and to his or her relational situation. For example, part of our psychoanalytic heritage has to do with clear distinctions of gender. However, each analytic pair, analyst and patient, creates an amalgam of gender reflections that it would be a mistake to discount.

A shift toward two-person psychology

The relational approach in psychoanalysis is unlike most approaches to psychoanalysis. Its origins, although stimulated by Freud's discoveries, are not directly rooted in his work. It began in the United States as an attempt to integrate American-originated interpersonal theory with British object relations theory. Adrienne Harris (2011) wrote that two-person psychology is "the most dramatic concept that inaugurated the relational turn" (p. 706). She stated that "minds emerge in the matrix of social relationship," and that the idea that mind is interpersonal "as well as individuated, has been central to the relational project" (pp. 706–707). Harris has reminded us that Emmanuel Ghent (1990, 2002), by bringing Winnicott's dynamic view of the transitional space and transitional object to the forefront of our attention, influenced the centrality of these ideas to the relational discourse. What is important to the discussion here is the understanding that relatedness is crucial to the formation of internal representations and to the establishment of distinctions between reality and fantasy.

The interpersonal approach benefited from the work of Sándor Ferenczi (1952, 1955), who was a member of Freud's original group and who experimented with original ideas and techniques that contributed to our understanding of what makes the therapeutic relationship helpful and how this occurs. For example, Ferenczi experimented with what we know as mutual analysis, in which the patient and the analyst explored each other's mind. This approach was controversial and risky, yet it opened our minds to the limitations of the one-person psychology in which the analyst is the all-knowing and abstinent presence in the consulting room, onto which a patient projects her fantasies and desires to reflect her unresolved unconscious infantile conflicts and desires in the transference. Ferenczi (1952, 1955) taught us to surrender, much as Ghent (1990) did, to the process rather than to hold back our countertransferential feelings and reactions as they are evoked through the analytic process.

Related to these changes in the process is the eradication of the idea that the analyst is or can be a blank screen that is capable of reflecting the patient's feelings without exposing elements of the person of the analyst (Arad, 2001). In contrast, an important aspect of two-person psychology assumes that there are two persons in the room who are in an irreducible relationship in which each member of the dyad contributes a whole range of feelings, actions, and contexts to the interactive work. It is assumed that this relationship provides not a cure, but more a grassroots platform through which a wider exploration of who the patient really is and potentially can become can take place, given an opportunity to slow down feelings and action in the transference and countertransference so they can flourish and then be understood. I find Donnel Stern's (2003) elaboration relevant here, as he has proposed that the analytic experience is often unformulated, more felt and experienced than understood and rationally verbalized, at least at first.

Prior to the current relational approach, there were others who developed an older tradition that attempted to look at ideas stemming from Sullivan's (1953) study of schizophrenic patients, which brought in the study of disturbed language and relationships, aspects essential to relational sensibilities (Aron and Lechich, 2012; Harris, 2011; Mitchell, 1999). Both the early interpersonal clinicians and scholars like Sullivan, Fromm, Fromm-Richmann, Thompson, and Horney, as well as those in the relational turn of psychoanalysis, are rooted in the study of psychology, sociology, anthropology, and philosophy, and are closely related to social constructionism in understanding the human mind in its relationships.

One of the basic elements of relational psychoanalytic thinking is its view that human motivation emerges from the need for relationality and striving to be in relationships with others, notably with caregivers at the dawn of life, which is then continued with others in the person's social network. This understanding, as opposed to the classic notion that having a relationship is more a function of utility and an outcome of intrapsychic drive, is a hallmark of relational thinking that leads to a belief that each personality is unique and was created in a relationship, and that therefore a relief of disturbances or anxiety in a patient's life can happen only in a relationship. In the analytic situation, the patient and the analyst examine the situation as it is recreated, indeed reconstructed, by both participants, given a portion of fantasy and reality elements. It is thus referred to as two-person psychology. It is a study in tandem.

While deemphasizing the role of the person of the therapist as an important participant in the EMDR therapy, an aspect of two-person psychology is inherent in the EMDR approach in which the work of both therapist and client feels collaborative without becoming authoritative, even when it is directive.

EMDR thus emphasizes the effect of actual relationships on the internal economy, themselves a result of relationships gone awry, and its process employs influences on the mind through the embodiment of the original experience, as in the case of trauma. EMDR also assesses and makes use of benign experiences committed to memory that contribute to resourcefulness and resiliency. These benign experiences can be expanded from a glimpse to a more prevalent presence with the combination of EMDR tapping into the somatic experience and relational psychoanalytic work.

Clinical vignette: Embodied trauma awakened and negotiated

Here is an everyday illustration of what happens when the body triggers a bottled-up memory that has had an influence on the mind and physical being. It is an example of a triggering that would not have come about without the (relational) intervention of another person.

Ronnie is a professional singer in training. Earlier today, her teacher asked her to hold both sides of her jaw to enable a more effective opening at the back of her throat as she struggled to open her mouth wide enough to allow certain sounds to emerge. As she began to sing with her fingers pressing against her jaws' gap, tears started flowing. Only when her teacher asked if she was in pain did Ronnie realize that she knew the feeling from her prehistory. A clear image came to mind of being a toddler strapped into her high chair. She could feel her grandmother's strong hold on her jaws, feeding her the last bit of applesauce, as she refused it. Ronnie felt a flush run through her body of the grandmother's frustration with her momentary refusal, and her own physical pain, muddled with shame over her beloved grandmother's treatment of her. This spontaneous trigger of physical body memory released the ancient feeling trapped in her, and—with her teacher's intervention—created a relational moment of reflection that made it possible to disarm the power of the flashback. No longer strapped in or bewildered, Ronnie no longer needed to clench her teeth lest an unsuspected intruder force herself on her.

The original traumatic event contained a broken trust caused by the grandmother overpowering the child. Ronnie was trapped in a situation in which the person who she could turn to in pain was now the person who inflicted pain. She needed to be seen not only for the limitation in her singing, but for the pain the seemingly benign correction invited. The teacher's awareness of the pain she inadvertently inflicted on Ronnie created a relational moment in which Ronnie's pain was acknowledged and remedied by the same person in real time. That was precisely what was missing from the original moment between Ronnie and her grandmother. In relational psychoanalysis, the ability to see one's influence on the other is an essential tool. EMDR can bring about the embodied experience of broken relational moments so that they can be dealt with within the relational matrix, including the transference and countertransference experience. At times, I find that out of an EMDR session a heightened resolution of the relational dynamic emerges and spills into the consulting room interaction between patient and therapist. Integrating EMDR with a relational sensibility enhances the effect of both. With Ronnie, during an EMDR session the image was again brought up to see if it carried any more emotional pain. Once the power of the image was at a low level, a BLS sequence was used to reinforce Ronnie's new feeling of relief, agency, and control over her wishes, and allowed her to project onto the future her choice to decide not only what comes into her mouth, but also what comes out of it. A note was made by relational scholars that although the idea of a two-person psychology is meant to emphasize the importance of each partner in the analytic work, it too may seem polarized and less fluid as there are other influences that enter the analytic room, such as others in the life of the patient or analyst as well as environmental influences (Altman, 2009). Others (Seligman, 2005; Stolorow, 1997, 2012a) prefer to emphasize the nonlinear dynamic system to highlight the multiple influences in each therapeutic relationship.

Recognizing less visible influences: The analytic third

Think of the analytic third as transcendence, a transcendence of such binary poles as analyst/patient, doer/done to, then and now, certainty and the revelation of blind spots. It is also an inevitable result of relationship that includes unwitting participation. It is found, if one can suspend disbelief, in the possibility of relational interactions that contain more than the eyes happen to see. It is a sea change as well in that, despite the wish to create a linear narrative, the complexity of a relationship, analytic or otherwise, defies the one-dimensional perspective of a moment in time or a life lived on a narrow path. As Harris (2011) notes, relating itself highlights the notion that a dyad is always more than twoness.

Harris (2011), following Jessica Benjamin's (1988, 1995, 1998) work on complementarity, has spoken about the process of both persons in the dyad forming attachments and negotiating separations. Thirdness may be seen as a new form of negotiating subjectivity and objectivity which, emerging from the state of twoness, may leave room for the participants to slip out of a symmetrical clinical encounter that can be experienced as sadomasochistic.

The concept of the third became popular across a variety of psychoanalytic schools. Scholar analysts such as Ogden, Benjamin, Green, and Lacan influenced writers by expanding the concept of the third (Aron and Lechich, 2012). Among the ways to think about the third are to imagine it to be the context in which we emerge from the dyadic interaction to something beyond the twoness that is the product of the dyadic interaction, as well as allowing for the creation of potential space for mindfulness and reflection. What is common among these attempts to name the process that creates the third is the understanding that each context in human interaction creates a potential for a new way of being that was not available prior to this particular meeting of embodied minds.

We may wonder whether the EMDR protocol in action facilitates the development of such a third. EMDR is instrumental to change. It maintains in its form a "something else," which is the holding space between two subjectivities, connected and mitigated at the same time. We can think of the EMDR tool as an observing, benevolent eye that allows for the relationship between different parts of the self (various negative cognition and positive cognition states in relation to an image) to interact, by creating the space in which each can thrive. It is a potential space for negotiating who the person feels themself to be authentically as all of his or her parts are experienced, contained, and explored. More recently, another approach to the reaching and release of embodied experiences is the linking of psyche and soma, as presented by Rappoport (2015), who describes a clinical case in which physical touch is used to create a *somatic third* that engages the explicit and implicit embodied states of both the patient and analyst, expanding and enriching the transference-countertransference matrix.

Arad (2002a, 2002b) and others (Harris, 2011; Stern, 2010) have written about the importance of witnessing the creation of a context that is then viable for the creation of a potential space in which the patient is witnessed with the full unfolding of the traumatic event in the presence of the analyst. Arad (2002a) also wrote that, at times, the patient's witnessing the analyst's advocacy of a disavowed part of the personality is crucial to the patient's willingness to embrace a piece of their past that is hard to digest. The two-person psychology, in which analyst and patient create an inner circle that can contain any aspect of the patient's personality, is a third in and of itself. This is a place in which EMDR, almost inadvertently, facilitates a similar function. Observing a patient in a process that encourages affective manifestation of the embodied, under-remembered links to trauma allows the patient a dream space in which the forbidden is allowed, at least once, while being witnessed, to experience a new path. And in such a moment, like the blossoming of a night-blooming cereus, comes a chance of seeing the world and being seen in a new light.

This particular quality of EMDR is already present in relational psychodynamic work, as the work often involves multiple thirds in the shape of subjective, more or less concrete influences in the minds of the participants. That space can be infused with a belief or vision of what the third might be, perhaps as an organizing principle through which most interactions are funneled. At other times the third may be sensed as a quality hovering around the participants, helping them to stay on task.

Although the third defies specification, as it is intricate and complex, I find patients wishing to name what it represents for them as they struggle with the ambiguity of the process. That temptation, however, may have the effect of conflating concepts into some known but flatter entity.

Clinical vignette: Discovering the third

The following vignette may elucidate some aspects of the concept of the analytic third.

A 50-year-old man who I see in analysis, who came to treatment in a crisis and who was severely depressed and suicidal, was for a period of a couple of months very quiet and tense in the session. He would lie down on the couch, close his eyes, and then, thrashing about, would make moaning, baby-like sounds. I was aware that when I would ask him about his actions or comment on what I saw in him, he would murmur angrily, or simply turn away from me, saying that I could not possibly understand his suffering. One day he came in distant and mildly antagonistic, as usual; he was in that familiar state of mind that seemed to shout at me, "I am here, but we have nothing in common, and there is no way that you or anybody will ever be able to pull me out of my trouble." I sat quietly, wondering about the purpose of this excruciating pain and the wall between us. I clearly felt helpless, and yet was aware of another feeling in me I had not previously noticed. I knew that I didn't need to worry about this man's trying to kill himself in session with me: I felt sure that he was in no physical danger as long as he stayed in the room with me. Needless to say, I thought I had better attend to my anxiety before it tainted my ability to work with this man.

As I ruminated about my realization regarding my need to make my own anxiety more conscious, and as I listened to the patient's continual moaning, I heard him mutter the word "babysitter." "Babysitter?" I said, to which he replied in a very matter-of-fact manner, "Yes. You are my babysitter. I come here and use the couch so you can watch me as I rest. I do not have this peace of mind elsewhere in my life. Here I feel safe, at least for a while." He proceeded to say that he was angry because he felt that by simply "resting" or being "baby-sat," he was not doing what he was supposed to do in analysis. He felt that he was failing by not following the rules of analysis, as he perceived them. We then discussed his sense of feeling sneaky whenever he wanted or needed something basic. As a child he experienced a great deal of loss; his only sibling died as a result of a violent crime, while he lost his father to cancer and his mother to mental illness. As a consequence, he never got the chance to relate candidly regarding his emotional needs—indeed, how could he allow himself the need to feel loved, when in a sense he had been abandoned by those who were supposedly designated with the responsibility of providing that love?! As an adult he found himself worrying that he might be found guilty by those from whom he "stole" love. In his mind, love had a cost, and someone had to pay the price, by feeling guilty and certainly unworthy.

What I realized was that where I had hoped that interpretation would help bring about an "ah ha!" experience that would help shift the indirect search for care and therefore reduce the level of guilt and persecutory feelings, the actual motivation for a shift happened to be an "um-hmm" context in which a need was met nonverbally and only later explored verbally. Without that better match, I believe, we would have stayed apart, searching for resolution out under the streetlight so to speak. That opening allowed both of us to reflect continuously on the patient's need for caring, and my anxious countertransferential tendency to rescue him. As we allowed for more of this to be in the open, the patient resumed his emotional and physical functioning in the world in a way I did not anticipate.

In this vignette, an analytic third was introduced inadvertently by the presence of embodied experience co-constructed by patient and psychoanalyst. As the relational matrix draws on various perspectives of the mind it allows the analytic dyad to venture into a transitional space necessary for unraveling a *protective swaddle*. Similarly, EMDR uses various theoretical and technical approaches to understand the traumatized mind and to develop and add clinical sensibilities to its therapeutic protocol, creating an alternative, less scathing embodied experience following the desensitization of the embodied traumatic experience. Mitchell (1988) concluded that current traditions of psychoanalytic thought were not isolated conceptual islands, but often integratable, and I feel that EMDR (Shapiro, 2001, 2002) is similarly integratable, most importantly with relational psychotherapy around the creation of a therapeutic third.

Mitchell (1988) wished to offer a third option to drive theory or theories of developmental arrest. I suggest that, as this is characteristic of the relational approach, it indeed offers a third option, but that this is not just a sequential third. Rather, it offers a third that is hovering as all options open to understanding, in a way similar to the concept of the *analytic third*, an entity that is palpable yet unseen. As such it offers the possibility of integration with other concepts and practices, like EMDR. Mitchell (1988) further suggested the relational-conflict model, as conflicts between desires, wishes, and fears do exist. However, as in developmental arrest models, it is relational configurations that are at the heart of conflict creation. Mitchell emphasized that it is a misconception to assume that all contemporary theories of the mind are rooted in drive theory. In addition, he claimed that much is lost by being wedded to a single theoretical model in lieu of integration efforts that can cross-fertilize our understanding of the human mind and therefore guide our approach in treatment.

Transference and countertransference in the relational tradition

In ways similar to those found in all other psychoanalytic persuasions, relational psychoanalysis shares a focus on the transference as a key element in the exploration of the patient's mind. However, relational psychoanalysis does not see transference as a mere projection of the patient's inner world onto the analyst who presents a neutral stance. According to the relational approach, the analyst's personality is relevant to the particular development and construction of the analytic situation. The transference and countertransference are an inseparable matrix in which one cannot exist without the other. This idea is grounded in the assumption that the person of the analyst cannot be hidden. It is conveyed in every word, tone of voice, cadence of speech, breathing pattern, mode of engagement, and indeed in interpretations, among other external and internal displays of personality (Grossmark, 2012; Arad, 2001).

It is therefore assumed that the patient will respond to who she feels the analyst to be in relation to herself, and the analyst will respond to the patient not objectively, but subjectively, meaning that the analyst will respond with his or her own complete being, given the context of his relational history and the myriad contexts that shape, motivate, and influence him. Indeed, Lewis Aron (1996) and Jessica Benjamin (1995) have seen the interpretation as the expression of the analyst's subjectivity. As Mitchell (1988) suggested, Fairbairn's (1952) object relations theory and American interpersonal psychoanalysis provided depth and greater consideration to the *other* as an actual interactional presence, as well as an intrapsychic internal presence that comprised the individual's psychic economy. He suggested that this was a broader interactive presence and context within which to understand self-organization and the individual's psychic economy (Mitchell, 1988).

Clinical work, like human development, is a fluid and dynamic process. We do observe repetition of behaviors that are persistent, seem to be immune to interpretation and rational thinking, and that are only modestly responsive to intervention. Aron and Lechich (2012) described how psychological change is nonlinear or discontinuous and noted that self-regulation leads to stable patterns or self-states of behavior. Strong perturbation is required to break that equilibrium. In relational psychoanalysis, this may mean paying close attention to the transference and countertransference. However, EMDR, with its interrupted sequence of going in and out of embodied experiences, paying special attention to the rising level of anxiety, and the locus of bodily reaction to disturbing images, can offer that interruption that did not exist in the original traumatic event. Though patients occasionally report feeling they were pried out of their process, noting that they wished to stay with it longer, they almost always feel empowered by their growing ability to start and stop their anxiety at will. We can think of this work not only as a strong perturbation, but also as a budding attempt at self-regulation with the help of the belief that they are not alone, and that the other in the room, the therapist, will help them by mitigating the need to be emotionally regulated.

Linking relational and systems theories, Seligman (2005) wrote that "Analytic therapists tolerate uncertainty, find meaning in apparently disordered communication, and embrace the unexpected twists and turns that emerge from intimate attention to the ordinary complexities of everyday life" (cited in Aron and Lechich, 2012, p. 215). Aron and Lechich further elaborate that "Co-creation emerges unexpectedly out of the chaos or sloppiness, as two minds interact to create something psychologically new" (p. 215).

According to Stolorow (1997), "change requires disorganization of the developing system"; it is only internal perturbation that can shake up old forms (p. 342). What is important is that the "patient–analyst dyad will be able to contain the painful and frightening affect states that accompany periods of destabilization," or what Stolorow (1997) called "the fear of structureless chaos" (p. 342). Stolorow (1997) and others (Slochower, 1996) have invoked the importance of a Winnicottian holding function and of Kohut's self-object concept, which allow the patient to suspend disbelief about change, with a somewhat reduced resistance against the change while a new systemic balance is in the making.

To illustrate, a patient may announce that they are taking time off for a vacation. On the surface that action may seem congruent with the time of year, and the importance of rest when the opportunity arises in connection with the work schedule and children being off school. However, if you add to the mix an announcement made hastily, while standing at the door as an afterthought, you may ask, "What system is in operation right now?" A relationalist may ask, "What just happened that may have triggered such an ever-so-slight variation on an otherwise reasonable comment?" Concurrently, there will be a crystallization of the person's dynamic system from *then* and *there*, in which care for the self is a threat to the parent, followed by retaliation against the patient as a child; another view might see the breaking of the anxious/enraged loyal tie to the analyst as an attempt to leave the analyst when the patient feels dropped by the analyst for any reason. Although EMDR therapy refrains from asking about the question of the therapist's contribution to the patient's response to the therapy, it does pay attention to dynamic shifts within the internal scenarios played out and evolved in the patient's process, and tends to ask questions about the shift and its current origins. The EMDR therapist will ask a question of clarification and may direct the patient to follow a certain element of the newly discovered dilemma.

For example, a patient who, after an agonizing delay, asks to change the appointment time can be confused by the analyst's accommodation. The whole gearing up for war that was necessary in other relationships to receive accommodation is now obsolete, and that difference by itself can raise a host of conflicting feelings. Helping the patient to develop curiosity, listening to their affective response to both receiving (the desired and unimaginable) and not receiving (the expected from their past), and reflection may help the patient to ask himself if this is the only way to respond to what they perceive the analyst to be doing. Perhaps the patient can begin to experiment in a relationship with a few less internally imposed conditions when offered an opportunity to change the seemingly permanent relational landscape. EMDR might use such a moment as an opportunity to embed the new experience in the patient's mind so that it can be recalled as a possible outcome in subsequent occasions. Over time, the patient may get accustomed to the possibility of more than one certain, and negative, outcome. Action in analysis represents a dynamic system that will reemerge throughout the work. Engagement with the dynamic system by speaking or acting in an unexpected way can put the dynamic system into imbalance, and thus bring into question the inevitability of its presumed trajectory.

As Aron and Lechich (2012) highlighted, repetition compulsion can be understood as the patient's *attractor state*. "Attractor state" is a term adopted from dynamic systems theory and refers to a pull toward a stable structure based on early experiences in development (Thelen and Smith, 1994). The idea is that out of chaotic, nonlinear elements, experiences are funneled into that structure. Minor disturbances to this form tend to not change the equilibrium of such a structure. To be able to escape this attractor state, significant perturbation is required. This can be in the form of an explicit interpretation or an implicit intimation (Aron and Lechich, 2012, p. 215). Although the behavior may appear repetitive, the analyst can detect minimal cues that are new or altered. As there is no well-defined process to follow, this can prove challenging. The analyst must be resourceful and allow themself to be thrown into trial-and-error situations without the certainty of knowing in order to co-create the opening for change (p. 215).

The repetition characteristic of this kind of highly stable system can only be disrupted by the most severe agitation. Stolorow (1997) suggested that psychopathology reoccurs not because of fixed intrapsychic mechanisms operating in an isolated mind, but "in consequence of relentlessly recurring, pathogenic patterns of early interaction—stable attractor states of the child-caregiver system—whose structure is cooperatively reassembled in all subsequent intersubjective systems, in which the individual participates" (p. 342). Thus, the patient–analyst interaction is understood to recreate that stable pattern in the transference, with the rigidly stable attractors functioning to increase the patient's fears of repetition of early experiences and again experiencing the threat of retraumatization.

For our purposes, it may be useful to mention the relevance of integrating EMDR into the mix. EMDR can be seen as a form of extreme perturbation in that, although the protocol is closely prescribed, the patient's process is nonlinear and thus has the capacity to move the patient from a rigidly stuck attractor state into newly formed alternate attractor states. Although the content is often anxiety provoking, it challenges the patient with unusually intense affect that the patient can learn to regulate in the holding environment. This is unlike what occurs in flashback states, for example, which the patient attempts to avoid because in the face of no effective intervention the threatening pattern persists.

The glimpse of newness in relation to remembering old and recurrent interaction during EMDR typically reduces the anxiety of delving into new anxiety-provoking moments in the analytic exploration process. The important point that Stolorow (1997) made was that change requires destabilization of the developing system. EMDR, which relies on a nonlinear process that is affective and in essence connects the body and the mind, offers a level of relatively secure, if not safe, destabilization of the original dynamic system. Unlike the chance moment of meeting that Seligman (2005) wrote about, EMDR intentionally creates such moments in which the patient encounters current attractor states, as well as mainly internal representational potential attractor states that may be captured by the analyst–patient pair.

The analyst's dystonic subjectivity tends to be disturbing and can even be derailing for the patient. The holding environment may help the patient experience a moment in which he or she feels protected from the object's separateness until it can be tolerated. At the beginning of the analytic work, EMDR can offer a way to not disrupt the need for being held, while allowing other more ego-syntonic states to be experienced that do not come directly from the analyst, but are being generated by the patient with the analyst *withnessing* (pun intended) through the EMDR journey.

Dissociation on a continuum

A sense of continuity of the self is an illusion that we maintain while interacting with others. It is taking place within a given interaction with a particular person, or in the presence of a particular environment that stimulates our mind, indeed our entire being, to respond in a manner that is congruent with this environment. This response is rooted in our relational history. We know when we feel comfortable, tense, or terrified. We know with whom we can risk that obscure catchphrase of "being ourselves" and with whom we are more careful. The *know* part is often unconscious. It is our body's response to triggers we are not necessarily aware of perceiving. When asked to portray how she felt and behaved the previous day, Jenny may not recall any of the details, and could only say "I was not myself." Not being one's self, not being privy to who they felt they were instead of themselves, is characteristic of people who have a feeling of being a separate, fragmented or whole, entity. This separate self-state has the quality of a different kind of awareness. Bodily and mental responses to events at the time of the original trauma are triggered repeatedly after the original self-state was created. They lack a reflecting capacity that can organize the self around a memory with its associated feelings and bodily sensations. With a meta-view of several dissociations or self-states, we can begin to understand the idea of multiplicity.

Dissociation is closely related to the handling of intense anxiety. More precisely, it is related to having so few emotional tools to handle the anxiety that one must endure it in recurrent interactions and their outcome. When a child experiences such overwhelming and reoccurring feelings in his interaction with a significant other, there is a wish to avoid or minimize the pain he experiences, which leads to his creating a self-state in which he experiences himself functioning in a protective mode. The fantasy that is developed is that the part that the child considers as *me* is different from the person who is experiencing that anxiety, and so he does not recognize the person who is feeling these unbearable feelings as part of the self. Sullivan (1953) dubbed this part of the self *not me*, a state that he believes helps the person feel wholesome by dismissing the horrified, hated, ashamed part of the self in interaction with a significant other as an unrecognized segment of the self. Sullivan also talked about a self-system in which one creates a worldview of oneself in interaction in order to avoid unbearable feelings at all cost, including that of forcing others to succumb to a particular way of interacting with him from his vantage point.

For the traumatized person in interaction, knowing how to manage a relationship by shifting to a whole new set of behaviors and expressions of emotion saves the person from decompensating emotionally. Think of a benign-enough situation in which a man encounters a uniformed armed representative at the border. This man likely feels some tension, based on past experience or fantasy of what could happen, and in an answer to a question may utter stiffly, "Yes, Sir," although the two have no superior/subordinate relationship. What drove that reaction can be of complex origin, but if the man responding formally learned in other relationships that it is safer for his physical and mental well-being to not mess with authority, his anxiety may lead him into a narrowing of his response to a style of military reply.

Philip Bromberg (1998), who wrote extensively on dissociative process, suggested that "an important function of dissociative processes is the management of relational space" (Harris, 2011, p. 713). Harris (2011) added:

> Paradoxically, dissociation is used in the service of certain kinds of false continuities and coherences. Intolerable and very shamed-based self-states must be kept split off in order for the individual to avoid dislocation from precious others. Again, in a paradoxical circumstance, dissociation may be the glue for attachment. (p. 713)

I find it helpful here to return to Sullivan's (1953) formulation of the source of self-states. For Sullivan, self-states arise from the "internalization of recurring patterns of interactions in our early significant relationships with others and are shaped by our distinctive patterns of avoiding or minimizing threats of anxiety activated by these relationships" (Aron and Lechich, 2012, p. 217).

If we now look at Jenny, mentioned earlier, who could feel that in an interaction she was "not herself" without being able to step back into that emotional space, we may get a sense of her dissociation into a particular self-state that is so congruent with its triggers and solutions that it feels as if it were another person that lived and operated on that particular occasion. It also feels familiar to Jenny, as it comes and goes often enough, but when it spirals out of one self-state into a new situation the quality of the experience feels as if it was not really she who experienced it. Perhaps she feels it happened to a distant relative. When she is in that state, it has the quality of a dream in which she is deeply engrossed, without the ability to leave the scene, and thus she feels compelled to just follow the path prescribed by past experiences. EMDR's added contribution is the ability to call upon such a self-state, in great emotional detail, when it shows up as a hint during the analytic session. It is particularly useful in moments when the patient feels but cannot verbally express a disturbing emotion. I find that when a patient has reverted to a nonverbal state, or a blocking of emotions, EMDR can engage the patient in a primary process that leads to consequent verbal engagement.

We can begin to wonder what might cause a person to relegate her rich emotional life to a caricature of a helpless child. Exploration may reveal that the patient experienced her mother as envious of her, or as someone who could not tolerate her child's youth, relationships to others, or success without launching a severe attack on her whole being. When the patient was very young, she learned to hide other relationships or even a wish for other relationships from her mother as those attacks were unbearable. Furthermore, revelation of such sentiments threatened the minute hope of having the mother recognize the patient as a worthy child. She learned to seem helpless in the presence of anybody in her life who needed to feel better than herself, or who needed any emotional support.

To use Sullivan's (1953) terms, her selective inattention helped her stay safe and keep a relationship that could not tolerate her in her own full colors. When she was out of that dissociated self-state, she wondered why she did not hold her own in a conversation, avoided talking about a recent promotion, and felt attacked for behaving helplessly. Now, although the patient is not a helpless child, when she is in a particular situation in which she feels compelled to dissociate, her helplessness feels real. Although it is a strategy of self-preservation, it is not a calculated tactic she chooses to apply. She is thrown into her-self state rather than choosing it.

On entering a traumatic event, the state of mind that existed prior to the creation of the *not me* state of mind is "dissociated, remaining completely unintegrated, unsymbolized, and unrecognized subjectively as a version of the self" (Aron and Lechich, 2012, p. 218). In addition Aron and Lechich invoke Sullivan's (1953) term *selective inattention* to describe the psychic processes that uphold dissociation of unaccepted elements of our being that otherwise might provoke unbearable anxiety if they entered into our awareness.

Bromberg (2006) suggested that, as a consequence of trauma, our reflexive mind is limited in order to preserve a seemingly coherent sense of self, while discordant self-states remain inaccessible to each other. The analyst's holding of the patient's various dissociated states allows the patient to increasingly retrieve the lost connection between these states. States of this kind are often comprised of intense shame that the analyst may inadvertently evoke. Recognizing the patient's self-state organization around shame and the analyst's reflection on his or her participation in such a relationally determined enactment, will help the patient increase her tolerance to her own psychologically threatening self-states created in earlier relationships. Bromberg emphasized the importance of being able to hold contrasting narratives simultaneously, which he called *standing in the spaces*. This idea refers to the therapist's ability to hold contradicting realities as they are expressed in different self-states with equal appreciation to each, which will foster similar acceptance in the patient toward her contradicting parts of the self.

Dynamically, dissociation flows between relational dyads, such as in analysis, as an effort to circumvent experiencing unbearable *not me* parts of the self and "landing" these unfavorable parts onto the analyst to hold and to be (see for example Stern, 2010). Similarly to Bromberg, Davies and Frawley (1994) suggested that allowing dissociated representations that originated in the trauma to thrive in therapy can serve as a pathway to integration of the dissociated parts into an accepted subjective experience. Although EMDR therapy does not encourage the flourishing and exploration of transference and countertransference enactments, it does encourage the patient to stay with the triggered self-state in the presence of the EMDR therapist, who provides the containment necessary in the early stages of the protocol. Later, as the process unfolds, the therapist invites potentiation of alternative self-states and pathways that are less self- or trauma-prescribed, along with an elaboration of bridge-building between self-states thus far kept dissociated.

Abridging multiplicity

To help illuminate the concept of multiplicity, consider observing any person in interaction with others in different contexts in everyday situations. The person observed may experience themselves to be a continuous self, having a sense of "me-ness" when speaking to their grandmother, their boss, or their child's high-school principal, while an observer of such interactions can detect significant variation in language, affect, body position, pitch and tone of voice, and a general sense of who the person feels themself to be in relation to the person they interact with at any given moment. Thus, the interactional context defines the sense of the self and its consequent articulation, while the person maintains the illusion of continual selfhood. In therapeutic situations, this observation can become more acute and articulated through actual interactions, indeed through the transference and countertransference exchange, in which each partner of the clinical dyad responds to the other with a host of changed displays of the self with its various components. These distinctive self-states can be organized, according to Davies (1996) "around a whole, part, or imaginary other" (Aron and Lechich, 2012, p. 217). Relational theory views the self as shifting between multiple self-states rather than being a unitary entity. Aron and Lechich (2012) write that the illusion of a cohesive self arises from our "fluid ability to maintain 'residence' in one self-state while maintaining awareness of others" (p. 217).

Bringing the patient to experience a particular self-state, while feeling its affective, bodily, developmental, and cognitive components, and "meeting" that person where she is relationally at that moment is a goal of both relational analysis and EMDR. Pertaining to EMDR, Davies's (1996) idea, that "self-states emerge around the internalization of the primary organizing relationships in our lives" is relevant (Aron and Lechich, 2012, p. 217).

Consequently, relational writers emphasize the centrality of the analyst's readiness to work with multiple self-states prompted by the analytic action and its inevitable transference and countertransference matrix (see, for example, Bromberg, 1998, and Davies, 1996). EMDR's formulation, save for the therapist and client transference-countertransference aspects, pays much attention to different internal scenarios that include developmental cognitive age, embodied experience, affective state, and perception of the self in relation to others, and, in particular, to traumatic scenarios that are activated in the here and now of the processing of disturbing images. Although the transferential relationship is not explored directly, within the processing of the disturbing image the EMDR therapist observes multiple self-states as they emerge. She helps the client to desensitize and reprocess the associated bodily, cognitive, affective, and self-representational aspects of given self-states, and to interweave the thus far disparate self-state with other multiple self-states so that over time these become part of the patient's recognizable tapestry.

We can think of therapy as a form of standing in the spaces between self-states. EMDR can be seen as another way to bridge self-states, especially those that are difficult to access otherwise. If we take gender as an example of this fluidity we can see that there are components that are biologically determined, yet much of what defines gender is comprised of intrapsychic representation, and has interpersonal and culturally determined aspects. Assisting patients to recognize various genderized self-states can help them become more comfortable with their gender fluidity.

Social constructionism, psychoanalytic feminism and queer theory's influence on relational thinking and practice

Relational thinking came to recognize the effect of cultural formation on the individual psyche (Harris, 2011). Feminist theory and feminist action challenged the traditional definition of the idea of who women are and who they should be as women, men, and the spectrum on which gender resides between these two dichotomies. Culturally defined roles, self-representations, and gendered interactions invited a critique of what could be regarded as an outsourced definition of self and the meaning of who a person might be to themselves and to others. Harris mentioned interpersonalist influences from Fromm (1941, 1947) and Levenson (2006), as well as Foucault (1961, 1976) from the field of critical theory, ideology critique, and political activism, all of which drew our attention to the ways in which cultural constructs impact the psyche. She also pointed to the importance of Foucault (1961, 1976) and Althusser (1970) to the thinking of those working in the area of gender and sexuality, as well as to the work of Zizek (1989) and Levinas (1974) in these realms, particularly on the attention paid to our own analytic tools that are not void of these cultural constructs and influences.

These psychological, political, and social aspects, and an analysis of how they reconstruct individual minds both consciously and unconsciously, are clearly present in the clinical work. Muriel Dimen's (2003) work on sexuality in its private and public dimensions is relevant here. She stresses the intersection between "disgust, excitement, and excess," which combine with the greed and power regulations that manage and produce sexuality (Harris, 2011, p. 709). As they explore in their relational writings on gender and sexuality, Dimen and Virginia Goldner (2002) recognize the points where relational theory and psychoanalytic feminism intersect.

Harris notes that it took a great deal of input from what was broadly described as psychoanalytic feminism, beyond relational understanding, "from a more Freudian and object-relational approach, and from Dimen, Goldner, Harris, Corbett, and others to alter the basic understandings in that political perspective" of feminism (p. 710). Specifically, Ken Corbett's work (1993, 1999, 2009) centered on the relational tradition and queer theory.[3] With the convergence of social critique and psychoanalysis, more complex ideas about what we experience in our offices with patients could now develop, through which attention to gender roles and their fluidity and gender power dynamics, including women's anxieties regarding aggression in sexuality, marked a shift away from focusing on traditional gender-role adaptation. Harris (2011) suggested that "queering psychoanalysis might be one way to describe the current projects in regard to gender, race, and class" as they include many relational ideas (p. 711). When describing social construction, Harris suggested that the social changes of the 1960s opened the door for relationalists working in the areas of sexuality, gender, and the ways family and other social power structures defined the individual, to explore these topics without the repression and even silencing that existed before.

In clinical terms, questions relevant to socially and culturally determined roles changed and expanded clinicians' ability to examine psychological tendencies and behavior not only as reflections of what was acceptable within the normal range, but also to help the patient recognize his or her acceptance of social norms and pressure, in part in adopting a view of his or her wishes and desires as being "sick" wishes, but also raising the question of "Why not?" when an off-gender wish was revealed. At times, the simplest wish can bring about lifelong emotional paralysis of some important aspects of the self in relation.

One patient, who was confused by a parent's overt sexuality along with an insistence on inhibiting any expression of sexuality in the developing child, felt in the throes of extreme anxiety about his attraction to both male and female objects of desire. His body, being short and stocky, became the focus of his anxiety, thanks to the help of cultural models, and led to his developing a fear of social interaction, as he imagined that others would associate him with the behavior of the parent of whom he was so ashamed and who he had learned to see as mirrored in himself. Feminist and queer critique opened the possibility of helping the patient explore a range of representations in the self and their context and relationally based fluidity. The following illustration gives a flavor of the complexity of gender and its possible shifting self-states.

Clinical vignette: The gender-fluid self

Brook is a woman in her thirties who believes she is a male in certain aspects of her psychological life. Her appearance is stereotypically feminine, yet she feels that with her male partner of seven years she is always the man. It is not just that Brook takes initiative, but she also feels as if she is the one penetrating, demanding, and conquering her partner's body, indeed his soul. Given the fluidity of gender (Harris, 2005, 2011), one can understand that psychologically, Brook shifts among traits that can be shared by any and all gender states. However, for Brook, having stereotypical male traits present in her relationship is quite disturbing. It is not just a trait or a behavior; it is her entire being that feels like a man. Since she can never trigger "a woman" during intimate interaction, she considers herself "filthy," but not confused. The trigger for such self-defamation is that in her mind she is not just a man, but a homosexual man, who is performing an act that is forbidden, a homosexual act.

Now, while the roots of preferences and self-loathing are complex and analyzable, this illustration is brought in here to highlight the depth of conviction felt while in a particular gendered self-state. In other parts of her life, Brook is a person who sees herself as a woman, at times interested in men and at other times in women. These latter states are psychologically perplexing for her. Being a woman with a sensual/sexual interest in other women brings about the horror of the homosexual sin. And as a woman, interest in men brings about the anxiety that she is unworthy of male attention because of her dark secrets or other self-states she recognizes, which in her view render her less than a full woman. You can see the shadows of shame glistening in the mirror of her self-states, adding to a sense of cohesion as well as to the lack of it. Relevant here is the formulation regarding body excitements and anxieties between mother and daughter (Elise, 2002; Harris, 2002). For example, the mother's arousal gazing at the baby daughter's body and the reciprocal baby daughter's gaze may be a sentiment that needs to be disavowed as it contains a "residue of shame and impossible, forbidden desires" (Harris, 2002, p. 283).

Can we ever list all the parts that might be in play at any given moment? Who is speaking from the patient's heart? Who is coming through the patient's mouth? To whom is he or she speaking? Can we live with the ever-shifting yet also definite parts of ourselves? Can we maintain our coherent yet illusionary mental skin as we hop between stances, often not knowing where we really are? Can we ever know who is in the field currently trading the ball? To be all, and none at all, the person of the patient and the person of the analyst need to be not fragmented but multiplied. Arad (2001) talked about the impact of self-states on the analyst during pregnancy being gendered by both the self and the patient.

This fluidity of gender—or any aspect of the personality, or subjectivities—could be expanding psychological plasticity when anxiety about its presence subsides. What the relational perspective helps us to see is that multiplicity is both a normal and a pathological phenomenon (Bromberg, 1998). It helps us analyze with our patients the intricacies of their lives in order to understand how, in certain ways, their experience came to be, and what invites them to stay in place as well as to identify what contexts trigger particular self-states. What EMDR can help do relationally is to assist the patient in bringing about a more isolated state of mind during a simulation of a dreaded situation in order to get familiar with it with impunity, befriending the hated in one's self. A further relational exploration is then important to integrate this state, not as a watered-down version of the self but more as a part of the ebb and flow of the self in interaction with others, internal or external, through representations of earlier object relations.

Enactment: Sharing the dissociated part of the self

It may be useful to keep in mind EMDR's specific understanding in relation to enactment. Part of the virtue of EMDR is that it helps the patient to bring himself to a relatively contained place. In this space, he can recall the troubling target event and reenact the emotionally embodied experience. Over several BLS iterations, the EMDR therapist helps the patient to reprocess and reconstruct the original image into a more positive and believable scenario, with its newly acquired associated thoughts and feelings, to allow for new neural pathways to develop. In turn, this will invite the patient to notice a trigger in his environment that in the past would set off an entire vortex of anxiety-based enactment, and instead allow him to abort the downward spiral path by having a plausible alternate path to follow in metabolizing the current experience.

Historically, *enactment*, and its linguistic and etiological cousins, acting in and acting out, was considered an active or passive action taken by the patient to bring about a primarily unconscious interruption in the analytic process, in an attempt to evoke a familiar dynamic in the analytic dyad (Aron and Lechich, 2012). This form of enactment was considered an outcome of the repetition compulsion stemming from unresolved conflicts and defenses against remembering. Over the years we have come to understand the concept of enactment quite differently. The idea that the language of speech and the language of action are expressions of each other was observed by Levenson (1983), as discussed by Aron and Lechich (2012).

In addition, the idea that there is only one person who acts in the analytic work is considered inadequate, at best, by relationalists (Arad, 2001; Aron, 1996; Benjamin, 2004; Cooper, 1998, 2000; Davies, 1998; Elise, 2007; Hoffman, 1996; Mitchell, 1988). Any interaction between patient and analyst contains a spoken or active language for both parties. When an analyst asks, comments, or responds, she is enacting or partaking in an "op-ed" that is interpreted by the patient, who, in turn, enacts based on her perception of what the analyst said or how she acted, and, more importantly, on what the analyst meant with her words or actions. It is a cyclical process that cannot easily be relegated only to the person who began it and the person who responded, as the ripple effect of the patient's and the analyst's representational history is added to the ramifications of the moment. Often new information that is presented in a session holds an analytic memory, which is what is remembered of the analytic action from the moment, but also perhaps from past sessions, last week or last month, and the present enactment is a reference to a previous analytic enactment, remembered or not.

It is useful to distinguish between body memory and cognitive memory for the purpose of explaining what may trigger an enactment. The body memory is acted out rather than cognitively remembered. Although recognition of acting out was considered a useful diagnostic tool, it was more generally considered a symptom of resistance to analysis. The acting out was seen as a compelling distraction on the part of the disavowed past intrapsychic conflict, brought into an action in the present. Stolorow (2012a), in a clinical vignette, described a case he supervised in which the patient presented two distinctive aspects when triggered by memories of past abuse or current life difficulties. These were accompanied by distinct bodily reactions. He suggested that engagement with the part that he suspected carried shame, rather than stressing the bodily manifestation of the traumatic reaction, opened the way to transference analysis, which in turn reduced the physical symptoms and allowed the patient to engage with the trauma (Stolorow, 2012a). Aron (1998) wrote about the role of the body in psychoanalysis, and the self-reflexive mind and its importance for the patient's capacity to experience, observe, and reflect on the self as both object and subject. Aron's (1998) effort was directed toward reintegrating the body into the understanding of self-reflection, whereas in the past the separation had connoted a cognitive process where the self was viewed as if from the outside. In EMDR, both the process and the body's response are integral to the protocol. One is shifting attention to the body's response as a thought or a feeling is generated, and, as in Stolorow's (2012a) clinical vignette, the attention to the body is part and parcel of the observation and opening for self-reflection. Developing mindfulness, first in enactment and then in real life, is an integral element of relational analysis as well. With the benefit that both approaches bring to the function of embodied experiences, integrating them seems to increase their efficacy.

Enactment is also the way in which an analyst may empathically respond to the patient. Something in the patient invites the analyst's affective response to the patient's nonverbal and often unconscious gestures that are typically disassociated and disavowed elements of the patient's personality that cannot be symbolized and reflected upon. These dissociated parts of the self are communicated to the analyst to experience subjectively and play out (Aron and Lechich, 2012; Bromberg, 2006; Stern, 2010). Keeping a vignette in mind may help elucidate this concept.

Clinical vignette: Mutual writing of the disavowed

It was at the end of a session when Margot stood up and enveloped herself in her coat; she looked at me and said, "Tough love." I thought what she meant was that something about how we constructed this session left her bereft of connection she yearned for, and I replied, rather spontaneously, "Pretend tough love." What I thought I meant to convey was that the tough part was for the purpose of exploration, not distancing. Seeing the expression on Margot's face told me that what I conveyed instead was "pretend love"—tough or otherwise. How could a relationalist begin to deconstruct this bundle of *oops*? The spoken communication, "tough love," perhaps held the patient's disavowed wish for love and fear of rejection by the analyst, me. The feeling evoked in me was one of a harsh parent who thought she was working on behalf of the patient but had to see that she failed her instead, by representing the original distancing parent.

In the exploration of this enactment, we can see value not only in realizing what had happened in the interaction, but also feel its mutative power in the experience itself, in which present events may appear identical to earlier events with important others. Yet the interpersonal engagement in and around the current event, the enactment, is generative, thus rendering it different from the original event (see Hoffman, 1998; Mitchell, 1988).

In thinking through this example of enactment in our session, Margot felt a lack of love that in her mind resembled her childhood interactions with her mother. She secretly yearned for a show of care that never presented itself. It was certainly "tough." Here the feeling was similar, by my being too analytic for example, and thus her cognition could not allow for "no love" to be associated with me, at least verbally, and instead it came to be "tough love." At least the word "love" was allowed to enter the discourse, which was very risky for Margot. To assume that anybody felt love toward her was a wild leap of faith. What was dissociated was two-fold. Her experience of failed love with her mother in childhood was always present and projected. But there was also love in the analytic relationship that she could experience now and constantly doubt, both her own and mine. In this moment of meeting, Margot noted to herself and to me, verbally for the first time, her wish for my care, and the deep fear of the lack of that possibility. Even when the moment was *real*, it was tough to believe in it. It was accepting and denying her current experience with me, based on her early interpersonal experiences.

In this enactment, I was pulled into action by Margot's words "tough love." In them was a statement that I, like her mother and others, treated her callously. While for me doggedly going after her anxiety was an expression of my care and wish to explore with her these dark places, for Margot I was a careless handler. The gap in our perception of what happened suddenly turned into a rift valley. She needed me to experience the loss she often felt in interaction, when what was dealt was a faded shadow of what she yearned for. I was pulled to participate in replicating an earlier experience in which she did not exist by re-creating a sense of being objectified for some extraneous good—the analytic process in this case—and what she could do to help the family in childhood, but never could she and her need for love be the center of attention as an object, or indeed of subjectivity (Benjamin, 1998). Here I was pulled to objectify her by exploration. Yet this mishap, because of Margot's revolt, helped us see how brave she was in saying what she wanted and needed to say, along with my own experiencing the horror of dropping her, despite my best efforts. Together this created a new, unfamiliar experience in which we were both able to listen to her better. We developed a set of clues she would leave—some were bodily expressions, some were verbal—to help both of us be better attuned to that fine line between being held and dropped.

Enactment is bound to happen in any relationship, and the analytic relationship is no different. It is mutually constructed, and can therefore be understood in tandem. Since it is first and foremost an embodied experience, it is accessible to EMDR's resurrection as a bridge to relational exploration. EMDR can be considered a form of restorative enactment, in which, in enacting internal representations, the patient is brought to consider various options to viewing herself and the dynamic of the enacted in order to increase mentalization and reflection (see Stolorow's (2012a, 2012b) writing on the somatic linguistic connection in the renewal of humanism in psychoanalytic therapy). In the case of the enactment between Margot and myself, we used EMDR in the following sessions to find Margot's disavowed wish for care that resided in her body and mind, while the canvas of rejection was primed. In addition, we used EMDR to unpack the enactment to see a part of Margot that could begin to consider that even a benign analyst could participate in an interaction that was perceived by her as malignant.

Recognizing bodily expression of emotional trauma and attending to the physical expression of shame is crucial (Stolorow, 2012a, p. 443). Furthermore, it has been suggested that without an enactment certain dyads can only go so far. In Abby Stein's (2011) post on "Faux Endings" from the IARPP Colloquium, she quoted Moreno (1987, p. 54), a proponent of psychodrama, as suggesting that what is often lacking for patients is the "binder" between analytic thought and action in the moment. Stein (2011) added that she believed that a more formalized kind of acting has provided such a binder in this and in other cases. She too suggested that without enactment a certain dyad may only go so far.

Summary

My intention, in presenting these concepts in this chapter is to help you, as you read forward, to keep in mind the embodied experience, the enactment, the capacity to dissociate, and also to understand the patient's need to lodge disavowed parts in the analyst's countertransference as manifested in her reaction to the patient, the enactment as it unfolds in any particular analytic pair, and in recognizing self-states not only in the patient but also in the self.

In this chapter we see that relational thinkers increasingly emphasize the importance of embodied phenomena as part of the development of a self-reflexive capacity that appreciates both objective and subjective experience in psychoanalysis (see for example Atlas, 2013; Atlas-Koch and Kuchuck, 2012). This growing interest in the nonverbal that is played out in the transference and countertransference lends itself to the possibility of integration between relational psychoanalysis and EMDR, as EMDR pays attention to the body's response to emotional triggers in a process that also supports observation and self-reflection. Enactment and its understanding in analysis, and as consequently reflected upon in real life, is an integral element of relational analysis and, albeit more implicitly, through what I term *restorative enactment*, in EMDR. Both approaches attempt to expand the function of embodied experiences and their influence on the mind. In the clinical chapters in Part II of this book, I hope to demonstrate that integrating the two approaches contributes to the efficacy of the treatment.

Notes

The epigraph is from an untitled poem by Israel Eliraz, in *How Much Time Is Left Is Not a Question but a Door* (Ben-Shemen, Israel: Modan-Helicon, 2013), 18. [Hebrew]

1 Beyond its outcome studies and prescribed protocol, EMDR allows for the particular and the unique in each exploration, although it deemphasizes the role of the practitioner as an involved entity. Of course, despite its best efforts, dyads do matter in the context of what Grossmark (2012) terms the *unobtrusive relational analyst*. The difference between thinking about a relationship and being in a relationship is particularly important. A patient who tries to understand his difficulties will benefit more from living in the experience of a relationship than by attempting to intellectually understand his situation (Grossmark, 2012).

2 Fairbairn served under Field Marshall Allenby during the Palestinian Campaign of 1915–1918. As Lazar (2012) writes, it is conceivable that these years with an eccentric commander who was brazen and extraordinarily creative gave Fairbairn the courage to not only serve in an unusual military unit where the relationship with the leader was more meaningful than military rules, but also allowed him to gain the necessary courage to present new and innovative ideas during his psychiatric/psychoanalytic career, despite considerable pressure to adhere to classic theory.

3 Queer theory is a field of post-structuralist critical theory that emerged in the early 1990s out of the fields of queer studies and women's studies. Queer theory includes both queer readings of texts and the theorization of "queerness" itself. Queer theory builds upon both feminist challenges to the idea that gender is part of the essential self, and upon gay/lesbian studies' close examination of the socially constructed nature of sexual acts and identities. Whereas gay/lesbian studies focused their inquiries into natural and unnatural behavior with respect to homosexual behavior, queer theory expands its focus to encompass any kind of sexual activity or identity that falls into normative and deviant categories.

Queer focuses on "mismatches" between sex, gender and desire. Queer has been associated most prominently with bisexual, lesbian, and gay subjects, but the analytic framework also includes such topics as cross-dressing, intersex, gender ambiguity, and gender-corrective surgery. (See http://en.wikipedia.org/wiki/Queer_theory (accessed 5-3-16).

References

Althusser, L. (1970). Ideology and ideological state apparatuses, in L. Althusser, editor, *Lenin and Philosophy and Other Essays*, 127–186. New York: Monthly Review Press, 1971.

Altman, N. (2009). *The Analyst in the Inner City: Race, Class, and Culture through a Psychoanalytic Lens*. 2nd ed. Hillsdale, NJ: Analytic Press.

Arad, H. (2001). *A Blank Rounded Screen*. Unpublished manuscript.

Arad, H. (2002a). Dialogue continues . . . (violence, terror, compassion, and forgiveness). *The Alliance Forum: The Newsletter of the Northwest Alliance for Psychoanalytic Study* April: 9–12. Seattle, WA.

Arad, H. (2002b). Focus on Violence. *Plenary Session: Focus on Violence*. Presentation at the 2002 Forum, On Violence. The Northwest Alliance for Psychoanalytic Study and Seattle Psychoanalytic Society and Institute Forum, April 27. Bellevue, WA.

Aron, L. (1996). *A Meeting of Minds: Mutuality in Psychoanalysis*. Vol. 4. Hillsdale, NJ: The Analytic Press.

Aron, L. (1998). The clinical body and the reflexive mind. In L. Aron and F. S. Anderson, editors, *Relational Perspectives on the Body*, 3–38. Hillsdale, NJ: The Analytic Press.

Aron, L., and M. Lechich. (2012). Relational psychoanalysis. In G. O. Gabbard, B. E. Litowitz, and P. Williams, editors, *Textbook of Psychoanalysis*, 211–224. 2nd ed. Washington, DC: American Psychiatric Publishing.

Atlas, G. (2013). What's love got to do with it? Sexuality, shame, and the use of the other. *Studies in Gender and Sexuality* 14(1): 51–58.

Atlas-Koch, G. and S. Kuchuck. (2012). To have and to hold: Psychoanalytic dialogues on the desire to own. *Psychoanalytic Dialogues* 22(1): 93–105.

Benjamin, J. (1988). *The Bonds of Love*. New York: Pantheon.

Benjamin, J. (1995). *Like Subjects, Love Objects*. New Haven, CT: Yale University Press.

Benjamin, J. (1998). *The Shadow of the Other: Intersubjectivity and Gender*. New York: Routledge.

Benjamin, J. (2004). Beyond doer and done to: An intersubjective view of thirdness. *Psychoanalytic Quarterly* 73: 5–46.

Bromberg, P. (1998). *Standing in the Spaces: Essays on Clinical Process, Trauma, and Dissociation*. Hillsdale, NJ: The Analytic Press.

Bromberg, P. (2006). *Awakening the Dreamer: Clinical Journeys*. Hillsdale, NJ: The Analytic Press.

Cooper, S. (1998). Analyst-subjectivity, analyst-disclosure, and the aims of psychoanalysis. *Psychoanalytic Quarterly* 67: 379–406.

Cooper, S. (2000). Mutual containment in the analytic situation. *Psychoanalytic Dialogues* 10(2): 169–194.

Corbett, K. (1993). The mystery of homosexuality. *Psychoanalytic Dialogues* 10: 345–357.

Corbett, K. (1999). Homosexual boyhood: Notes on girlyboys. In M. Rottnek, editor, *Sissies and Tomboys: Gender Nonconformity and Homosexual Childhood*, 107–139. New York: New York University Press.

Corbett, K. (2009). *Boyhoods*. New Haven, CT: Yale University Press.

Davies, J. (1996). Linking the "pre-analytic" with the postclassical: Integration, dissociation, and the multiplicity of unconscious process. *Contemporary Psychoanalysis* 32: 553–576.

Davies, J. (1998). Between the disclosure and foreclosure of erotic transference-countertransference: Can psychoanalytic find a place for adult sexuality? *Psychoanalytic Dialogues* 8(6): 747–766.

Davies, J., and M. Frawley. (1994). *Treating the Adult Survivor of Childhood Sexual Abuse: A Psychoanalytic Perspective*. New York: Basic Books.

Dimen, M. (2003). *Sexuality, Intimacy, Power*. Hillsdale, NJ: The Analytic Press.

Dimen, M., and V. Goldner, editors. (2002). *Gender in Psychoanalytic Space: Between Clinic and Culture*. New York: Other Press.

Elise, D. (2002). The primary maternal Oedipal situation and female homerotic desire. *Psychoanalytic Inquiry* 22: 209–228.
Elise, D. (2007). The black man and the mermaid: Desire and disruption in the analytic relationship. *Psychoanalytic Dialogues* 17(6): 791–809.
Fairbairn, W. R. D. (1952). *An Object-Relations Theory of the Personality.* New York: Basic Books.
Ferenczi, S. (1952). *First Contributions to Psycho-analysis*, translated by E. Jones. London: Hogarth, 1952. Reprinted: London: Karnac, 1994.
Ferenczi, S. (1955). *Final Contributions to the Problems and Methods of Psycho-analysis*, edited by M. Balint, translated by E. Mosbacher et al. London: Hogarth, 1955. Reprinted: London: Karnac, 1994.
Foucault, M. (1961). *Madness and Civilization: A History of Insanity in the Age of Reason*, translated by R. Howard. New York: Vintage Books.
Foucault, M. (1976). *The History of Sexuality*. Vol. I. *An Introduction*, translated by R. Howard. New York: Vintage Books.
Fromm, E. (1941). *Escape from Freedom*. New York: Rinehart. Reprinted: New York: Avon, 1965.
Fromm, E. (1947). *Man for Himself.* Greenwich, CT: Fawcett.
Ghent, E. (1990). Masochism, submission, surrender: Masochism as a perversion of surrender. *Contemporary Psychoanalysis* 26: 108–136.
Ghent, E. (2002). Wish, need, drive: Motive in the light of dynamic systems theory and Edelman's selectionist theory. *Psychoanalytic Dialogues* 12: 763–808.
Greenberg, J., and S. Mitchell. (1983). *Object Relations in Psychoanalytic Theory*. Cambridge, MA: Harvard University Press.
Grossmark, R. (2012). The unobtrusive relational analyst. *Psychoanalytic Dialogues* 22: 629–646.
Harris, A. (1997). Aggression, envy, and ambition: Circulating tensions in women's psychic life. *Gender and Psychoanalysis* 2: 291–325.
Harris, A. (2002). Mothers, monsters, mentors. *Studies in Gender and Sexuality* 3: 281–295.
Harris, A. (2005). *Gender as Soft Assembly*. Hillsdale, NJ: The Analytic Press.
Harris, A. (2011). The relational tradition: Landscape and canon. *Journal of the American Psychoanalytic Association* 59(4): 701–735.
Hoffman, I. Z. (1996). The intimate and ironic authority of the analyst's presence. *Psychoanalytic Quarterly* 65: 102–136.
Hoffman, I. Z. (1998). *Ritual and Spontaneity in the Psychoanalytic Process*. Hillsdale, NJ: The Analytic Press.
Lazar, H. (2012). *Six Singular Individuals*. Tel Aviv, Israel: Hakibbutz Hameuchad [Hebrew].
Levenson, E. A. (1983). *The Ambiguity of Change*. New York: Basic Books.
Levenson, E. A. (2006). Fifty years of evolving interpersonal psychoanalysis. *Contemporary Psychoanalysis* 42: 557–564.
Levinas, E. (1974). *Otherwise than Being, or Beyond Essence*, translated by A. Lingas. Pittsburgh: Duquensne University Press.
Mitchell, S. (1988). *Relational Concepts in Psychoanalysis: An Integration*. Cambridge, MA: Harvard University Press.
Mitchell, S. (1999). Preface. In S. Mitchell and L. Aron, editors, *Relational Psychoanalysis*, ix–xx. Hillsdale, NJ: The Analytic Press.

Moreno, J. L. (1987). *The Essential Moreno: Writings on Psychodrama, Group Method, and Spontaneity*. J. Fox, editor. New York: Springer Publishing.
Orange, D., G. Atwood, and R. Stolorow. (1997). *Working Intersubjectively: Contextualism in Psychoanalytic Practice*. Hillsdale, NJ: The Analytic Press.
Rappoport, E. (2015). Dynamic linking of psyche and soma: Somatic experiencing and embodied mentalization. In J. Bresler and K. Starr, editors, *Relational Psychoanalysis and Psychotherapy Integration: An Evolving Synergy*, 136–158. New York: Routledge.
Seligman, S. (2005). Dynamic systems theories as a metaframework for psychoanalysis. *Psychoanalytic Dialogues* 15: 285–319.
Shapiro, F. (2001). *Eye Movement Desensitization and Reprocessing: Basic Principles, Protocols, and Procedures*. 2nd ed. New York: Guilford.
Shapiro, F. (2002). EMDR treatment: Overview and integration. In F. Shapiro, editor, *EMDR as an Integrative Psychotherapy Approach: Experts of Diverse Orientations Explore the Paradigm Prism*, 27–56. Washington, DC: American Psychological Association.
Slochower, J. (1992). A hateful borderline patient and the holding environment. *International Journal of Psychoanalysis* 28: 72–88.
Slochower, J. (1994). The evolution of object usage and the holding environment. *Contemporary Psychoanalysis* 30: 135–151.
Slochower, J. (1996). Holding and the evolving maternal metaphor. *Psychoanalytic Review* 83: 195–218.
Stein, A. (2011). Faux Endings. Presented at International Association for Relational Psychoanalysis and Psychotherapy, Colloquium Series No. 19, Good enough endings: Contemporary perspectives on termination, December 5–18.
Stern, D. B. (2003). *Unformulated Experience: From Dissociation to Imagination in Psychoanalysis*. Hillsdale, NJ: The Analytic Press.
Stern, D. B. (2010). *Partners in Thought: Working with Unformulated Experience, Dissociation, and Enactment*. New York: Routledge.
Stolorow, R. (1997). Dynamic, dyadic, intersubjective systems: An evolving paradigm. *Psychoanalytic Psychology* 14(3): 337–346.
Stolorow, R. (2012a). The renewal of humanism in psychoanalytic therapy. *Psychotherapy* 49: 442–444.
Stolorow, R. (2012b). Toward a renewal of personology in psychotherapy research. *Psychotherapy* 49: 471–472.
Stolorow, R., G. Atwood, and D. Orange. (2002). *Worlds of Experience: Interweaving Philosophical and Clinical Dimensions in Psychoanalysis*. New York: Basic Books.
Sullivan, H. S. (1953). *The Interpersonal Theory of Psychiatry*. New York: Norton.
Thelen, E. and L. Smith. (1994). *A Dynamic Systems Approach to the Development of Cognition and Action*. Cambridge, MA: MIT Press.
Zizek, S. (1989). *The Sublime Object of Ideology*. London: Verso.

Chapter 4

Attachment

Companionship in action

> Here is an infallible test. Imagine yourself in a situation where you are alone, wholly alone on earth, and you are offered one of the two, books or men. I often hear men prizing their solitude but that is only because there are still men somewhere on earth even though in the far distance. I knew nothing of books when I came forth from the womb of my mother, and I shall die without books, with another human hand in my own. I do, indeed, close my door at times and surrender myself to a book, but only because I can open the door again and see a human being looking at me.
>
> — Martin Buber

In this chapter, I make a case for the ways in which relational psychoanalysis, EMDR, and attachment theory may be valuable in dialogue. My goal here is to outline the importance of attention given to minimal cues, failures of attunement, small *t* and big *T* trauma, to use EMDR terminology, and their potential use in therapy. Because many psychotherapists draw on attachment theory to conduct therapy with their patients, I explore how understanding and giving attention to minute changes in self-states may provide cues for the therapist to shift from verbal to nonverbal intervention.

Attachment-focused EMDR

EMDR recognizes the importance of close interpersonal communication. This is communication that underlies and escapes verbal communication alone, and that is conveyed through the use of our bodies in therapy, allowing us to receive bodily information about our patients. This view of communication is similar to the way relational psychoanalysts have thought about their countertransference, and how infant researchers have understood the communication between infants and caregivers from the dawn of life. Using these innate and developed feelings of our own body's responses can be of particular value when working with patients who learned to dissociate in response to early trauma.

EMDR, especially with this focus on attachment, finds relational trauma to be wide-ranging in its occurrence. Laurel Parnell (2013) referred to trauma as including any trauma taking place in a relational context that involved doing or not doing something that caused harm to the patient. She provided a list of possible sources of harm, ranging from actual abuse, "neglect, abandonment, lack of mirroring and attunement," to "unconscious absorption of parents' trauma, early loss of a parent or caretaker," and "parents' mental or physical illness or drug and/or alcohol abuse" (p. 6). She added that the trauma can also include a parent's lack of responsiveness to an abusive situation. Big *T* trauma and small *t* trauma can be highly influential in establishing the patient's self-perception and their relationships. It is possible to conclude that most mental trauma is attachment or relationally based.

Parnell (2013) uses the attachment styles developed by Mary Main (1992) and her Adult Attachment Interview (AAI) to describe schematic relational types in relation to attachment focused EMDR. These styles are not purely matches made to a given classification, as a personal attachment style is assembled and congeals through attachment to various caregivers throughout childhood and develops into a unique attachment style in adolescence. Thus, attachment styles become implicit. A key element on which attachment-focused EMDR and relational psychoanalysis agree is that, later in life, these patterns can be altered through new relational attachments to others. Here, I describe these four common attachment styles (secure, avoidant/dismissive, ambivalent/preoccupied, and disorganized), together with suggested EMDR approaches, along with some findings from Lyons-Ruth's studies with her colleagues regarding nuanced disorganized attachment strategies as they manifest in infancy as well as in later years of childhood beyond infancy through young adulthood (Lyons-Ruth, 2012).

Secure attachment

Secure attachment manifests itself in relationships that have flexibility, following early experiences that seem to be metabolized and have become a base for future engagements. Secure attachment can be based on relational history or acquired through later relationships, including therapeutic ones. Both relational work in the transference and countertransference and EMDR therapy may leverage secure attachment in the patient at times of crisis in order to amend an overwhelming affective state, and to help the patient return to a place of relative objectivity regarding their current situation and relationship.

Avoidant/dismissive attachment

Avoidant/dismissive attachment presents as a consequence of unresponsive or neglectful parenting. Here patients may be unconnected to their emotions or their bodies, a state leading to being cut off from self and others. Attachment-focused EMDR suggests that it is useful to help a patient find connection to their right-brain activity as an antidote to their linear thinking and lack of memory, and to enhance self-reflection. This can be done through integrating new relationship information by learning to pay attention to bodily signals. Parnell (2013) has suggested the use of "art, movement, psychodrama, guided imagery, body-based work, and resource tapping[1] with imagery" to achieve this (p. 9).

Because these patients tend to have limited access to emotionally rich incidents, an EMDR approach can add in new relational circuits. It is my experience that with the creation of new emotional and relational circuits some emotionally laden memories arise. The use of bilateral stimuli to encourage a focus on nonverbal signals helps to increase body awareness. Adding awareness to a memory of relational connection with other persons or in the therapeutic dyad helps in making that sense of connection explicit in body and in mind (Parnell, 2013).

Ambivalent/preoccupied attachment

Ambivalent and preoccupied parenting in which the parents were inconsistent or unavailable may result in a person's anxiety about others' availability to them. Other parents may have been intrusive. In these cases, the patient may be desperate for others, yet worry that their needs may not be met by a significant other, or that they will be occupied by the other. Here, it is assumed that they struggle to self-sooth, as well as have a persistent feeling that something is wrong with them as their needs are not met consistently. With EMDR and the co-constructed holding environment of the consistent object-regulation of therapy, self-regulation in the patient will develop. Over time, these new experiences, along with resource tapping, will calm the right hemisphere and promote the activation of new neural pathways that in turn contribute to reduced anxiety and the entertaining of different interpretations to familiar internal and environmental triggers (Kitchur, 2005; Parnell, 2013).

Disorganized attachment

A disorganized pattern of attachment develops in those whose parents or caregivers are overwhelmed and frightened, and who created chaos in their child's mind, as manifested in a disorganized attachment pattern, or with an unresolved sense of trauma and loss. This trauma often results in fragmentation arising from both the self and others. Patients may present with "flashbacks, frightening body memories," difficulty with social communication, and with impaired reasoning, and they tend to dissociate (Parnell, 2013, p. 10). Thus, dissociation is an attempt to keep the good parent representation from the frightening disorganizing one, as aspects of the entire spectrum of attunement and interaction, from the caring to the horrific, are found in the single parenting figure. Since self-regulation is developed through object-regulation (Schore, 2003), when this precious object-regulation is disrupted, the child resorts to a survival mode of engagement, as by evacuating the self into a compromised dissociated mode of emotional operation with its unique set of sensations, cognitive functioning, and interaction with others.

Relevant to the clinical understanding of adult attachment styles and their influence on patients' relationships, including in the analytic setting, is Lyons-Ruth's research on disorganized attachment. For her and her colleagues, disorganized attachment in infancy is a risk factor for later psychopathology in childhood and adolescence (Lyons-Ruth and Jacobvitz, 1999), one beyond the avoidant or ambivalent strategies that have been observed in infants as a response to a slightly insensitive caregiver. As Lyons-Ruth and Spielman (2004) pointed out, and contrary to earlier studies, "parental behavior that is somewhat insensitive is not correlated with infant disorganized attachment behavior since studies using Ainsworth's global rating scale for sensitivity (Ainsworth, Blehar, Waters, and Wall, 1978) have generated only a small association between parental behavior and infant disorganization" (p. 321). Rather, Lyons-Ruth and Spielman (2004) argued that it is disruptive parental affective communication with the infant such as "parental withdrawing responses, negative-intrusive responses, role-confused responses, disoriented responses," and "affective communication errors" that lead to a disorganized response by the infant (p. 321). They suggested that as cognitive capacities "for taking account of others' states of mind" advance during the preschool years, the "disorganized strategies often become organized into controlling strategies in which the child takes over the initiative to maintain the parent's involvement through caregiving or punitive behaviors" (pp. 320–321).

The EMDR method emphasizes the importance of stabilization of patients whose attachment strategy is disorganized and dissociated, as there is little self-regulation on which to rely (Parnell, 2013). Establishing a therapeutic alliance is important in any analytic dyad, yet before employing the EMDR protocol, in which embodied traumatic events are approached, a secure therapeutic bond must be sufficiently established. EMDR therapists gently introduce resource tapping to increase self-regulatory capacities through the addition of new neural pathways and the patient's trust in his or her ability to handle previously challenging situations outside of the consulting room. To reduce the risk of further dissociation and decompensation once traumatic experiences are processed, the highly skilled therapist should proceed with great care and expect the need to intervene when patients have difficulty believing that the future may be different and less anxiety-producing. The therapist's attunement should help detect further dissociation and the potential need to change in the course of processing to refocus on the patient's self-regulation. As with relational psychoanalysts, EMDR therapists are similarly attuned to their own emotional response, highlighting the need to stay grounded, emphatically staying with the patient's current state of mind while holding onto the patient as a whole person, and by believing in their ability to heal (Parnell, 2013, p. 11).

Before I describe the relationship between attachment theory and research and psychoanalysis, it is important to note that attachment-focused EMDR taps into attachment research to help guide the therapist in understanding the patient and finding the right approach for each individual. While the relational approach sees the work as centered on the patient as well, the core of the work is in the dyadic interaction. A safe, nurturing therapeutic relationship is key to a successful EMDR approach. However, for relational psychoanalysts, transference and countertransference, along with rupture and repair in the analytic relationship, are significant focal points of the therapeutic work. In these areas lie new opportunities that can emerge to create emotionally rich embodied experiences that parallel—but also change—paradigmatic relational bonds.

Attachment and psychoanalysis

For decades, attachment theory and psychoanalysis were seen as being opposed in their focus, each often contradicting the other's intention to find pathways to understanding the human mind. Over time, the areas of empirical research and psychoanalytic hermeneutics have been recognized as mutually beneficial. The history of postwar infant observation in England included a range of older attachment theories, while in the past twenty-five years, alongside the infant observation of the past, there has been a surge of renewed interest in attachment research. Greater precision in the observation of early attachment patterns has been documented through research, allowing for the development of a more subtle theory and practice. Infant observation has taught us much about the future development of human relatedness through its study of the quality of dyadic bodily and synergetic interaction taking place long before speech could turn the actors into verbally willing participants.

Attachment theory emerged out of a particular tradition that followed John Bowlby's (1969, 1980, 1988) observations of children and his study of the influence of separation and loss. Bowlby was interested in observing actual interactions in families as well as the cross-generational transmission of troublesome patterns of attachment. Subsequently, Bowlby developed theories about the importance of the child's attachment to his or her primary caregivers. Most importantly, Bowlby suggested, based on his observations and theoretical formulations, that children's adaptive and maladaptive attachment patterns were the result of real experiences with their parent and not an outcome of their fantasies, a view held by many in the traditional psychoanalytic milieu (Seligman and Harrison, 2012).

From a psychoanalytically oriented infant-research standpoint, what is central to the discussion of human development and an effective therapeutic relationship are social relationships that are understood from a transactional perspective in which individuals, each with their own developmental system, are engaged with another's (Seligman and Harrison, 2012). This perspective assumes that psychosocial development takes place through intersubjective interactions and includes at its core nonverbal communication.

Developmental researchers agree that the relationship between infant and parent is the base on which development takes place, and that infants are motivated to form and maintain ties to other people (Seligman and Harrison, 2012). In addition, Seligman and Harrison (2012) suggested that "over time, through evolving sequences of signals and responses, infants and caregivers continually influence and regulate each other's internal states and behaviors" (p. 240). They cite Ekman and Friesen (1969) and Stern (1985), who were among the scholars who suggested that humans are prepared from birth for communication in order to promote caregiving and form significant emotional ties. Infants from an early age are capable of mirroring their caregiver's mimetic expressions. The pleasure the parent takes in their child's ability to coo in response to being looked at and spoken to results in the infant's repetition of this conversation, which in turn encourages the parent to express pleasure and wish to continue the conversation. There is the creation of an expectation that there will be interaction, that there will be expected behaviors and play. This repertoire then grows in detail and complexity, and will include some surprising or new elements yet unknown to the dyad. The possibility of mediating communication, both verbal and nonverbal, that allows the parent and child to negotiate a variety of situations throughout childhood and into adulthood, is also present in this dynamic circuit. These interactions are co-constructed by both parties. Each is active and influential, contributes to the mutual regulation of the other's emotional, bodily, and mental states, and helps build intrapersonal meanings.

The systems and transactional perspectives

Therapeutic action, as well as infant–caregiver relationships, evolve through interpersonal engagement. This mutual influence system motivates change in both parties. Early developmental research demonstrates that each infant–caregiver dyad develops a unique interpersonal system, which suggests that a similar system is constructed in each psychotherapy dyad as well (Seligman and Harrison, 2012). In relational psychoanalysis, Seligman and Harrison note the current interest "in the inextricability of transference and countertransference" that "parallels the infancy researchers' dyadic focus" (p. 244). They suggest that "just as the infant activates the maternal capacities as he or she is sustained by them, the analytic therapist finds reflections of his or her own personality in the patient's relational dilemmas" (p. 244). As Aron and Lechich (2012) and others (Sameroff and Emde, 1989) suggested, a nonlinear transferential and countertransferential relationship exists in each therapeutic dyad.

Seligman and Harrison (2012) posit that the transactional perspective proposes that dynamic nonlinear process is at the core of development. It offers the idea that relationships are at the base of both developmental and clinical theory (p. 240).

To give an example, imagine an infant who is carried by and born to a mother who feels rejected by loved ones for her own historical reasons. It is plausible to imagine that the infant senses early on that in order to receive care from the mother he must constantly make the mother feel that she is loved. The infant quickly learns to be an admiring partner to the mother, overlooking his own emotional needs (for example, by refraining from crying too often) to keep the mother functioning on some level. The mother returns to the infant to give some partial care as long as the infant avoids behaving in a way that makes the mother feel rejected. Another infant may turn away from the mother, increasing his sense of abandonment, while the mother will, over time, treat the child as disappointing. The child may get fewer of his emotional needs met, and begin to see himself as the mother's trouble child, to which the mother responds in kind. It is easy to see the different trajectories that the docile or rebellious infant may take into older childhood and adulthood with different complex relational consequences.

Seligman and Harrison (2012) point out that infant researchers have found how individual identity and the sense of connection with others are predicated up on relationships with others, and by being recognized by others who see the person as he is. Similarly, in psychoanalysis the intersubjective perspective stresses the idea of mutual recognition when one person can understand another while feeling separate yet without losing the awareness of connection (p. 240).

Clinical vignette: Renegotiating attachment patterns

Here is an example of an attachment pattern that was developed in the past and renegotiated in the painstaking relationship in analysis.

Megan was changing. Recently, ambivalence was gradually replacing her blocking off any possibility of spontaneous human relations. She used to say, "Thank you, but no" to most attempts to create closeness. Businesslike, she came to her sessions ready to work. Closeness was out of the question. She paid me so that she could receive its value in kind. She was perplexed by the change in which she benefited more than she felt she paid for. She was about to have her first child, and finally she was able to feel the ambivalence she could no longer hide. Ambivalence in full bloom showed up now in every meeting. It was about the proverbial mother in her marriage, work, and therapy, and indeed in her relationship with the original mother. At times she would meet it at the side of negation, at other times at the corner of welcome, but now she was always swayed to recognize the angst of wanting a fuller spectrum of her paradoxical wish. For example, she yearned for the special time of her new family—herself, her partner, and the child—to be uninterrupted. Yet she also longed to have her mother take care of her and her baby, in a hope for a corrective experience of the kind she had never had with her mother earlier. The hope for reconciliation and reuniting with her reflection in her infant–mother interaction, watching herself as her mother correcting what went awry in her own relationship during childhood, was precious.

Toni Morrison's comment, from an on-stage interview at Oberlin College, March 14, 2012, comes to mind, following a reading from her then forthcoming novel, *Home* (2012). She was responding to a question from moderator Johnnetta Cole (now director of the Smithsonian National Museum of African Art), who asked Morrison "What does Home mean to you? A place? A feeling?" Morrison answered, "Memory."[2] In the example here, Megan needed to recreate the memory of a nonmalignant time with her mother in early childhood in order to create a bond with her mother, and to accept the permission to have a nonmalignant connection with her own daughter as her mother witnessed her mothering her newborn and herself. That experience brought gentleness in each mother–daughter pair in this three-generation rebonding and remembering.

EMDR provided the space in which Megan could defend less against her early and current wished-for connection with a mother who could focus solely on her needs without demanding care in return. This clarification, through repeated BLS cycles, saw Megan try many iterations, both in the past and projected into the future, in which her need was no longer modified to prefer that of the mother. It could help Megan to create, for the first time in her life, boundaries that could preempt the all too familiar rage she had come to expect as the first precursor to her understanding that something wasn't right. EMDR helped in the renegotiating of old dynamic patterns that were represented within Megan's embodied memory. Such an experience opens the possibility of being able to renegotiate known systemic patterns in actual relationships that previously seemed to lack any potential for relational change. It is not surprising that EMDR helps change the analytic dynamic as well, in allowing for the deepening of the connection as patients' sense of agency begins to emerge, or from an attachment theory perspective, as Megan experienced a subtle shift from a disorganized attachment pattern to a more secure one.

Infancy research and the changes that followed have suggested a number of distinctive implications for clinical theory and technique. When we think of the psychoanalytic relationship as a relational dyad, as described in the previous chapter, we make use of infant research, holding the image of infant and parent within a mutual influence system, as we listen to the patient in relation to the analyst while simultaneously being in the experience.

Affect attunement

In research on the earliest infant attachment we find affect attunement is a core principal. It can be defined "as the cross-modal matching of intensity, timing, and 'shape' (contour) of behavior, based on dynamic, micromomentary shifts over time, perceived as patterns of change that are similar in self and other" (Beebe, Sorter, Rustin, and Knoblauch, 2003, p. 793). Beebe et al. (2003) discussed researchers such as Meltzoff (1985; Meltzoff and Moore, 1998), Stern (1971, 1985), and Trevarthen (1993, 1998), who have been key figures in the tradition of microanalysis of mother–infant interactions. This research has focused on how infants can sense the state of the other, and has offered theories on how intersubjectivity evolves in infants. Beebe et al.'s (2003) comparison of the approaches of Meltzoff, Stern, and Trevarthen helps us recognize the importance of early development, although each one emphasizes a slightly different angle of research and understanding. The comparison of their approaches is relevant to the understanding of their individual intersubjective forms, as well as for their contribution to adult forms of intersubjectivity and psychoanalysis (Beebe et al., 2003).

Coming from an experimental tradition, Meltzoff (1985; Meltzoff and Moore, 1998) has studied infant imitation behavior, drawing on it as a basis for broader inferences about the origins of representation and self. Meltzoff's formulation is that representations created in infancy through self–other interactions, by means of proprioception and *like me* perception, will be embedded in the self, and then be triggered, without the need for actual interaction with the original partner, in transferring these representations to new situations with others. Meltzoff's description of the timing and the special mechanisms employed through the cross-modal mapping that is simultaneous for both partners, and which the infant and the mother employ in the first six months of life, is helpful in understanding the importance of attention to micro-signals in the analytic relationship, as well as in recognizing them when they appear during EMDR sessions. The emphasis is on the infant's reading and mapping of the interaction with the mother, as both are involved and contributing to the interaction for the infant's development.

Trevarthen (1993, 1998) focuses more on the dyad as innately primed for intersubjective interaction, using their *mutually sensitive minds* in a work between partners. Both Meltzoff (1985) and Trevarthen (1993, 1998) agree that the innate ability to connect exists from birth, and that imitation is an essential mechanism in increasing interaction. However, Trevarthen (1993, 1998) suggests that humans do not need cognitive thinking and words to immediately perceive their partner's impulse. Understanding that the human mind can interact "knowingly" pre-verbally is crucial to therapeutic work, as both EMDR and relational methods make use of that inherent ability by creating either an internal or an interactional environment in which other possibilities can flourish. It is useful to think about Trevarthen's idea that instead of attachment, which may imply directionality and intention by the infant to the mother, we should think about companionship in action, which implies mutual influence and growth for both partners through their interaction. This fits with Seligman and Harrison's (2012) emphasis on the mutuality in both the infant–caregiver relationship and its parallel in relational psychoanalytic treatment, where both partners impact the relationship and are changed by it.

Stern (1971, 1985) described how, around the age of 9 to 12 months, inner subjective states can be shared, and the stage where overt behavior shifts to inner states when a mental self and a mental other are interfaced. Like Meltzoff (1985; Meltzoff and Moore, 1998), Stern (1985) sees the infant's capacity to perceive cross-modally as the mechanism by which both partners capture the quality of the other's inner state. However, unlike Meltzoff (1985), but similar to Trevarthen (1993, 1998), Stern (1985) sees the correspondence as a reciprocal dyadic process across time. Like Trevarthen (1993, 1998), Stern (1985) uses the categories of form, timing, and intensity to define the dimensions of these correspondences. From my clinical experience, including infant–mother observation, I tend to agree with Trevarthen (1993, 1998) and Meltzoff (1985; Meltzoff and Moore, 1998) that from early on and at a preverbal stage the baby is present in the interaction and capable of recognizing the other and self, while contributing to the interaction. Like Trevarthen (1993, 1998) and Stern (1985), I see the mutuality in and the transformation of each partner in the dyad. I agree with all three that intersubjectivity is innate.

As Beebe et al. (2003) relate, Stern's studies brought him to believe that affect attunement helps secure the process of attachment and creates a sense of security in the baby, thus helping develop "the capacity for psychic intimacy" while increasing the ability to symbolize (p. 795). It is postulated that if at the beginning of life the focus was on mutual regulation of behavior, that there was then a shift to the mutual sharing of experience (p. 795). This view lends itself well to the assumptions of both EMDR and relational psychoanalysis, in which change is taking place when there is an attunement of affect. In EMDR, this process takes place through minute attention to shifts in affect, while in psychoanalysis this process occurs through the co-constructed *now* moments of meeting of the transferential-countertransferential affect attunement and misattunment. However devastating moments of misattunment can be, they also offer the opportunity to recognize that even when attachment is fairly secured, a therapist and patient's subjective states may not match at all times. At times, in clinical situations, when a patient is unskilled in the to and fro of interaction, they still leave traces of recognition of the therapist, as well as of themselves, in however faint form, in both timing and intensity. The following clinical example illustrates elements of such dynamics.

Clinical vignette: Mutual recognition

Keith enters my office late after a break of ten days. He was on vacation with a beloved friend. He uses the couch without his usual introductory seated, checking-in position. He reports his emotional well-being during the vacation and his sadness over its ending. Then he pauses and asks, “Are you angry with me?” I inquire about his feeling, and the possible reasons I might feel angry at him. He says, “I don’t know, I just feel something different in the air.” Quickly he is willing to foreclose discussion and move on.

I invite him to listen more carefully to the discrepancy he feels between his account and where he finds me to be. Although I did not feel anger toward his tardiness, perhaps Keith sensed something he was quick to take on as guilt over some crime he must have committed in our relationship for which he should be reprimanded. There was a lot to discuss about that habit of putting himself in harm’s way by provoking in the other some personal expression.

We talk for a while about his sense of guilt for missing our conversations for the sake of having fun with another person. I then ask him to think for a moment about the possibility that he did not provoke negative feeling in me, but still picked up on my being different at that moment. He is surprised by the possibility that I might be less attuned than otherwise, and hesitantly says, “I don’t know, maybe something bad happened to a family member.” I encourage Keith to imagine other possibilities. He mentions a possible broken car, a difficult situation with a patient before him.

Keith’s funneling of the absorbed emotional reading of me as applying to himself was a recurrent theme he inhabited much of his life. It was inconceivable that his feeling would stem from his relationship or be a mutual contribution to the affect and its sufficient or insufficient regulation. Cooper (2000) wrote about the mutual regulation in the analytic dyad, and Hopkins (2011), writing about Masud Khan, spoke about the consequences of the analyst’s failure to regulate himself, and hence the patient. Here Keith, being accustomed to a tolerable level of attunement/misattunement in our mutual influence system, felt abandoned. His solution was to gather it all into his single influence system.

However, unbeknownst to him, Keith was slowly shifting to a mutual influence system, and only noticed it through my shift of attunement. He could track the reduced verbal interaction, yet with exploration could detect some embodied reaction at the shift. This occurrence was an improvement of sorts. Keith felt he wanted out of the emotionally uneasy situation in which he felt dismembered by my response to him. Although he suggested that I might have been angry with him, he could also see that he might have been angry at me for not being there the way he had learned to expect, especially upon his leaving and returning on his own terms (taking a vacation and being late). He also had to find out that, at times, I may not be responsive in the same way because of other mutual influence systems I might be a part of, and that the intersection between our system and other regulatory systems might be at odds, with a failed attunement being its casualty.

Although detailed self-disclosure was not warranted in this case, Keith got to widen the range of possibilities to include the, thus far, improbability of misattunement. Of course through the years there were other times, but they went under the radar of awareness. Keith's pulling on my proverbial apron to get my attention when I was otherwise occupied brought us back into full engagement, a task of every mutual influence system but one that, for Keith, was skewed most of his early life.

What he regained in analysis was the right to notice openly, inquire about, and demand that full attention and focus be on his needs, knowing that there would be an echo and response even at times of failure. To know who he was, Keith needed to feel who I was in our relationship. With Keith, EMDR was a welcome companion. I imagined that, at times, I deprived him when I did not offer to use EMDR at his sessions. It was as if it served as an extension into a connection that felt more real to him than conversations alone. With Keith the use of EMDR was more about attachment. It was tangible, making him feel something in his body and mind, and that rendered it believable and real.

The co-creation of therapeutic interaction by observing, in real time, each participant's contribution to an enactment could not be achieved without careful attunement to minimal cues on the part of both participants, much as an infant and mother are influencing each other continuously. The change in cadence in my reaction to Keith was picked up as a disruption of the formerly predictable to and fro that was possibly invisible to us both until there was a discrepancy that created discomfort. All Keith could say when I inquired about his feeling was, "I don't know, but something is different." He knew it without being able to name the shift in my interaction with him.

In the example of my actual interaction with Keith, understanding was made nonverbally. The behavioral expression of declaring not-knowing contained the effect of implicitly knowing something that was held back until a safer moment arrived—typically, in a later session following the affective exploration in the current session of the danger behind *knowing*. Interaction and interpretation are not intrinsically opposed. Related to this observation is the view that the present is as significant as the past is relevant to the therapy (Seligman and Harrison, 2012). "The past is carried into the present so as to be *expressed and transformed at the same time*" (p. 246). Seligman and Harrison added that the psychoanalytic approach outpaces developmental research in asserting the connection between childhood and adulthood. The manifestations of these connections are multiple, and include actual enactments, "along with internal representations" such as "images, affects, bodily states, interpersonal expectations, fantasies, dreams, memories, and more" (p. 246). These representations are reflected in interpersonal transactions as moments in development move into the next developmental step, "both transformed and preserved" with the moving time (p. 246). EMDR sessions too can bring about embodied experiences that represent affective representations from various places in the patient's developmental turning points.

In EMDR processing, both the therapist's attention to minute shifts in affect in the patient, to which the therapist responds with minute affective cues, and her helping the patient recognize his affective reaction to an affective image, allow the patient an opportunity to develop recognition of triggers that are related to misattunement, and his embodied reaction to this failure. It is a research lab of sorts in which the patient can *see* and experience certain intersubjective moments, and then imagine altered variations of the remembered original scenario with a more desired interaction and outcome. Relational affective engagement is enhanced by an affective transference-countertransference interaction that has a base in the EMDR affective experience.

Here, the order of appearance is not essential. The psychoanalyst's attunement to minimal affective cues that stem either out of misattunement in the dyadic interaction, or precisely because the patient felt the therapist was cueing in on the utmost need of the patient to be heard in a particular way, can be moments leading to the use of EMDR to make the affect more pronounced and to elaborate it with greater emotional detail. Oftentimes, patients who had to bottle up their feelings for the sake of safety will, in the aftermath of trauma, fight any signal of budding expressive emotion. I find that offering EMDR action at such moments helps the patient stay with the affective moment with reduced shame, while affectively it offers the patient a renewed attempt at better attunement, from the restored other, malignant or benign, as well as from a renewable care-object within themselves.

The relational baby

The work of Brazelton, Koslowski, and Main (1971), Brazelton (1982), Malloch (1999), and Tronick (2007) has suggested that, in the dyad, expression of a coordinated emotional dance occurs through the motion, cadence, sounds, timing, intensity, and gestures of each participant, both alone and in interaction, just as in imitation and attunement, and that these elements form the ground of co-constructing subjective experience.

Following Wallin (2007) and others who researched the developmental neuroscience that describes the brain's architecture and physiology as "organized to orient the infant to the interpersonal world from the beginning of life," Seligman and Harrison (2012) gave the example of mirror neurons, which allow the observer of an action to feel as if they were "making the motion while knowing it is made by another" (p. 241). Solms and Turnbull (2002) suggested that this mechanism of the infant observing the parent in action helps the baby to passively learn that such behavior can later turn into their own action. Simultaneously, the infant learns to think about the action without executing what they learned when observing the parent. As Seligman (1998) wrote, "understanding is not about experience. It is itself an experience, and this experience involves the crucial presence of another person with whom one feels secure, in part by virtue of feeling understood by that person" (p. 84).

Developmental thinking in psychoanalysis emerged around two main lines of understanding of infant development and motivation, and the consequences of these in adult psychopathology.

The classic notion is that infants are geared toward satisfying an urge to fulfill basic primitive needs at all costs, and then through stages of development find ways to deal with the reality of having to curb such desires. Seligman and Harrison (2012) used the term *drive instinct baby* to refer to the view of infants as "primitive, motivated to reduce internal tension," and having "few, if any, interpersonal boundaries" (p. 242). From the drive-instinct baby point of view, psychopathology goes hand in hand with early development as suggested by Freudian and Kleinian theorists and clinicians with their observations of adult patients.

The other line of understanding sees the baby as relational. The *relational baby* is "oriented to the outside world from the beginning," and is "particularly prepared for human interaction" (Seligman and Harrison, 2012, p. 243). From this perspective, the baby's interest in "social relations are a primary motive" (p. 243). While the infant is dependent on her caregivers she is primed to engage interactively with the complex familial environment. Although the relational baby is immature, its "early development is seen as more continuous with later development," as "similar processes organize adult personality," in contrast to the drive-instinct baby formulation. (p. 243). What is crucial to the way psychotherapy is conducted is that psychopathology is not analogous to infancy, because "normally developing infants are not disorganized or primitive, just less organized and more dependent" (p. 243). Instead, the relational infant perspective suggests that "psychopathology is a variant of development rather than a fixation to an early developmental stage" (p. 243). In turn, proponents of this theoretical model, such as the variants of ego psychology as seen by Hartmann (1956) and Erikson (1950), as well as interpersonal psychoanalysis, self psychology, and attachment theory, have been partial to infant and child observation that demonstrates this (Seligman and Harrison, 2012, p. 243).

Changes in the perception of what contributes to psychopathology piqued interest in motives and child development beyond the drives, including an interest in the relational aspect of development. Patients with less severe complaints increased researchers' propensity to understand developmental needs and what was lacking in development, including preoedipal dynamics (Kumin, 1995; Seligman and Harrison, 2012). As a consequence, in both research and therapy there was a shift toward seeing the caregiver–infant and clinician–patient dyadic relationship as an organizing principle of mental life and main focus of therapy, rather than the drive-based fantasy life of the infant or patient as it is projected onto its environment. The idea, following general relational sensibility, was that psychic structure was organized in a two-person system that could manifest "internally, externally, or in the intersubjective spaces between," and that it was comprised of a mutually influential system that intersects both the relational psychoanalytic clinical observation and practice and attachment theory and research.

Over time, these ideas found their way to other psychoanalytic persuasions (Seligman and Harrison, 2012, p. 243).

It is widely accepted in the relational psychoanalytic milieu that engagement, rather than external observation, is central to the therapeutic action (Racker, 1957). Even within EMDR, the sense of engagement must precede the EMDR work on the traumatic event. Although practitioners may want to see this feeling as a precursor to an internal embodied experience of the traumatic experience, establishing the basis of engagement that allows the patient to entrust her deepest emotional experiences to the practitioner is essential.

In a way that is similar to Meltzoff's description of the infant's preference for faces, and its searching for *like me* in the caregiver's disposition in early relational interactions during infancy, patients search for minimal cues in the therapist's verbal and nonverbal embodied expression. For example, they may seek to be reassured by a particular echo or careful about what they express in a session if they find signs they interpret as psychologically dangerous (Beebe et al., 2003). Using the couch oftentimes releases the patient from this natural tendency of seeing and following by reducing the "noise" created by the analyst's countertransferential account. I use the term countertransference loosely here to describe the human influence of the analyst on the person of the analysand, not necessarily to indicate productive or counterproductive reactions of the analyst to the patient's expressions. Of course, at other times patients may need to read the analyst through these same expressions, especially if they are more disorganized in their attachment in early stages of the treatment.

A similar response can be found in the EMDR session. Although it is not a requirement, many patients choose to shut their eyes when venturing into an anxiety-inducing internal journey, thus creating an inadvertent veil that allows only limited content from the practitioner to permeate their mind, while at the same time being aware of the EMDR practitioner's presence. In both modalities, the patient has exposure to limited yet crucial intervention from the therapist. In EMDR, there is a conscious effort to reduce the influence of the practitioner on the patient's process, although voice and presence allow the patient to feel more secure in venturing into frightening realms. By comparison, in relational psychoanalysis there is less of an effort of this sort, but more of an acceptance of the mutual influence in the dyadic system.

Nonverbal embodied dimensions

Therapists regard the nonverbal nuance that is shared with patients—and that arises from actual interactions in the therapeutic situation—as essential (Seligman and Harrison, 2012). This nuance helps the analytic dyad gain understanding of their interaction as it represents both conscious and unconscious inner workings. Seligman and Harrison (2012) spoke of the source of this greater attention to nonverbal detail in the therapeutic interaction as stemming from infant research observation and microanalysis of videotaped psychotherapy sessions. For example, they evoked processes such as *disruption and despair* and *chase and dodge* as formulated and described by Beebe and Lachmann (2002), and *affect attunement* as described by Stern (1985), and made the observation that such patterned interactions can be observed in psychotherapeutic interactions as do *projective identification* and *mentalization* (Seligman, 1999, 2008), that are considered more "reformulated processes" often discussed by intersubjectively leaning therapists (Seligman and Harrison, 2012, p. 244).

Infants rely on nonverbal cues such as gestures, sound, and affect to make sense of relationships, as we learned from neuroscience (see for example Trevarthen, 2009). Sounds and motion as well as change in physiological cues are tools that help infants communicate their needs and preferences, and in turn assist the caregiver in deciphering what the child may be asking for. Nonverbal cues, for example in the register and pace of sound, continue to be central to human communication, in conveying as well as receiving throughout life (see for example Damasio, 1999; Trevarthen, 1993, 1998, 2009). Knoblauch (2000, 2012) and colleagues (Beebe et al., 2005), in privileging nonverbal embodied communication in clinical practice, have drawn on the importance of rhythm, tone, and gesture in jazz improvisation. Knoblauch (2012) claimed that a similar process was taking place in the clinical situation, one with a rich potential for recognition and expression when words are not being used, as in the communication of unspeakable trauma (p. 184). Improv-isation is predicated upon attunement. Thus, change can occur through improved implicit attunement between the two participants, in a dance of sorts.

In the following clinical example I show how, with some patients who are hypersensitive to cues either due to temperament or to experiences throughout their development, the use of the couch reduces such sensitivity, either while they are interacting verbally or during integrative EMDR sequences.

Clinical vignette: The couch and EMDR: From hypersensitivity to relationality

Lisbeth is lying on the couch. She is speaking softly about her difficulty in feeling anything in her body. She wants to connect, she is hunting for a feeling, but cannot detect any. Nonetheless, her hands and her voice say she is feeling something. She caresses her hands in a slow motion, telling us that something is being provoked. When I point to the discrepancy in her words and motion, she quickly covers one hand with the other, as if ashamed to be caught doing something that is forbidden.

Lisbeth's early emotional mirrors told her she was not desirable. When she looked at her mirror reflection all she could see was ugly. Ugly body, ugly mind. She was certain she was a bad person with bad thoughts to be eradicated. If she were to describe herself to me as she felt herself to be before we met, I would expect a monster. She walked through the world feeling a lot but aware only of the channel that was guilty and ashamed to be. When she was sitting up in the first year of her treatment Lisbeth would carefully check my face for hints of disapproval. Then, if her hunt found the slightest sign, she would revert to *not knowing* how she felt, a safe and lonely mode of operation.

With the intentional use of EMDR, initiated by the patient and myself alternately, such embodied experiences became a parenthetical pause in which we could focus on enhancing an embodied experience that was essential to the patient's affect regulation at a time of need but that was kept away from her conscious and reflective mind. It was a dissociation of want, as she learned from an early age to push away desire for her caregiver's intimate closeness because this longing conflicted with the mother's projected disappointment in her daughter. Neither was able to live comfortably with the ambivalence of the relationship. For Lisbeth a deep desire for connection went underground, as she gave up even the slightest belief in the possibility of meaningful intimate engagement.

When I commented on the discrepancy between Lisbeth's words of emptiness and her hand stroking, shame was introduced. Feeling that perhaps repeating the motion would bring emotions, I suggested the use of EMDR to continue the pacing Lisbeth naturally began with her hands. She used the tappers in several BLS cycles, with each hand, now feeling more the longing she felt as a young child to be held and comforted yet had never had, as her parents were preoccupied with several young siblings, and were distancing owing to their own histories of relational deficiency.

Lisbeth, who typically did not show emotions, talked about the little girl she was in gentler terms. Although in the following sessions it seemed that Lisbeth crusted over what she had let herself feel, there was an ever so slight shift in her speech, as if for the first time she believed, for certain moments, that she had an equal place in the consultation room. The manifestation was in her speech flow, in her making decisions about what she wanted out of our work relationship, and the way she decided to occupy the couch, or to try to tolerate having direct eye contact.

What led her now was a wish to feel, and with it a preoccupation with the conditions that fostered such engagement with me and with herself. The playground grew into a forest. She could walk alone as long as she believed I was watching, listening, and remembering who she was before she entered the Pardes,[3] as she strolled into it, and sometimes ventured out. She would strategically probe about the use of EMDR as she felt something. It became a tool of attachment. I had it, but we could both reach out and use it.

As this example highlights, nonverbal communication is an important organizer of experience that lingers from the dawn of life onward. Its continuation is a premise on which EMDR operates. Trusting that what was installed in the body and mind in the meaningful interactions of infancy and childhood will carry on throughout life means that these can be retrieved through that process, as reexperiencing these interactions opens paths through reduced or closed-circuit patterns. Relational psychoanalysis similarly carries the belief that nonverbal engagement, which includes both the patient's and the analyst's embodied experiences of each other at the moment of engagement, has the power to transform old patterns by reengaging in the action and reflecting on the process of enactment to find pathways not yet etched in the patient's realm of possibilities, or for that matter, in the analyst's (Racker, 1957).

Composing new tunes

EMDR employs musicality not as a primary goal but as a useful outcome. We can appreciate the ways in which rhythmic motion, either through hand movement followed by the eye, knee tapping, or feeling the alternate gentle electric buzz in the palm of the hand, can offer a nudge similar to a mother's stimulation. In addition, the EMDR protocol, in particular during BLS sets, sends the patient into an internal dialogue that resembles early or significant communication with a caregiver. As a consequence, the patient engages with negative representations, sourced from the small *t* trauma of daily misattunement every child experiences, or the big *T* trauma of gross violations of the mind and body by a person in the life of the child. Both repetitive imagery and the reconstructed imagery in the EMDR protocol evoke a mini-idiosyncratic world determined by their own rhythmic cadence. It is within these all-encompassing affective dances that the possibility of distinguishing between a dance that seems to be to the only tune possible, and other variations of the musical building blocks that can potentially spell a new, more adaptive tune of the self in relation to the other and its environment can emerge.

Relational psychoanalysis offers the possibility of creating a new musicality by having the therapist not conform to the expected tune every time, but instead create that discrepancy in the transference-countertransference matrix that once more demands that the gap between the expected dance and a new one be bridged. Each dyad creates music, be it dissonant or harmonious. This opens the couple to endless variations on the theme of attachment. Even when the transferential dance resembles the original dance of childhood for the patient, the analyst will be able to reflect on the dynamics as it is enacted, or more likely following the collapse of such a cadenza.

Trevarthen's theory of intersubjectivity is essential to an understanding of EMDR's usefulness as a precursor to the analytic work. In EMDR, the practitioner invites the patient to process an image, with its associated negative and positive cognition. All the while, the practitioner pays close attention to the patient's minimal cues, which register shifts in the emotional response to the scenario being played out. On the other hand, the practitioner reciprocates minimally with her presence, sounds, or the words she uses that help or at times disrupt the patient's process. Although it is not a declared aim, the dyadic interaction fosters attachment. This process reassures the patient that he or she can rely on the presence of a caring other who can feel where they are and monitor their level of tolerance to painful relational material. What is first felt during EMDR's embodied experience can then be brought over to allow for a relational examination that is affect based. Following Trevarthen's (1998) theoretical formulation, we may assume that, at the same time, the patient is aware of the therapist's attentive quiet presence and follows the containing environment to reduce his or her stress, both within the self and in the interaction with the therapist.

Clinical vignette: Unwitting mirroring

Frances is lying on the couch speaking, and her voice suddenly cracks. She is emotional about being understood, and for all the years she did not feel mirrored. Wishing to convey that I hear that she has suddenly become sad, I conflate, voicing my presence with her with an analytic inquiry. "What is going on, Frances?" I ask, aware that I am using her name, not that common in our work together. "You *get* me, and I do not have this kind of caring outside of here," she says. The next day, Frances tells me how she felt cared for at that moment, then distanced by my expression. It reminded her of a close friend who was critical of her months earlier, using these same words, in conjunction with her name, thus telling her she was now dropped out of her friend's mind and care. Frances's budding sense of attachment was intruded upon by that memory, following many moments of failed attunement in early life. There was a discrepancy between my words that channeled early interactions, and the tone of voice which sounded to her nonmalicious. She caught the nuanced split response, one that was loyal to old disappointing relationships, the other to newly formed, and still surprising, attunement. The evolving representation, in which Frances could expect to be mirrored more or less accurately by her analyst, was still shaky, yet she was now autonomous enough to inquire about the meaning of my words.

Being the constant victim, and expecting that, was beginning to change into some semblance of agency in the analytic relationship. The question "Who am I to the person of the analyst?" replaced her certainty that "I cannot expect anyone to take the time to get to know who I really am." As Martin Buber (1974) suggested, "all journeys have secret destinations of which the traveler is unaware" (p. 36). Through the *Thou*, a person becomes *I*.

With Frances, EMDR was helpful as she tried on newly projected paths following BLS cycles in which she traveled first to the familiar place of belonging to no one and deserving no personal relationship, before trying to meet a positive cognition in which she was worthy of such connection. The idea of this possibility, at first foreign to her, reduced her anxiety in trying to connect, first in my office, then with co-workers, family, and friends. Sometimes, the intensity Trevarthen (1998) pointed to, in relation to an infant mirroring her caregiver, is off-kilter. For example, with

Frances, anger was amplified in interactions, as when it overwhelmed her friend and caused Frances shame and embarrassment, while at other times she expressed more closeness than the relationship could support. What she was experiencing is what I call *dissociation into action*, in which the associated context for this behavior as found via EMDR is not immediately transferred to the renewed relational environment. Often, going back to the current real-life scenario helps the patient to find a more nuanced articulation of what she feels, and to develop some empathy not only for her own needs but those of the other.

Relevant psychologically interactive contributors are identified as involved in the process. Seligman and Harrison (2012) mention several such therapeutic actions as

> insight, interruption of old relational patterns, creation of new conditions of safety . . . containment and holding, empathy and the working through of disruptions in the therapeutic tie (Beebe and Lachmann, 2002; Kohut, 1977), enhancement of reflective functioning, interpretation . . . negotiation of paradox (Pizer, 1992) and the transformative "now moment" (Stern, 2004). (Seligman and Harrison, 2012, p. 246)

Therapeutic action is not only a reflection of the inner intersubjective world, it is also a reconstruction of the past with the contribution of the present through therapy. In EMDR a weaving together of internal convictions related to affective misattunement due to small *t* or big *T* trauma with more recent generative representations takes place. Through repeated cycles of BLS, the patient finds affect attunement in the self and new expressions beyond the grip of the tenacious negative perceptions of their intersubjective capacity possible.

What relational analysis has to offer through enactment in the here and now of an interaction, EMDR has to offer with the embodied return to early experiences, and their reflection in current relationships. The combination of the two modes of working helps secure something much like the state of the original intersubjective moments before they went awry. Both relational psychoanalysis, through enactment in the analytic relationship, and EMDR, through the process of evoking difficult intersubjective scenarios alongside potentially renewed intersubjective attachment scenarios, offer the elaboration of a *like me* experience, and hence the possibility of change.

Developed and redeveloped we-ness

Karlen Lyons-Ruth (2006) found that by the end of their first year human infants, unlike babies of other primates, develop the awareness that others have subjective states like their own (p. 142). She posited that this awareness leads to negotiation and greater complexity of the *we-ness* or shared orientation toward the world that in turn allows the child to create collaborative relationships with others (p. 142). Lyons-Ruth wrote that joint "pretend" play in early childhood is essential for the elaboration of such strategic negotiation of meaning creation (p. 142). A view suggested earlier by Margaret Mead (1939) in her book *Growing Up in New Guinea: A Comparative Study of Primitive Education*, was that in the course of child development, meaning is created differently in various cultural groups. She found that play is essential to meaning-making, with its presence or absence having consequences for the further development of the child. Mead's study also suggested that, along with environmental, cultural, and other influences, meaning is created in relationships.

I offer that theory, when combined with empirical evidence of physical and mental correspondence, suggests that the addition of embodied experiences through EMDR and affective connection in the psychoanalytical environment may help replicate natural relational tendencies, while allowing for the creation of experiences that are containable for the analytic pair, and ultimately by the patient in her significant relationships outside our offices. Here, I suggest that, like joint pretend play, both psychoanalysis and EMDR offer an *as if* environment necessary for the creation and expansion of meaning. They do so by inviting the patient to entertain, in an affect-enriched way, the possibility of being open to strategic changes in relationships, both in play form and in real life outside of the consulting room, a space that had earlier been foreclosed by relational trauma and its aftermath.

Clinical vignette: Embodied experience and chaperoning of a sense of agency

Dana, an adult patient, reports that she had requested certain care from her mother, but that it was denied. The mother asserted she could not possibly provide any. Rationally, and when viewed apart from the dynamic history between mother and daughter, the patient's deep upset is puzzling. In the same breath, the patient's mother was asking the daughter to provide an attentive care of her. Dana, who is used to the disappointment of any wish but feels overwhelmed by the implicit and explicit requests of care from her mother, becomes depressed. Dana also does not understand the underlying connection between these two events. Her partner, on the other hand, is enraged at the mother and is able to articulate the narcissistic dynamic in which this is yet another wall blocking the path to amending the early relationship Dana is so wishing for at a crossroads in her family life.

Following exploration of the dyadic dance with the mother, now and in the past, Dana's depression and displaced rage about the need to keep some limited relationship with her mother is no longer so foreign and perplexing. This was a moment in which EMDR became an addition that propelled the emergence of affect that could not be expressed in early childhood and had to be dissociated repeatedly throughout Dana's life. Asking Dana to bring to mind the negative cognition of the power of her rage to kill off the mother, along with her belief in her inherent badness, and then adding a few sets of BLS to raise and desensitize the related anxiety and level of belief in her negative cognition, was followed by a rise in positive cognition that it was possible to feel, and to replace the negative feeling in relation to the image of her enraged self in this situation with her mother. What emerged was a deep sadness over her inability to access her mother's emotional attunement to her own need, regardless of her mother's ability to feel empathy toward Dana (Stern, 1985). Another emotion triggered in this session was shame over failing to elicit her mother's attunement. In both, EMDR was instrumental in helping the patient see and feel that the emotion she feared would destroy relational ties was not the only response. With the observing presence of the therapist with EMDR, Dana retrieved and experienced a missing element of benevolence.

The action in EMDR first allowed Dana to experience her dissociated rage, which was mirrored in her partner's anger. To proprioceptively experience the rage in her partner through the EMDR BLS cycles, the patient returned to the image of her partner by imitating them, in effect finding her own displaced feelings. Once Dana could recognize the rage as an emotion that was held in the spousal dyad had originated in her, she recognized and reclaimed it verbally, and more importantly nonverbally. Dana came to trust her embodied experience better. We used BLS rounds to return to the current moment and move through layers of space and time in Dana's history to the bedrock of her remembered relational life to help make the experience her own again.

The EMDR protocol assisted Dana to begin to locate and trust her now embodied memory that was awakened with new interactions with others. The new connection between experience and words had the potential to reshape her current experiences with less fear. Another benefit of using EMDR at this juncture was in helping Dana see that she was no longer a baby elephant tethered to a pole from which she could not move away. She could use both EMDR and a relational psychoanalytic process to experiment with other solutions, rather than having to fall back on her well-engrained eradication of part of herself to maintain her relationships. In the integration element of the EMDR process, Dana experienced similar situations with a different, more desirable, outcome more like what she had seen and felt through the embodied experience of EMDR.

Oftentimes, as happened here, the patient feels confident that she can try out a different interaction outside the consulting room, in this case in a situation in which she recognized how it feels to be enraged at a love object without losing the other person, and also while keeping a larger part of her subjectivity intact. That confidence comes in addition to gaining an understanding that the rage is in reaction to a sense of helplessness, which can now be transformed through alternative potential scenarios. EMDR embodied experience helps Dana to sense signals that clue her into the source of the negative emotion, and give her a chance to use her growing reflexive capacities to change the course of the interaction, and her reaction to her budding anxiety.

Back to the mother here, Dana reported that in another attempt to interact with her mother in a different way she experienced less anxiety at trying to make her needs heard, and in setting a better boundary with her mother. EMDR in this case allowed the patient to imagine other possibilities of interaction in ways she could execute without forgetting important aspects of her self. It is often surprising to patients to find out that they can feel differently about a situation, even when the building blocks have not changed much at the time of the interaction.

We can speculate from what we have learned from infant attachment research that had the patient felt early in life the sense of the to and fro of a relationship, in which part of the time, during play for example, pleasure is experienced and expressed by both parties—until one of them needs a break, say, because the play got too rough, and a limit is introduced—the sense of being dropped would not have been as palpable for the adult patient who is denied care, as in fact was the case. The ability to differentiate between what one person feels and what another person feels grows from an experience with a caregiver who is able to commiserate with the child at times of pain without making the pain their own. A parent who makes the pain their own might confuse the child with regard to who is the one who suffers over something that happened to the child. When an empathic response is demonstrated, the child feels that the caregiver is with him, without becoming him. When this process is heavily skewed, the patient may relate to others primarily by projection (Seligman and Harrison, 2012).

Hypothetically, if the mother, with the patient in infancy, had been able to negotiate how much demand she could contain from her baby, they could then learn from each other how to regulate their needs as well as the ability to contain emotional demands. In the reality of this particular dyad, following the mother's feeling of being emotionally and physically overwhelmed by her infant, Dana learned to choke back her needs, and attempted to contain the mother's impending breakdown that had not been attended to in the marital bond, nor probably in the mother's childhood, and therefore had been transmitted into the relationship with her daughter. She could also understand the rage her partner felt on her behalf as rage she had had to give up early on to sustain the relationship with her mother.

Intersubjective engagement and change

Rules of intersubjective engagement are written by both parties as they are experienced. Every dyad combines a unique set of traits that define the relationship from early in life.

In the example with Dana, elements of early childhood intersubjective interactions and their modification to preserve the relationship with the mother were triggered in current interactions with her. Proprioceptively, the patient's partner displayed her emotions. In therapy, the patient reported a narrative without much emotion. Using EMDR, the patient had a chance to move through her interaction with her mother, including returning to the bedrock of the earliest experience she could recall, and then begin to see and experience her partner's reaction. Then, through the rehashing of observing her partner's rage at her mother, she was able to find her own anger, and finally feel sadness for the lost connection. A sense of agency was in the making.

Stern (1985) concluded that although developmental theories abound, clinicians seldom apply developmental understanding to their therapeutic work at the pre-symbolic stages. EMDR helps by engaging the patient not only in remembered historical excavations and their relevance to the current difficulties in the patient's relational bonds, but also in the nonverbal, embodied sensations that follow their screen memories.

Stern, Sander, Nahum, Harrison, et al. (1998) wrote that for therapeutic change to occur something more than interpretation is needed (p. 903). Based on mother–infant research, Stern et al. (1998) proposed that the *something more* resides in the interactional intersubjective process that allows for what they term *implicit relational knowing*. This relational intrapsychic process is different than the symbolic one. Its implications for the analytical situation are that, in the analytic dyad, there will be reorganization of the patient's implicit procedural knowledge, in addition to the change in the interaction between the analyst and the patient. What EMDR adds, though this is not explicitly a goal, is a third element, forming a triangle between the therapist, the patient, and the old and new relational constructs that creates the new, believable implicit procedural knowledge that will invite the patient to respond differently to situations outside the consulting room. Perhaps the configuration that Stern et al. (1998) suggest may help illustrate this idea. They noted that a therapeutic relationship similar to the mother–infant interaction helped develop implicit relational knowing in both the analyst and the patient. The moments of meeting helped to organize, or reorganize, earlier ways of relating, so that when the new environment was created the response to it would be new as well. Such moments of meeting in the establishment of the EMDR sequence similarly help to effectively change the environment in a way that allows the patient to respond to it in a new way, as opposed to the dissociated response prescribed by a trauma reaction.

In the presence of the therapist, the patient is encouraged to again engage with environments associated with the old and the new relational responses. At the beginning, it is as if the patient is *meeting the self as other*. Gradually the patient reorganizes the engraved internal relational reaction into a more mutative landscape through implicit relational knowing. This knowing is based on believable moments of meeting initially created by the EMDR experience of self-regulation, which are then elaborated upon in the relational engagement in the psychoanalytic process through transference and countertransference. Mental action follows this implicit relational knowing and subsequent reorganization of reactions to past events. EMDR and the analytic situation contribute to changes in action and behavior that arise from this new context. Stern and his colleagues (1998) stressed that the intersubjective environment would "create progressively more coherent implicit relational knowledge" that included "what each member understands to be their own and the other's experience of the relationship" (p. 906). They described how research by Freeman (1994) suggested that a change in the olfactory context in rabbits changes not only the neural firing and spatial pattern in the brain for the new odor, but also alters neural responses to all other previously established odors. A new context brings about change in pre-existing elements (Stern et al., 1998). Stern et al. (1998), based on Sander (1962, 1987) and Nahum (1994), believed that well-timed interpretation was an attempt to grasp aspects of the idea of the *moment of meeting* as an adaptive process in development that were key to state shifts and organismic reorganization (p. 906).

Trauma versus fantasy

In many of our patients, trauma plays a formidable role in their relational difficulties. This realization finds its way into the minds of psychodynamic therapists in both theory and therapeutic action. With the feminist critique of Freud's change of mind about what he knew to be the reality of his patients' real trauma, and more recent accounts of psychoanalysts' clinical observations, along with the now recognized impact of trauma on the developing brain contributed by neuroscience, a shift occurred in the treatment paradigm. Focusing on the impact of trauma expressed in the relational situation came to the forefront of the therapeutic approach, while the more classical psychoanalytic slant, in which fantasy was sourced at conflicted wishes of the forbidden in early childhood, descended to the background and was no longer seen as the primary contributor to psychological difficulties. As Longden (2013) asserted, "the important question in psychiatry should be not 'What's wrong with you?' but rather, 'What's happened to you?' " (n.p.).

Stern (2010), in his discussion of the early social life of the baby, pointed to the difference between stimulus strength that was too low or too strong. The former might create a baby that was not very aroused and interested, while if a stimulus was too strong, creating infant arousal that was too high, the infant would try to reduce the overstimulation. Following this formulation—speaking of the baby's engaging as a real partner to the parent—may help clinicians to recognize patterns of interaction as they attempt to see which aspect can best show the specifics of the interaction, in order to help guide treatment (p. 107).

We may want to consider the dynamics of a patient who as a young child experienced neglect and weak stimulus by one parent, and a strong stimulus by another parent, or another person in the child's environment who took advantage of the child's need for interaction. Alternatively, the effect on a child who is understimulated in some situations and over-stimulated in other situations by the same parent can be just as significant. In our clinical work, this information, arising from that interaction, can be particularly helpful in assessing the source of interactive distress, as it was in the example with Keith presented earlier in this chapter. Then, a shift in my attentiveness created a sense of low stimulus, which left him feeling too alone and wishing for more, and that in turn created an internal dynamic to which he was accustomed, which took the form of his fantasy of my being angry with him. When he felt me to be unengaged, he turned the engagement into a familiar one in which he experienced an over-whelmingly strong stimulus. Each response represented a fear of being rejected by the same parent. This kind of oscillation mirrored Keith's early experience, when the stimulus was too low or too high. With other patients who are severely abused, this kind of movement back to the familiar is further pronounced in the transference-countertransference interaction, causing both parties to feel thrashed as they attempt to steer their relational boat.

The recognition of the reality of abuse is interwoven with the relational attention to real experience, both in the patient's past and in the therapeutic relationship, and without judging the subjective account as being distorted. This understanding is diagnostically and clinically relevant as trauma tends to defy meaning by attending to the greater need of survival through dissociation and the development of post-traumatic stress symptoms.

I have found that EMDR is an ally in bridging the gap of incongruence between needs and reality that often appears where several options of the ideal and the wished for, the reality and its failures, exist. Similarly, it can assist in investigating other states, including parapraxis and the narratives one adheres to in order to maintain an important illusion of connection and integration with loved and needed objects.

Summary

In this chapter, we saw the importance of early attachment between infants and their caregivers at the dawn of life, and its implications for all other relationships, including the therapeutic relationship. We saw that well-being and trouble develop in the context of the to and fro negotiation of needs and wishes, that participation of both partners in an interaction is essential and influential, and that infants from the very first hours after their birth, perhaps even before birth, contribute significantly to their relationship with their mothers and others in their lives. These interactions are nuanced yet profound, and span the range from bodily to verbal expression through stages of meaningful sound-making communication. We saw that interactions that are repeatedly disrupted, as they are in trauma situations, carry their intricate implication into therapy, in which they are reenacted and hopefully, over time, can be drawn on to create new language, both verbal and nonverbal, through a believable relational discourse that allows for uncharted paths to be explored in the therapeutic and extra-therapeutic realms. Knowledge about attachment can inform therapists diagnostically, and help them use their countertransferential responses and reactions to the patient as a guide to what has happened. Modification of the EMDR protocol to include attachment-focused steps that enhance the safety needed for the therapeutic work may be necessary in order to meet patients who suffered relational trauma, on the path to repairing their attachment capabilities (Parnell, 2013).

Attachment studies and their related theory shed light on the important focus of EMDR on the embodied experience as a critical step in increasing auto-regulation through interaction with both the original and new internal objects in order to re-create a more benevolent presence. Relational work uses its knowledge of research on attachment and its conceptual theory to improve the relational regulation between the patient and therapist while richly developing new ways of being in relationship through the examination of the transference and countertransference.

Notes

The statement in the epigraph is from Martin Buber's *Meetings: Autobiographical Fragments*, first published in 1967 (La Salle, IL: Open Court); here it is cited from the third edition (London: Routledge, 2002), 72–73.

1 Resource tapping is a relatively low-risk EMDR technique that amplifies positive experiences acquired from previous experience, or experiences that were newly learned through EMDR or other forms of therapy. These resources can then be drawn on while the patient imagines current or future stressful situations and can increase the patient's ability to respond adaptively.

2 This is one of the quotes from Evelyn Schreiber's description of Morrison's interview that Schreiber presented at a New Directions Writing Conference, May 3–5, 2013, and from a personal communication following the conference.

3 *Pardes* literally means "orchard," in Hebrew and refers to different levels of interpretive depth originally developed for reading Jewish texts. Four levels of interpretation are combined in the acronym:

P for direct or simple meaning (Pshat = simple)
R for symbolic hinted meaning, deeper beyond the literal in the narrative (Remez = hint)
D for inquiry, or exploration, seeking precedents in other similar earlier texts, for the purpose of comparative interpretation, recognition of metaphors in the texts (Drash = inquire)
S for the uncanny that is hidden in the text's many folds and is revealing of its deeper, higher or mysterious meaning (Sod = secret).
(As adapted from http://en.wikipedia.org/wiki/Pardes_(Jewish_exegesis, n.p.))

References

Ainsworth, M. D. S., M. Blehar, M. E. Waters, and S. Wall. (1978). *Patterns of Attachment*. Hillsdale, NJ: Erlbaum.

Aron, L., and M. Lechich. (2012). Relational psychoanalysis. In G. O. Gabbard, B. E. Litowitz, and P. Williams, editors, *Textbook of Psychoanalysis*, 211–224. 2nd ed. Washington, DC: American Psychiatric Publishing.

Beebe, B., S. Knoblauch, J. Rustin, and D. Sorter. (2005). *Forms of Intersubjectivity in Infant Research and Adult Treatment*. New York: Other Press.

Beebe, B., and F. Lachmann. (2002). *Infant Research and Adult Treatment*. Hillsdale, NJ: The Analytic Press.

Beebe, B., D. Sorter, J. Rustin, and S. Knoblauch. (2003). A comparison of Meltzoff, Trevarthen, and Stern. *Psychoanalytic Dialogues* 13: 777–804.

Bowlby, J. (1969). *Attachment and Loss: Attachment*. Vol. 1. London: Hogarth Press and the Institute of Psycho-Analysis.

Bowlby, J. (1980). *Attachment and Loss: Sadness and Depression*. Vol. 3. London: Hogarth Press and the Institute of Psycho-Analysis.

Bowlby, J. (1988). *A Secure Base: Parent-child Attachment and Healthy Human Development*. New York: Basic Books.

Brazelton, T. B. (1982). Joint regulation of neonate-parent behavior. In E. Z. Tronick, editor, *Social Interchange in Infancy*, 7–22. Baltimore, MD: University Park Press.

Brazelton, T. B., B. Koslowski, and M. Main. (1974). The origins of reciprocity: The early mother-infant interaction. In I. Lewis, L. A. Rosenberg, and M. Main, editors, *The Effects of the Infant on Its Caregiver*, 49–76. New York: Wiley.

Buber, M. (1974). *The Legend of the Baal-Shem*, M. Friedman, translator. New York: Schocken. Reprinted: Princeton, NJ: Princeton University Press, 1975.

Cooper, S. H. (2000). Mutual containment in the analytic situation. *Psychoanalytic Dialogues* 10(2): 169–194.

Damasio, A. (1999). *The Feeling of What Happens: Body and Emotion in the Making of Consciousness*. Orlando, FL: Harcourt.

Ekman, P., and W. V. Friesen. (1969). The repertoire of non-verbal behavior categories, origins, usage, and coding. *Semiotica* 1: 49–98.

Erikson, E. (1950). *Childhood and Society*. New York: Norton.

Freeman, W. (1994). *Societies of Brains*. Hillsdale, NJ: Erlbaum.

Hartmann, H. (1956). Notes on the reality priniciple. *Psychoanalytic Study of the Child* 11: 31–53.

Hopkins, L. (2011). Cocreated idealization in the Winnicott/Khan analysis: Commentary on paper by Joyce Slochower. *Psychoanalytic Dialogues* 21(1): 28–32.

Kitchur, M. (2005). The strategic developmental model for EMDR. In R. Shapiro, editor, *EMDR Solutions: Pathways to Healing*, 8–56. New York: Norton.

Knoblauch, S. (2000). *The Musical Edge of Therapeutic Dialogue*. Hillsdale, NJ: The Analytic Press.

Knoblauch, S. (2012). Body rhythms and the unconscious: Expanding clinical attention with the polyrhythmic weave. In L. Aron and A. Harris, editors, *Relational Psychoanalysis: Evolution of Process*. Vol. 5, 183–204. New York: Routledge.

Kohut, H. (1977). *The Restoration of the Self*. New York: International Universities Press.

Kumin, I. (1995). *Pre-object Relatedness: Early Attachment and the Psychoanalytic Situation*. New York: Guilford.

Longden, E. (2013). The voices in my head: Presenter: TED Talks. www.ted.com/speakers/eleanor_longden (accessed on 5-21-2013, n.p.).

Lyons-Ruth, K. (2006). Play, precariousness, and the negotiation of shared meaning: A developmental research perspective on child psychotherapy. *Journal of Infant, Child, and Adolescent Psychotherapy* 5: 142–159.

Lyons-Ruth, K. (2012). When love goes awry: Varieties of adaptation in the early attachment relationship. Human Evolution and Human Development Symposium 2012. University of Notre Dame Shaw Center for Children & Families. www.youtube.com/watch?v=3IxCB4lpTBI (accessed on 1-25-2017).

Lyons-Ruth, K. and D. Jacobvitz. (1999). Attachment disorganization: Unresolved loss, relational violence, and lapses in behavioral and attentional strategies. In J. Cassidy and P. Shaver, editors, *Handbook of Attachment: Theory, Research, and Clinical Implications*, 520–554. New York: Guilford.

Lyons-Ruth, K., and E. Spielman. (2004). Disorganized infant attachment strategies and helpless-fearful profiles of parenting: Integrating attachment research with clinical intervention. *Infant Mental Health Journal* 25(4): 318–335.

Main, M. (1992). Attachment: Overview with implications for clinical work. In R. Muir and J. Kerr, editors, *Attachment Theory: Social, Developmental and Clinical Perspectives*, 407–474. Hillsdale, NJ: Erlbaum.

Malloch, S. (1999). Mothers and infants and communicative musicality. In I. Deliege, editor, *Rhythms, Musical Narrative and the Origins of Human Communication*, 29–57. Liege, Belgium: European Society for the Cognitive Sciences of Music.

Mead, M. (1939). *Growing Up in New Guinea: A Comparative Study of Primitive Education*. New York: Morrow. Reprinted: New York: Harper Perennial Modern Classics, 2001.

Meltzoff, A. (1985). The roots of social and cognitive development: Models of man's original nature. In T. Field and N. Fox, editors, *Social Perception in Infants*, 1–30. Norwood, NJ: Ablex.

Meltzoff, A., and M. Moore. (1998). Infant intersubjectivity: Broadening the dialogue to include imitation, identity and intention. In S. Braten, editor, *Intersubjective Communication and Emotion in Early Ontogeny*, 47–62. Cambridge, UK: Cambridge University Press.

Morrison, T. (2012). *Home*. New York: Vintage Books.

Nahum, J. (1994). New theoretical vistas in psychoanalysis: Louis Sander's theory of early development. *Psychoanalysis Psychology* 11: 1–19.

Pardes. from http://en.wikipedia.org/wiki/Pardes_(Jewish_exegesis) (accessed on 11-12-2013).

Parnell, L. (2013). *Attachment-focused EMDR: Healing Relational Trauma*. New York: Norton.

Pizer, S. (1992). The negotiation of paradox in the analytic process. *Psychoanalytic Dialogues* 2: 215–240.

Racker, H. (1957). The meanings and uses of countertransference. *Psychoanalytic Quarterly* 26(3): 303–357.

Sameroff, A. J., and R. N. Emde. (1989). *Relational Disturbances in Early Childhood: A Developmental Approach*. New York: Basic Books.

Sander, L. (1962). Issues in early mother-child interaction. *Journal of the American Academy of Child Psychiatry* 1: 141–166.

Sander, L. (1987). Awareness of inner experience. *Child Abuse and Neglect* 2: 339–346.

Seligman, S. (1998). Child psychoanalysis, adult psychoanalysis, and developmental psychology: Introduction to symposium on child analysis, part II. *Psychoanalytic Dialogues* 8: 79–86.

Seligman, S. (1999). Integrating Kleinian theory and intersubjective infant research: Observing projective identification. *Psychoanalytic Dialogues* 9: 129–159.

Seligman, S. (2008). Metaphor, activity, acknowledgement, grief: Forms of transformation in the reflective space. In E. L. Jurist, A. Slade, and S. Bergner, editors, *Mind to Mind: Infant Research, Neuroscience, and Psychoanalysis*, 353–372. New York: Other Press.

Seligman, S., and A. Harrison. (2012). Infant research and adult psychotherapy. In G. O. Gabbard, B. E. Litowitz, and P. Williams, editors, *Textbook of Psychoanalysis*. 2nd ed., 239–254. Washington DC: American Psychiatric Publishing.

Schore, A. (2003). *Affect Regulation and the Repair of the Self*. New York: Norton.

Solms, M., and O. Turnbull. (2002). *The Brain and the Inner World: An Introduction to the Neuroscience of Subjective Experience*. New York: Other Press.

Stern, D. N. (1971). A micro-analysis of mother-infant interaction: Behavior regulating social contact between a mother and her 3 1/2 month-old twins. *Journal of the American Academy of Child and Adolescent Psychiatry* 10: 501–517.

Stern, D. N. (1985). *The Interpersonal World of the Infant*. New York: Basic Books.

Stern, D. N. (2004). *The Present Moment in Psychotherapy and Everyday Life*. New York: Norton.

Stern, D. N. (2010). *Forms of Vitality: Exploring Dynamic Experience in Psychology, the Arts, Psychotherapy, and Development*. New York: Oxford University Press.

Stern, D. N., L. W. Sander, J. P. Nahum, A. Harrison, K. Lyons-Ruth, A. C. Morgan, and E. Z. Tronick. (1998). Non-interpretive mechanisms in psychoanalytic therapy: The "something more" than interpretation. *International Journal of Psychoanalysis* 79(5): 903–921.

Trevarthen, C. (1993). The function of emotions in early infant communication and development. In J. Nadel and L. Camaioni, editors, *New Perspectives in Early Communicative Development*, 48–81. London: Routledge.

Trevarthen, C. (1998). The concept and foundations of infant intersubjectivity. In S. Braten, editor, *Intersubjective Communication and Emotion in Early Ontogeny*, 15–46. Cambridge, UK: Cambridge University Press.

Trevarthen, C. (2009). The intersubjective psychobiology of human meaning: Learning of culture depends on interests for co-operative practical work—and affection for the joyful art of good company. *Psychoanalytic Dialogues* 19: 507–518.

Tronick, E. (2007). *The Neurobehavioral and Social-Emotional Development of Infants and Children*. New York: Norton.

Wallin, D. J. (2007). *Attachment in Psychotherapy*. New York: Guilford.

Part II

Case studies using both relational psychoanalysis and EMDR

Chapter 5

In the trenches

Digging for lost passions—The use of EMDR in psychoanalytic work

> But most hearts say, I want, I want,
> I want, I want. My heart
> is more duplicitous,
> though no twin as I once thought.
> It says, I want, I don't want, I
> want, and then a pause.
> It forces me to listen, . . .
> — Margaret Atwood

In this chapter I describe my work with a woman during the progress of which, a number of characteristics that emerged as we proceeded led to my decision to introduce some modifications of treatment, based on EMDR technique to our regular sessions. Here, in order to enhance our analytic work, EMDR was used not to replace but as an adjunct to analytic work, in order to help bridge the patient's splitting and fragmentation. That is, before bringing EMDR into our work, part of what I considered was my personal experience of being with this patient in the room, which was quite palpable, as the patient's dissociation could not be mediated simply by verbal exchange.

Sheila is a woman in her mid-fifties. She lost her husband five years ago in a single-engine airplane crash, and has felt stuck and unable to move ahead in her emotional life ever since. Although she describes her marriage as the center of her universe for nearly three decades, Sheila also struggles to reconcile the gap between her idealization and certain truths about the circumstances that led to the creation of her marital bond, and the important losses that also endured through this marriage.

Although her presentation seemed ego-syntonic, I had a persistent sense, in the first phase of our work, that Sheila was sanitizing a much more complicated and perplexing reality than she wanted me to believe or know about. I was unsure whether she liked the tidy psychic and external reality she created for herself, or whether she actually suffered the deep losses she had to endure, and covered this with the superficial ways in which she expressed herself.

Referred to me by a colleague, Sheila's initial complaint was about her difficulty in dealing with a tumultuous relationship with her only son, who was himself dealing with a recurrence of a life-threatening complications of his congenital heart disease. The focus of our work has been for her to find a way to reach and accept her own personal level of separation between herself and others, whom she experiences as part of herself, so that she can develop an internal sense of herself as an independent person.

One important manifestation of the self-eradication of herself I felt in Sheila was her heavy dependency on her son for decision making. She would call him on a weekly basis with imaginary crises that she demanded be addressed promptly. A simple decision on her son's part to act autonomously has been met by her bewilderment, as well as a barrage of prophesies of immanent disasters.

One element became clear early on. Sheila had no sense of psychological mindfulness to call on. She had no cogent understanding of how she was impacted by significant events in her life and has few clues and very little insight into her impact on others, although a vague sense of loneliness creeps in. Part of my experience with Sheila seems unremarkable. I have found myself from time to time asking myself, "What is Sheila doing in analysis?" Yet with more exploration that notion faded.

Sheila does not have an in-depth understanding of her emotional life. In addition, she perceives the many contradictory allegiances that have kept her relations split as necessary in her effort to maintain the image of perfection intact. It is this instability between actuality and the appearance of the perfect in relationships that commonly brings about the most obvious instances of fragmentation. I often feel that Sheila is somehow still in the bunker, hoping to be rescued from something that she cannot comprehend, where two-dimensional images of good, evil, and indifference threaten her fragile sense of sanity. In particular, envy over her lost youth takes over when she is in the presence of the vivacious youth in family members. She then alternately attempts to fuse with the youthful image, or wishes to destroy the person who shows her how imperfect her picture of herself is. She constantly struggles to hold any negative feelings about herself steady; they threaten to overwhelm her.

After several months during which I attempted to work with her via relational psychoanalysis, and particularly when I felt the less than effective struggle to connect affectively, I realized that there was some decline in cognitive function associated with instances of anxiety. It was at that point that I suggested to Sheila that we try EMDR, both because we could engage her anxiety more consistently in a measured and contained way, and because I had already seen her respond affectively to a tactile stimulus.

EMDR helps refine this capability for response a step at a time. Typically, when we followed a fragmentation, Sheila commented on how difficult it was to stay with one theme or even to recognize an emotion. She began such a session recently by saying that she felt good, as if she had "licked off all her son's problems," and then worried about becoming dispensable. I asked, "Licked?" and wanted to offer the BLS tappers to start an EMDR session.

Today, after some months of work, this introduction isn't needed, as Sheila spontaneously continues with much emotion in her voice. She realizes the loaded term, and goes on, "Yes, like a mother in nature will lick her newborn baby (Image). I should have done it more to my baby, but I didn't. I was a bad mother (NC—Negative Cognition). I should have licked him more." She sends her tongue out, and pulls it back with a slurp (Bodily Expression and New Image). Her hands follow to grab an imaginary infant.

She then slips into an emotional state of mind that in earlier sessions had been reserved for work that included an EMDR component. Now she can move spontaneously into that space, feeling, musing, and able to use metaphor and reflect on her experience. I feel it is possible that the EMDR experience has ignited a previously dormant ability, and that she no longer needs to be dissociated during her analytic experience—and, more importantly, in her real world outside analysis.

In this session, she talks about being touched by her women friends, hugged, and the gift she got in developing these relationships following the accidental death of her husband (Integration with the Now). She says she has never had that level of closeness. Now she wonders, if she had been able to keep close relationships with her women friends during her child-rearing years, whether they would have served as models to her (Elements of both Positive Cognition and Negative Cognition, to be separated and defined). Feeling cared for, she might have become a better-connected mother. Daniel Stern (1995) has spoken about new mothers who need the company of other women and mothers after giving birth, and at the start of motherhood, rather than just the company of men.

Given the women in Sheila's early world, one dense with complex envy, disappointment, and lack of ambition in the external world, disengagement from women also meant rejection of the demand to become domestic and depressed. Instead, males and the male working world became the turf on which she competed and against which she measured her success. As with women, her relatedness to her child took a back seat at best. Most of the time, she has been oblivious to the possibility of developing such relationships, and gaining something valuable for herself, in addition to the satisfaction of being involved in her child's development.

With EMDR and analytic exploration, Sheila has begun to remember that she was once a younger, wilder person. This self is now long gone, gone and veiled so completely that when she sees it in others she feels as if she is looking at a foreign object that must be condemned.

What good did it bring her to be so wild? She and her husband became one flesh; nothing got in between them, certainly not the child. As long as she conformed there was no punishment. But where had all the passion gone?

Sheila pours her aggression and sense of bewilderment, as well as her disowned and lonely self, onto others, while assuming an aloof, seemingly submissive stance toward the world.

Therefore, it was an act of great courage for Sheila to enter analysis. Much of what she had been dealing with, once she found her emotional self, was mourning over elements in her life that she can no longer change, as someone in their thirties or forties can often manage to do.

In one session, as she described a spontaneous embrace with her son that they both seemed to enjoy, Sheila commented, "I wish I had hugged him more when he was little. I see now that he needed it." She adds, "and probably me too." She continues, "Why didn't I see that?! How could I have missed it?" I say, "To see his pain would mean you would need to feel your own pain over not being held enough." She sighs, "He was just a little boy who needed me, and I left him behind, alone. I didn't pay any attention." She adds, "How horrible. I want to hug him, that little boy, right now." She pauses, and we sit with the weight. I am silent. She says, "It is too late now, huh?"

Sheila can now work with her wishes and treat them as just wishes. She can now often feel her emotions without manipulating a situation into a fight or emotional blackmail as an alternative.

In another session, Sheila spoke about a tender infant she met who seemed to be lost without his parent, and said, "This is what I did to my son; he was standing there at the door as I left, wanting me to stay with him, and I just turned my back and went away, just saying goodbye. How could I do this to him? He was so young. Of course he is mad at me. Because of the pain he had to suffer for so many years, because I did not pay any attention, he isn't well."

Her murderous feelings toward herself, often projected toward others, shift between a sense of defeat for being reminded of not being a good mother and guilt over that. Much of our work has been in locating her neglected self, as a step on the way to developing compassion toward others.

In her effort to repair her fragmented internal landscape, Sheila instead directs substantial attention to efforts to keep up external appearances of health and beauty, while at the same time relating to her body by evading it in a deeply narcissistic way. She puts constant pressure on her body, and treats signs of deterioration in muscle tone and joint flexibility as temporary. For example, she was enraged when a wrist injury made her skip an opportunity to play tennis in a regional tournament.

During our work, it was possible to see a parallel and a link between her beloved son's medical crisis and Sheila's concern about her body, which EMDR work has helped address. Perhaps one of the most important realizations is that she experiences her frailty more keenly when her son is ill and needs her. She feels both triumphant thanks to her superior genes, but is also reminded of her own deteriorating bodily function. And, looking forward, she is in part dreading being unable to assist in her son's care.

What has unfolded in this psychoanalysis, and in what I have come to understand about Sheila, is that her longing for human connection is much stronger than her wish to control others. Both Sheila and her loved ones are trapped in the repetitive process of searching for secure attachment that is only somewhat reparative. There, short bouts of new emotional and satisfying physical connectedness can feel healing, yet she longs for more.

Early tactile exploration

At the beginning of our work, Sheila's emotions arose almost exclusively out of her tactile associations to her childhood pleasures. Words were used to create elliptic defensive arguments that increased the level of fragmentation and splitting of emotional reality by blaming others or feeling guilt. Occasional openings to emotional opportunities represented very dangerous situations that threatened to shatter her vulnerable perfect self-image.

In fact, the idea that a shift between complete emotional numbness and the thought that an analytic exploration might be possible came out of the following observation of Sheila's link to her sense of touch. At the end of one session, Sheila stood up and seemed to notice for the first time a glass sand-tray in my office. She picked a woman figure out of the sand, and with gentle hand motions stroked the sand-frosted glass body of the figurine, first with a finger, then her entire palm.

She then asked the glass woman questions about her origin and whereabouts. She pretended to get answers, and continued the short conversation in a gentle voice, almost as a mother talks to her newborn child, all the while stroking gently. I had never seen her that calm and dreamy. But she was then startled out of her dissociative mode by her self-conscious thought that she had gotten too emotional. She pulled her hand out of the sand, leaving a sand trail on the carpet. Her dead father's name resembles the object she happened to pick up and gently touch. Then she said, "How silly of me" before leaving the table. Here we can see that the potential for relationship is there, but the question is how do you get to a more lively, caring person who soldiers up rather than having to risk a breakdown over all that is lost?

Now a little more of Sheila's history. In the summer following her third year of college, she went to work in a remote community in South America. She loved working outdoors, the simple rigorous life, and the people she met. Moreover, she fell in love with a fellow worker who planned to stay long-term in this remote community. Sheila wrote to her parents about her decision to stay in South America another year and the reason for her choice.

She subsequently received a reply in which her parents demanded that she return home, complete her college degree, and marry the wonderful man she had met prior to leaving on her trip, whom she found eligible, yet not that exciting. The tone of the letter left no room for negotiation. She either returned home or risked being disowned.

Heartbroken, Sheila returned home, dated the man for several months, and married him. Although she did not think consciously about this loss until the beginning of her analysis with me, the first two years of her marriage were tumultuous for her.

The layers of truths regarding whom Sheila loved, and who loved her were not always clear. For example, during her first year of marriage she responded to her employer's overtures and secretly dated him. Her husband never acknowledged knowing anything about this, and the issue was never mentioned, although on at least one occasion Sheila feared he might strike her in his rage over a petty disagreement.

She left the marriage several times, but returned after short separations. Her loneliness was greater than her discontent. She resolved this struggle by deciding to participate fully in her marriage, and from then on did just that.

As a result of this decision to adhere to the marriage, Sheila lived her life with little examination. She just left all her wishes and doubts behind her. It took many regrounding efforts to bring back memories locked in her body and mind and to move from that oblivion into a fairly active analytic exploration.

Why EMDR with Sheila?

In addition to the significant trauma in her family of origin and its impact on Sheila's psychological development, two separate occasions brought me to consider using EMDR with her. The first was the incident by the sandtray in which Sheila was so moved by stroking an object that it brought her to tears.

On the second occasion, Sheila engaged in emotional grief for a man she loved. For the first time, she did not need me to mediate her feelings and thoughts in her reverie. Sheila was able to find tenderness in her mind toward others in her life for whom she had earlier expressed, over several months, projected ridicule, rage, and exasperation. On that day, she forgot my presence and was deeply engaged in a conversation about an emotional experience she had never noticed consciously or discussed before.

This rich moment revealed one of many disavowed truths in Sheila's relationships, not the least of which was the disavowed connection between mother and son. It was at this meeting that, until I employed EMDR, for the first time I observed Sheila's ability to articulate, symbolize, and use metaphors to describe her earlier emotional state, and not only that but to also engage with her grief richly in the here and now.

By that time, I had realized that because of the high level of dissociation she was experiencing, an analytic approach alone was not likely to be successful, as access to words that conveyed emotions was threatening all by itself. Sheila felt unprotected. With the mitigation of BLS, Sheila could control the emotional gush, hence allowing herself to dissociate *into* her emotions rather than *out of* her emotions. In other words, EMDR forced her into a messy state of mind that she could tolerate.

In the countertransference, the issue of time was not unimportant. The seriousness of her son's unstable heart condition was knocking at the family's door with an impressive tap. What would happen the next time that mother and son must support one another, emotionally and physically? The off-ramp last time had led her to my office. What if there wasn't an off-ramp this time?

This time Sheila had the opportunity to explore and understand some of her wishes and concerns. Although she is still relatively young and highly active, some signs of physical and mental decline are negatively marking her sense of invincibility, which in turn has had an impact on my own sense of pressure in sensing time draining quickly in her hourglass. I have felt that the therapeutic goal must take precedence over the psychoanalytic goal, to borrow Owen Renik's (2001) discussion of priorities.

The main question I have been concerned about is whether Sheila could and would manage to change something important in her relationships before it was too late. Here I continue to think about the effect of a possible change, both on Sheila and on her close relations, while they are still well enough to find an emotional connection. I am also keenly aware of the potential melancholy Sheila may experience, alongside and in addition to her mourning over lost connections in the past.

I have felt compelled to help her locate the place of truthfulness that is congruent with more layers of her psychic life, yet at the same time have realized how resistant she would be to verbal exploration of her experience following half a century of emotional silence.

Attachment and reflective function: Integrating the methods

With Sheila's growing ability to feel and contain her emotional states, and with EMDR embedded in individual psychodynamic work, she has experienced less emotional volatility in her interactions with others (Fonagy and Target, 1997).

In their attachment research, Fonagy and Target (1997) maintained that the parent's most important task in infancy is to help the child regulate its affective states by lending his or her mature nervous system to assist the child's development of the capacity for self-regulation. This process is nonverbal for the most part. Adding EMDR to relational work has helped Sheila find her emotional maturity and a new ability to contain the anxiety that has affected her actual relationships for years.

To paraphrase what Eldredge and Cole (2008) have written, it is their belief, gathered from insights derived from attachment studies, affect research, and the breakthroughs in neuroscience, that the body and mind are mutually inter-implicated (p. 81–82). For example, they mention the "Boston Process of Change Study Group, in its investigation of how non-interpretive mechanisms lead to change and the question of what changes" (p. 83). The Boston Process of Change Study Group (also known as the Boston Change Process Study Group) looked "to cognitive developmental studies, neuropsychological data, and attachment studies to 'refashion a psychoanalytic meta-theory that is consistent both with the new research base and with a more fluid, mutual, and constructivist view of relational change in adulthood' (Lyons-Ruth, 1999, p. 579)" (Eldredge and Cole, 2008, p. 83). As Eldredge and Cole (2008) stated, "Lyons-Ruth contends that 'enactive knowing develops and changes by processes that are intrinsic to this system of representation and that do not rely on translation of procedures into reflective (symbolized) knowledge' (p. 579)" (Eldredge and Cole, 2008, p. 83).

Harris (1998) emphasized the difference between simple imitation and mimesis. Mimetic identifications are points of transfer of affective states through interaction. Identifications like this are a "responsive, imitative encounter with another being that can lead to mutually induced affective experiences" (p. 46). Harris has reminded us of "Fromm Reichmann's suggestion, described by [Sue] Shapiro (S. Shapiro, 1996), that one might imaginatively grasp the patient's affective state by assuming the patient's posture" (Harris, 1998, p. 46). The ideas of identity contouring, and of contouring the skin-ego of the speaker, borrowed from Anzieu (1990), help us understand the intricate creation of connections that are both affirming and rejecting of the self (Harris, 1998). Harris (1998) suggested that because the listening was never simply caring, it also contained some contempt and irritation and could be seen as part of a process of installation of misattunement, or even more so the creation of a *masochistic envelope*, as Anzieu (1990) would call it, through the gaze of the other. The masochistic envelope is a "psychic representation of certain modes of connection in which the adhesion or glue connecting self and other is shared experiences of pain, crisis, or anguish" (Harris, 1998, p. 55).

From attachment research (Seligman and Harrison, 2012), we know that infants respond to the emotional and bodily positions of their parents, in part by assuming these positions. These mimetic experiences are imbued with anxieties among many other qualities.

We humans sense each other's self-state through gaze, body posture, movement, and the sound of the voices directed at us. Within this range of states we tend to fall back into known patterns of bodily sensation, as well as uniquely complementary self-states. Sheila's self-states are triggered both in her imagined or actual connections, as these sensations of misattunement, learned long ago, launch her on a neural pathway that she must ride for its entire, often destructive, course. These familiar sensations encapsulated many memories and interpretations of experiences, and explained the continuous negative triggering of early traumatic interactions. To disengage from those unpleasant bonding experiences, the patient must have an opportunity to reengage in mimetic experience by disassociating some of the negatively coded information, and reassociating with the barely remembered experience of approval of the self-experience.

The goal of EMDR, in mimetic terms, is to help develop that positive body representation and also to turn it internally so that other less-positive parts of the self can refer back to it. In a way, EMDR invites the patient to assume a new schema that feels foreign to her. It encourages the creation of body memory by inducing sensation and mentalization that are somewhat disengaged from the hateful negative identification established through the negative interactions that the child had with the original caregiver. In this way EMDR aims to help the patient feel and imagine mimetic experiences as projected into a future scenario by binding a reality-based scenario with a different, positive imitative experience.

Let me expand that idea a bit. I suggest that EMDR creates a situation in which the patient engages in mimetic experience with existing parts of herself, and where the therapist primarily serves as an important holding shell and a relational container. This allows the patient to find within herself a positive voice, even if it is minor, that can be amplified through the desensitization and reprocessing of negative cognition that originated in trauma, while at the same time integrating positive cognitions as a reference point matched by a bodily position integrating a less-anxious parental figure. This assumes that each surviving patient has a positive mimetic experience within them, however faint or seemingly lost due to excessive trauma.

EMDR assists the patient to gradually disengage from pain felt as identity while finding another more viable psychic envelope to hold the identity with less pain and greater connectedness. It's important to note that this process is different from disavowing the person's awareness of the trauma. Instead, the patient is invited to enter a new enveloping dyadic relatedness with the self.

Clinicians tend to apply psychodynamic treatment with individual variation, supplementing it as needed with multidisciplinary approaches. I look at the use of EMDR similarly, in an undoctrinal way. It is a skill in my toolbox that I found helpful in this case because of the patient's unacknowledged fragmentation that originated both in known and in obscure trauma.

Some feel strongly about using EMDR almost exclusively, and with very clear structure. Other clinicians hesitate to integrate EMDR with a psychodynamic approach, assuming their premises are too far apart or perhaps even contradictory. Both are purists of sorts, concerned about contamination.

For me, EMDR involves some important overlap with analytic work, especially with regard to the association process. The actual travel into thought, feeling, or pain during EMDR sets is dynamic in nature, and resembles a deep primary process in analysis. On its various levels, the structure of the procedure is somewhat different. It is directive and deliberate, contains interruptions of the associative process, and also redirects the stream of consciousness. EMDR practitioners (Parnell, 1997; F. Shapiro, 2001, 2002), like analysts, follow the patient's anxiety. EMDR abundantly uses cognitive reframing and guided imagery, along with intermittent occupation of the cerebral cortex through the use of BLS in order to release arrested amygdala function, and to create bridges between emotions and memory.

EMDR is different than psychoanalysis in some additional ways as well. In psychoanalysis we strive to provide a potential space in which affect-rich associations and projections can thrive, where transference can be addressed, and where countertransference can be used as a diagnostic and analytic tool. With certain limitations there is time for exploration to occur. Sometimes inadvertently, or at least unconsciously, a less-careful interpretation can hasten or slow down the analytic process by inflammation of the transference and countertransference dynamics. If the analyst believes she understood the patient to say one thing and responds from the perspective of that perception, this response, accurate or mistaken, can trigger a reaction in the patient when she feels it means something else. (See the example of tough love in Chapter 3 of this book, in which the process was hastened in order to deal with a deep issue, one not consciously approached but occurring through an enactment in the transference and countertransference at the door.) Yet in most psychoanalytic work there is little attempt to hasten the process to get to therapeutic results.

EMDR on the other hand strives to help with trauma and its aftermath through a concentrated effort to remove resistance to affective engagement. It expressly negotiates a path in which trauma can be desensitized and reprocessed in a way that allows the creation of an internal mastery of potentially repeated attacks on the psyche. It involves a directive approach, and expressly focuses the therapy's attention on the patient's process, rather than on the transference.

A large part of EMDR is nonverbal. The patient is instructed to limit the verbal description to a brief description of an anxiety-producing situation, the related negative cognition, a related desired positive cognition, and a goal, and has to report their emotional and physical position in between sets of BLS intervention. They are also asked to rate their level of discomfort, and of belief in both negative and positive cognitions. The goal of EMDR is therapeutic, rather than explorational, whereas psychoanalysis carries a constant tension between the analytic and the therapeutic.

Although a central goal of EMDR is to reach affect regulation, the work of *reprocessing* is crucial. Reprocessing resembles dynamic psychoanalytic approaches in that it strives to engage emotions that are locked up or dissociated in the body, a state that inhibits psychological flexibility in relationship both to self and others. The use of EMDR can propel the autonomous analytic association by training the body and mind of certain patients with significant fragmentation in order to enable them to tolerate moderate affect.

Without being too technical, merging EMDR into the psychoanalytic framework raises the question of touch. EMDR accepts certain touches like tapping as part of the work whereas psychoanalysis does not. In Sheila's case, I had to make a decision with regard to using a tactile device, as I realized that for this patient using eye movement had some limitations.

When I introduced EMDR to Sheila, I first talked with her about the BLS options. We once tried the eye-movement option, but she could only keep following briefly and it thus did not provide access to affective material. Here, there were other considerations of difficulty, as for example in following the movement of my hand, typically a signal that suggested even greater dissociation owing to her trauma, but that also indicated certain physical limitations, such as fatigued eyes.

I suggested tapping. Although the patient was able to follow her thoughts and affect more effectively with this option, I felt the frame was changing in a way that made me uncomfortable. I think the fact that the analytic frame, with its certain boundaries, had already been established made the shift into a tactile BLS involving my touching of the patient a problematic technique to bring in. Thinking of Sheila's longing for touch, in general and in friendship with me outside our work, made me suggest an alternative approach, perhaps headphones or a set of electronic tappers that are held in the patient's own hands. Sheila found the latter to be least intrusive and most effective.

EMDR illustration

Here is an example of our work during which I heard a metaphor expressed flatly one day and decided to suggest the use of EMDR. Sheila agreed.

> Sheila opens one of our sessions saying, "My purse was hungry, so I fed it." She then shifts to talking about the new balance she found in her relationship with a close friend. She adds, "I guess it is because I behaved. I hope I am able to continue with this good behavior." I ask about her concern. She replies that she is not concerned. Then mentions a trip she is planning with this close friend. "I hope I don't mess

> it up" she says. [Now adding a tactile device, she is lying on the couch holding the tappers.] She continues, "The warm water of the Caribbean Sea relaxes me. . . . Seeing the crocodiles lying motionless, only their eyes above water . . . so relaxed. They can be dangerous too, you know . . . sometimes. If they see someone . . . or if a big juicy fish swims by. Then they open their mouth, and that's it! . . . but I guess they need to have nourishment too . . . everybody does."
>
> "Even your purse," I say. "Yes," she laughs, "and even me."
>
> I reply, "When you are hungry, you are not always sure you will be able to control your own calm crocodile, when it needs to devour somebody."
>
> "That is true," Sheila says. "I never know when it will attack. I hope I do not do that to my friend. I do not want to mess it up."

When Sheila is tormented by her fear of violence, either coming from the outside by way of projection (my friend will attack me) or from within (a new idea, that she will say the wrong thing to hurt her friend) she retreats to a flat affect. Her internal crocodile raises its head and threatens to hurt her, even before it takes a bite.

Bromberg's (1998) concept of thinking about dissociation as a self-regulatory function of traumatic sensation that threatens the sense of sanity is useful here. I suggested EMDR to help Sheila stay in her body. In this way she could dissociate into a place where she could circumvent punitive reflection, where she could even be hostile momentarily, and still feel it in her body.

As we brought back the image of calm water and the crocodile, Sheila imagined being in a situation in which she might attack. She imagined this friend talking to a mutual acquaintance. Her close friend seemed more interested in the other acquaintance than in her. She felt envious, and lonely, and thought she might come by and say something critical about her close friend, with a smile. She would enjoy her close friend's attention, but is scared of her own reaction when the acquaintance moves on. She follows her anger with loneliness and then fear.

> I invite her back to the room. When she scans her body for sensation, her throat is constricted. She does not breathe. She is expecting an attack. She is still afraid she will do something bad; her friend will

> find her and punish her. She is bad. She will never be a good and loyal friend. [She believes in her badness at a level of 10 on a Subjective Units of Disturbances scale (SUDs) of 0–10, with 10 being the highest disturbance.]
>
> We start a second round of BLS by tactile buzzing. What to do with the wild animal? How to keep her wild self helpful, the one that can plan a trip to build a clinic in a remote village for the general good, while keeping the dangerous part of the crocodile at bay?
>
> Sheila goes into her second round of EMDR BLS sets, hauling her reptile into a back closet, providing him with a pool to wade in and a dark environment to keep him calm. She is significantly calmer when we check in. She goes back into herself, to look at her friend talking to their acquaintance. She is able to enjoy the view of bringing two persons she loves together, and sees the invisible umbilical cord connecting them all, as she is relieved to notice that the way to maintain her relations requires no sharp teeth. The relationship is there, if she cares to trust it.
>
> In the third round of tactile bilateral stimulation, Sheila goes back to a calming place of her childhood, playing in the dirt. She can now see her friend's interest in geology as wishing to be close to her, rather than as a distancing measure.
>
> That night when her friend appears a day early to help with the trip planning, they embrace and laugh. They count their blessings. Still, during the session, Sheila confides her wish that her friend were a bit more organized, and less stressed, yet she associates to times in which she makes similar mistakes, and forgives both for being simply more human than otherwise. More importantly, there is a greater flow between her distinct self-states. Perhaps these are buds of integration within, and her way of sensing less of a blurry outline between self and others. Subjectivity is in the making.

The trauma of feeling evil can be quite compelling and hard to shake off (Grand, 2002). For Sheila, finding a path she can walk without her self-hatred is a necessary step in her willingness to admit her deep aggressive intentions, reflect on their origins and purpose, and stay connected more often than not to her emotional grounding. EMDR allows us to move in and out of these difficult emotions.

When Sheila is in one of her nonreflective, dissociated self-states, EMDR helps ground her in a feeling state that otherwise is prohibited from entering her consciousness. She can then talk about her envy of her talented younger sister, who took her mother's attention away from her, never to be returned. She can feel the guilt of loving her father, being the boy he never had.

With these encouraging results, Sheila and I have developed a language that allows us to use these states diagnostically, and to explore the source of her anxiety.

I would like to elaborate here on my decision to use a nonanalytic technique. Why this technique? Why now and why with this patient? Sheila's age, combined with her son's illness, made me choose the therapeutic goal over the analytic one. In the process, I discovered that this route was beneficial for the analytic goal as well.

I decided to use the EMDR technique with Sheila to help her find a *physical* grounding base that she could turn to. With the help of EMDR, Sheila and I have found a path back into her memories and dreams, as well as to her intelligent, bright self. Needless to say, this recognition and memory is accompanied by some unhappy and angry segments of her personality, unrecognized thus far. Sheila has had great difficulty in feeling and knowing what she feels. She has lived the experience of her life as if she had had a happy childhood. Finding out that her judgment is superficial and the reality very different is difficult to digest. EMDR helps contain each segment so that it can later be woven into an integrative tapestry of the self, adding segments as we go.

In the context of very deep psychoanalytic engagement and through an evolving treatment, we are meeting her needs of integration. What EMDR has helped to do is to summon up the images she could not let herself remember while also providing a bypass around her concreteness and simplistic understanding of herself. Following our EMDR sessions, more dreams have started to show up and richer discussions of experiences have taken place, whether in the moment on the couch, in the room, or as the seasons change outside the windows.

Sheila now has a greater awareness that it's possible to consider what might cause a disruptive effect in an interaction. Specifically, when she realizes that her son has a medical need, she might mention a potential remedy but now will not push it as if it is the only way to deal with a situation, respecting her son's separateness and recognizing her potential intrusive urges, without resentment. She stays tuned in. We both stay tuned in.

Summary

In conclusion, this chapter delineates the narrative that first brought me to think about EMDR as integratable with my relational analytic practice, which occurred when I noticed a patient's spontaneously finding a natural BLS in an inanimate object in my office. That, in turn, resulted in my observing the patient's genuine emotional response for the first time in our work together. In this chapter, I have described how time-sensitive considerations also prompted me to relinquish a generally segregated approach for EMDR and psychoanalysis. I then described the case with some detail, and showed how I intertwined EMDR into relational psychoanalysis, including a discussion of the tapping tools I found most compatible. I also discussed the limitation each working approach imposes on the other. Here, I made the case of employing EMDR to make the depth of the relational psychoanalytic approach possible for the patient and for her clinical benefit.

Note

The lines of poetry in the epigraph are from "The Woman Who Could Not Live With Her Faulty Heart," a poem by Margaret Atwood, from *Selected Poems II: Poems Selected and New 1976–1986*. (Boston: Houghton Mifflin Company, 1987), 5–6.

References

Anzieu, D. (1990). *A Skin for Thought: Interviews with Gilbert Tarrab on Psychology and Psychoanalysis*, translated by D. N. Briggs. London: Karnac.

Bromberg, P. (1998). *Standing in the Spaces: Essays on Clinical Process, Trauma, and Dissociation*. Hillsdale, NJ: The Analytic Press.

Eldredge, C., and G. W. Cole. (2008). Learning from work with individuals with a history of trauma: Some thoughts on integrating body-oriented techniques and relational psychoanalysis. In F. S. Anderson, editor, *Bodies in Treatment: The Unspoken Dimension*, 79–102. New York: The Analytic Press.

Fonagy, P., and M. Target. (1997). Attachment and reflective function: Their role in self-organization. *Development and Psychopathology* 9: 679–700.

Grand, S. (2002). *The Reproduction of Evil*. New York: Routledge.

Harris, A. (1998). Psychic envelopes and sonorous baths. In L. Aron and F. S. Anderson, editors, *Relational Perspectives on the Body*, 39–64. Hillsdale, NJ: The Analytic Press.

Lyons-Ruth, K. (1999). The two-person unconscious: Intersubjective dialogue, enactive relational representation, and the emergence of new forms of relational organization. *Psychoanalytic Inquiry* 19: 576–617. Reprinted in L. Aron and A. Harris, editors, *Relational Psychoanalysis: Innovation and Expansion*. Vol. 2, 311–349. Hillsdale, NJ: The Analytic Press.

Parnell, L. (1997). *Transforming Trauma: EMDR*. New York: Norton.

Renik, O. (2001). The patient's experience of therapeutic benefit. *Psychoanalytic Quarterly* 70(1): 231–241.

Seligman, S., and A. Harrison. (2012). Infant research and adult psychotherapy. In G. O. Gabbard, B. E. Litowitz, and P. Williams, editors, *Textbook of Psychoanalysis*, 239–254. 2nd ed. Washington, DC: American Psychiatric Publishing.

Shapiro, F. (2001). *Eye Movement Desensitization and Reprocessing: Basic Principles, Protocols, and Procedures*. 2nd ed. New York: Guilford.

Shapiro, F. (2002). EMDR treatment: Overview and integration. In F. Shapiro, editor, *EMDR as an Integrative Psychotherapy Approach: Experts of Diverse Orientations Explore the Paradigm Prism*, 27–56. Washington, DC: American Psychological Association.

Shapiro, S. (1996). The embodied analyst in the Victorian consulting room. *Gender and Psychoanalysis* 1: 297–322.

Stern, D. N. (1995). *The Motherhood Constellation: A Unified View of Parent–Infant Psychotherapy*. New York: Basic Books.

Chapter 6

Working in tandem

In his book, *Landscape Painted with Tea*, Milorad Pavić (1990) sketches in moving images and lines an allegoric reflection related to the extreme perturbation that must often be suffered to reach beyond a physical and mental cage. In this metaphor, when a bird's gaze is set beyond the cage it notices an elusive but desired natural future. A nightingale may peck repeatedly at the door without much impact, yet a sparrow hawk will force its way to freedom in one burst.

In this chapter, I focus on my work with couples who were lost in old unspoken relational trauma. Finding them mired in their respective old pain now being reenacted in their relationship, I introduced them to activities they could mutually perform outside of the consulting room. More specifically, this chapter describes the mutual activities that served as a natural individual bilateral stimulation (BLS) that helped release emotions that had been frozen in their body. I describe here how this highly modified BLS allowed a renewed intimacy and a more spontaneous exchange. I then describe how the relational psychodynamic approach set the tone for attention to containing the emotional whole, thus increasing the attachment bond in the couple. This renewed bond provided a ground on which each could support the other's early unmet needs, and a space for the beginning of trauma recovery to emerge.

In considering the formulation of this process, I suggest that working with couples oftentimes resembles the work done with a person who suffers from dissociative identity disorder, as self-states shift between partners in an effort to share the unbearable emotional stress. Consideration is given to the idea that EMDR sessions done individually, as well as while each partner is present in his/her partner's processing, can increase both empathy and support in the observing partner. This observing participation can also help in the couple's relationship outside of the consulting room.

In this chapter, I discuss how helping couples experience themselves in relation, not only with words but also with attention to their nonverbal communication, will bring a better use of words once an attuned connection is made possible, both individually and by the couple.

Conceptual and clinical considerations

Familiarity with both theoretical and technical disciplines in their pure form is an asset in coming to grips with the reality of a couple's basic themes, which offer clarity and a respite from the hum when approaching multiple disciplines at once. As clinicians, we at times tend to prefer to stay with one approach to a clinical application. Yet over time adhering to a known technique can become a religion of sorts, leading to rejection of other options that may seem different and/or too specific. Thus, for dynamic therapists EMDR may appear to be mainly a trauma protocol, and so be dismissed as a tool helpful for deep-seated relational challenges. Similarly, EMDR practitioners may perceive dynamic psychotherapy as digging too deeply into the past and so miss the opportunity to help patients arrive at some relief from symptoms with less delay. Transference and countertransference may be perceived by the EMDR therapist as focusing on extraneous aspects of the patients' relationality, thus distracting from the therapeutic central goals. Yet working with couples, perhaps more than working with individuals, brings out the need for an approach that is appropriate for each individual within the couple while still focusing on the couple as the main patient.

Having patients tell their stories in their own words is an approach consistent with both EMDR and relational work with couples. Here, both techniques join when we listen to family of origin stories and for multigenerational histories. However, they may be modified when used in conjunction with each other, as EMDR prefers a short, focused approach. In couples therapy, the length and depth of the family history that is detailed will depend on the issue at hand. To deal with character structure, a more in-depth psychoanalytic approach may be applied, with EMDR supporting the engagement through its physical and emotional dimensions, while a wish to change a particular cluster of behaviors may use family history as a base for engaging the source of that behavior. In this case, EMDR takes the lead in targeting family and relational history in the service of desired change. EMDR helps to quickly locate emotional blocks and trauma in order to focus on current situations and the altered cognitive belief system to which they are related.

Working with couples offers a unique perspective and a challenge to the therapist. Over the years, listening to couples describe situations they have struggled with often made me feel as if I were working with a person with dissociative identity disorder. Each partner in a couple told an idiosyncratic tale, one that could not possibly represent an accurate picture of what happened, but that also held a whole subjective truth, while at the same time being void of any awareness of their counterpart's intentions, actions, or needs. From brain research we learn that the observing person is both the observer of external reality and internal cues, but also that this person is what Solms and Turnbull (2002) call the *observing machine*. In this process, an observation is based on selective attention given to certain elements in the environment that are important to the need or wish-fulfillment of the observer, while he or she overlooks aspects that may be important, or indeed essential, to their partner. I have often found that couples listening to their partner in a session feel hurt by and perplexed at the little attention given to their needs in their partner's account of an event. When this is compounded by one spouse having a deep need to have their views heard, the other may feel completely dropped, feeling that they have already used all the words in their vocabulary to express their need to no avail.

Because needs and desires that are only partly known to the individual are often unconscious, an approach that bypasses the need to explain what these are can tap into those deeper needs and wishes, creating a nonverbal dance that may help the couple feel—rather than understand—the real location of a need and be able to meet their partner there. This process is akin to that of a mother who is trying to decipher her infant's needs based on her child's nonverbal vocal and action cues. But it is important to add that, at times, what a partner may ask for will only partially represent what they wish for, as their intention is not only hidden from their partner's awareness, but from their own. Moreover, in the brain the activity having to do with seeking is located in a different area than that having to do with what it is the person is searching for (Solms and Turnbull, 2002).

One attempt to combine treatment modalities in family treatment was presented by Kaslow, Nurse, and Thompson (2002), who described the use of EMDR in conjunction with systems theory. Their view was that adhering to a purist theoretical view and technical application would inevitably miss some individuals and their unique ways of communicating best. Making the case for integrating EMDR and family systems therapy, they argued that both in its conception and application EMDR was itself constructed from various theoretical paradigms. As they wrote,

> Its underlying practice rationale actually connects to several of the theories. EMDR's focus on and concern for people's historic relational past and original trauma are similar to components of multigenerational and family-of-origin approaches. From psychoanalytical family therapy comes the premise that early traumatic events or interactions became points of arrested development and need to be resolved for a healthier developmental trajectory of concentrating on the core problem identified by patients and working toward its resolution without being diverted by other issues. Having patients tell their story in their own way is derived from both psychoanalytical and narrative approaches, whereas attempting to help patients rewrite what will occur in the next chapters of their lives is an intervention strategy primarily derived from the narrative approach and social constructionist thoughts about fashioning a new reality. (Kaslow et al., 2002, p. 293)

Their experience with EMDR showed that, in addition to individual talk therapy, the use of EMDR allowed a patient to integrate the gained cognitive understanding with emotional aspects of the couple's relationship, as well as with the physical manifestations of early trauma that linger on in the marital relationship. Their strategy was to tackle the difficulty in working with a couple through individual EMDR sessions with one partner at a time. Below I describe the benefit of approaching couples with individual EMDR in the service of conjoint therapy, while highlighting the importance of an individual EMDR approach in the presence of both partners.

Also pertaining to a case I present in the following passages are power and gender roles in the couple's relationship, which are embedded both consciously and unconsciously in each partner, weighing on their relationship and compounding the dynamic burdens imported from their families of origin. This is further complicated by the fact that each partner carries an unavowed shadow of the opposite gender that is active dynamically, desired and refused at once by each individual and in the other partner. Muriel Dimen (2003) has written astutely about the power relations in couples and their complexity, of which we see only a sliver in our offices (p. 206). She has described the multiple sources of the intricate relationships between power, sexuality, and intimacy, and their impact on the relational realm between men and women, in the singular or plural, either personally related or randomly engaged. Kaslow et al. (2002) paid tribute to the importance of the gender power difference, and described the ways in which he and his colleagues attended to this relevant issue in their case example and its formulation.

Adding to the confusion in couples therapy is the fact that two of the most powerful transference-prone relationships in the patient's life—the marital and the therapeutic—coexist there (Ringstrom, 1994). The therapist must be attuned to each partner, yet their conflict creates a special situation in which the therapist must partially fail in her effort to understand both the individuals' and the couple's needs. This point is well described by Virginia Goldner (2014), who proposed the use of mixed modalities for couples and family therapy. Her integrated model relies on intersubjective and systems theory and technique, and is informed by current brain and developmental research to understand the relational matrix in couples. Goldner equated conjoint therapy to the work with people who are described as suffering from borderline personality disorder (pp. 402–403).

Something in the work with the couples therapist, who is originally perceived as the God/parent/authority figure, triggers competition for the therapist's attention, and the desire for recognition of the truth according to each partner in the couple. Once there is an attunement or recognition of one partner's point of view, the other partner invariably feels dropped, even traumatized, by the situation, by their partner, and now by their completely biased therapist. At times, this feeling is represented in a bodily sensation or minimal cues; or at other times by a full-blown savage-looking attack on the partner or the therapist, or the presentation of a defensive reaction. Goldner has employed brain research in addition to developmental and systems theories to untangle the firing of trauma responses between couples during sessions, and the induction of a secondary trauma in the therapist, emphasizing that primary process is often accessed by the couple during sessions without sufficient reflective function. This type of reaction in couples therapy, and the feeling of stalemate that brings about a sense of impossibility no matter what modality is used in working with the couple, is what has brought me to believe that using the verbal method alone is insufficient.

EMDR and other methods that engage the resisting mind directly seem to work better. The idea of meeting the mind where it is, instead of attempting to drag it to the place we want it to be, can be seen metaphorically as a ladder. It is a playground that is not too scary. It conveys to the couple that there is a time where all time seems to disappear. It has gentleness where aberration seems to be the norm in every interaction. It represents the possibility of self-soothing, and with that the idea that emotional reset is possible even in the midst of turmoil. In other words, it demonstrates that the drama that is created can be abated when the mind is occupied enough so that the trauma reaction is deactivated through bilateral stimulation (BLS).

To give an example of a couple's work that has benefited from a combined approach using psychoanalytically informed psychotherapy and a modified use of EMDR, I present the following case.

Clinical illustration

Lee and Isaac were referred by a colleague for couples therapy. They are in their late thirties, pursuing their careers after graduate school. They met in law school, but were friends for some time before they started their courtship. Lee's family immigrated to the East Coast of the United States from Southeast Asia in the early twentieth century. Isaac was raised in New York City's Lower East Side in an assimilated Jewish family. Lee's judicial clerkship took her away to the West Coast, and the couple's relationship was based on bimonthly weekend visits. Now they are living together for the first time and have found that keeping a daily routine is different from what they anticipated.

The excitement of the on-again, off-again is wearing off quickly, their time alone with friends is minimal, and they are struggling to find a common language for mutual joy. Instead, resentment and competition are taking over. To deal with their disappointment they retreat to competitiveness and criticism. Not much intimate talk is possible before they find themselves in the thralls of a fight, blaming each other for all that is lacking in their lives.

Lee takes her disappointment to a place like Cinderella after midnight, waiting to be found by her prince, but the prince goes to bed alone since he is tired and cannot wait another hour for her to become available. Exhausted, they have found intimacy a chore they both dread, with Lee mourning the days before they got married when they seemed to enjoy intimacy with each other. "It was much more fun before we got married," she says. Frankly, she feels cheated. The pre- and post-nuptial courtship were so quickly juxtaposed that she suspects Isaac was motivated to draw her away from other men, but lost interest shortly after they took their vows.

Isaac for his part is afraid that he is a man without emotions, as he feels no desire. He remembers desiring Lee when they were still dating, he knows that he loves her, but he is unaware of any strong sensations he can recognize as desire. In contrast, his anxiety, anger, envy, and despondency are palpable. He says, "I do not feel anything, I do not want anything, and I just feel irritable and worried most of the time." That these are markers of depression and post-traumatic stress come as a relief to Isaac when he learns about them. He has felt under siege and anticipates an attack at any moment at home, at work, and in his family of origin. He can hardly breathe. These symptoms can be associated with childhood trauma, a factor that suggests that EMDR can be a particularly effective tool. This is because at first it bypasses verbal articulation, instead engaging primary processes that are too horrible to remember and utter, while providing the emotional, parent-like container of an empathic witnessing while the guards are down for processing.

The couple has no children and is ambivalent about whether they want to have a child. However, throughout this turmoil, Isaac shows Lee his love at times of distress, and she seems to respond, although with less fervor. Lee confesses she loves Isaac, but adds that as the day draws to an end her anxiety increases. She is weary of her anxious anticipation of Isaac's angry outbursts at the end of the day, which are followed by his bouts of depression. Would he be happy with the meal she prepares, with the level of the house's cleanliness, with how she performs when taking their cat to the veterinarian? When he doesn't approve of her management, she tries to defend her choices, and then retreats while Isaac feels deserted. She yearns to have some unexamined areas, places that are private and inaccessible to him. Kulish (2002) wrote about the importance of secrets in women's life. Lee craves having secrets both because her past is filled with private places, and because these are places where she can contemplate possibilities. These nightly events are taxing to her, and she feels trapped in a relationship that resembles her parents' miserable years together until her mother's death when she was 10 years old.

Lee is interested in having better communication and greater intimacy. She feels lonely in the relationship. Worse, she feels isolated at times. Isaac wants Lee to be happier and he struggles with her use of pot, which makes her seem unaware of her surroundings. He is embarrassed, he is angry, and he is worried about her, about their social relationships, about the future of their fetus if they are ever to conceive one. He is concerned that they are repeating his family of origin's terrible saga of addiction and the accompanying humiliation, in which he seems to be the centerpiece. Lee admits that she is worn down by Isaac's micromanagement of her in every minute detail, as well as by his outbursts of rage that frighten her and remind her of her father's drunken stupors.

Lee, a little over five feet tall, walks into my office, trotting on her bright-red high-heeled shoes, flashing a shy and hesitant smile. Isaac follows her, his dark eyes wide, his head slightly bent forward. They settle on the couch, and, when prompted, Lee says that they want—in fact, that she wants—to work on their intimacy, that they have been together for a decade, yet she feels the courtship ceased with marriage and she misses it. I make a note of Isaac's jaw.

It is working hard, as he looks at Lee intently, blinking slowly. It takes us several sessions to articulate what that communication is about. Shifts in his voice and a sense of despondency often accompany these moments. Isaac sounds as if he is talking out of a hollow barrel. He never verbally negates Lee but retreats instead. When I comment on the shift in his mood and ask if he is aware of the change, and what he thinks is going on for him, he replies, "Nothing. Nothing is going on. I am just fine." However, there are noticeable changes to his nonverbal communication that are indicating a shift in mood. For example, the tempo of his speech slows down, while he uses fewer, yet carefully chosen, words. He is clenching his teeth and his jaw muscles are contracting and releasing in a measured pace, serving as his unconscious BLS device, helping him momentarily gain control over his overwhelming emotional response, which it is yet unsafe to expose. Nebbiosi and Federici-Nebbiosi (2008) highlighted the importance of the quality of expression and the way it relates to both acoustic and bodily rhythm, as well as the way in which different rhythms express different qualities, all of which in turn impact the dynamically involved partner's response.

Michael Eigen (1993) wrote about the face as symbolic of the personality. He reminded us of the effect of mirroring in the clinical sense. This takes a unique turn in couples work, as facial expression, along with other nonverbal bodily cues, is perceived in the other partner as an invitation to act or to fear the other's act. In the case of Isaac and Lee, I often have the feeling that Isaac's facial expression changes when he fears Lee's words will expose him as a villain, or, worse yet, as a man with no power. Lee's facial expression seems as if she is about to be rejected again, as in her childhood, unless she engages in some repair of Isaac's shattered sense of control.

This bodily blocking of awareness signals to me that words alone could not bring us any closer to insight. The more I interpret and probe, the more Isaac retreats, his voice thinner and hollower. Lee watches intently, tight-muscled, sometimes offering her own observation. Isaac looks at her and shrugs away her concerns. Something needs to shift, but what?

Although Lee is intelligent and an educated professional, I sometimes wonder whether she appreciates her own value in the family. Growing up with her father and grandparents, since she entered middle school, as her mother died from medical complications following the birth of her younger brother, she is sensitive, almost vigilant around Isaac. I once suggested that perhaps Isaac was afraid to know what he wanted out of his life, given his stepfather's overshadowing presence in the family and the community. Lee chimed in, saying that Isaac is just overworked, but that of course he knows where he is going. That comment surprised me. Oftentimes, Lee will be the one to highlight Isaac's lack of assertiveness, as when one of his stepfather's suggestions had become a rule for the couple, raising tension between them. Lee's sensitivity translates to my understanding that she knows something important about Isaac's ego strength, and she helps her husband keep his equilibrium, as well as the couple's, by protecting Isaac's ego when she senses it might be threatened.

Couples come to treatment with their complex individual interpersonal skills and needs mixed together with their ability to support the relationship with what they learned in their family of origin. Here, Lee is using what she had learned in her own family. If she asserted her needs and wishes she would get hurt. However, if she protected the potentially volatile grandmother or brother she might walk away without a scratch. This approach was costly of course. I notice that Lee's words seem carefully chosen, and while verbally conveying caring, her tone suggests caution and distance. The more I listen to her, the greater my wish becomes to decipher the discrepancy between the content and the tone. Asking both to reflect on my observation yielded little at this time.

Isaac is too hurt to admit feeling dropped, and Lee is too shaken to confess her fear of Isaac's control over her life. This dynamic plays itself out in the many moments that have felt potentially dangerous, moments they have avoided by gingerly dancing around the threatening other. The constant need to be vigilant has resulted in one person's hyperarousal (anger, criticism, and obsession on the part of Isaac) or hypoarousal (cold communication, suppressed desire, and passivity on the part of Lee) much of the time. Since their mutual disappointment is rarely articulated directly, nothing seems to be wrong except for the mutual avoidance of intimacy. In therapy, when Isaac gets pale and quiet, Lee's breathing becomes shallow and she will glance at Isaac and me, unsure if we want her to intervene or stay away. As Eigen (1993) wrote, "It is surprising to think what little role the experience of breathing has played in Western accounts of personality, considering the importance of breathing in Eastern systems of personality change and the age-old association of breath with psyche, spirit or soul" (p. 43).

What EMDR offers, much as do some other healing methods such as psychodrama, is the therapist's fine tuning in to the patient's bodily shifts, a training that when combined with the analytic approach is directed toward understanding more about those shifts. I often find that early in this exploration a patient may not be aware of his or her breathing pattern, as for example when they hold their breath, but over time there is a shift in which the patient will recognize it subconsciously and later might notice the change spontaneously. In this context, it is of interest to mention the animated film *Belleville Rendez-vous* (Stein, 2007) in which the entire communication between the protagonist, as a boy—now become a young man—and his grandmother process their sorrows and the aftermath of trauma with a series of sighs, syncopated breathing, and an arrest of breathing. In listening to the sounds of breathing without the interference of words, one feels in the presence of a whole conversation, without the need for words of explanation. Another reason to consider this film is its unwitting provision of BLS for the growing child in the form of competitive, indeed compulsive, bicycling that takes the youngster's mind off the loss of his beloved mother.

Dissociative process within a relationship

As mentioned earlier, sometimes it helps to think about couples work as work done with individuals who suffer from dissociative identity disorder. All of the necessary emotional components are present, but are held by an alter ego with the other partner.

To illustrate this phenomenon, consider the following account, about another couple I worked with who came to therapy after the loss of a daughter in a car accident, the couple's only child. Originally, they had made a contract that they would conceive and raise only one child in this marriage. When that child died, the bereaved mother said that she would like to get pregnant again, while her husband maintained that he agreed to have only one child and they had had that child, even though he was now deceased. The mother, greatly frustrated and hurt, held that they agreed to raise one child and that the father did not keep his side of their agreement. I noticed after a while that the husband's main complaint was that he suffered from a lack of intimacy with his wife for over a year after their child died. He wanted more out of the relationship. However, his spouse said she would not be intimate with him until he agreed to have another child.

It occurred to me at that moment that they were holding complex emotions together by sharing the burden. The father said he was sad about the loss of his child. He was also relieved to a degree, both because the child did not suffer long, and also because—since their child had been born—he felt that he took second place in his wife's heart. Her relationship with their child, which both of them perceived to be cathectically more her daughter than his, became so central that the couple's relationship took a lesser priority. He felt shunned, unimportant, and betrayed. After their daughter's passing, he felt that there was a chance they could find each other again as a couple. She, on the other hand, refused to have any intimate contact with him and preferred not to be found alone with her husband.

I suggested that without intimate interaction, from which she retreated, it would be impossible to conceive a baby. Similarly, as he pursued greater physical intimacy between them, the possibility of conceiving a baby increased. Examining the ways in which they both wanted and dreaded the prospect of becoming parents once more evolved into an affecting dialogue. Up to this point and beyond their relational pain, they could not observe the yearning and the loss they each endured alone, and as a form of self-preservation polarized the relationship until their more complex desires were locked out of their consciousness. In this case, integration of the conflicting wishes within each spouse led to months of renegotiation of the terms of endearment and led them eventually to having a second daughter.

The couple had each shifted the dissociated and disavowed traumatic pain by evacuating it into the other. This dynamic act can be seen as projective identification gone awry, or perhaps a form of dissociation in which the marital unit itself held all the pain and desire each individual in the couple could not hold alone because of their ambivalence. Here the internal conflict had to do with replacing one child with another child, and desiring each other despite the loss of the child. Her thought was "How can I get over it when my daughter was fatally injured?" while his thoughts were, "How can I have another child when I know life can be perilous and something bad can happen again? Therefore let's enjoy the life we do have despite the loss. Later he said, "I am so thrilled and relieved that I found my wife again after the loss of our beloved Kayla."

When emotional scaffoldings were offered through therapy to hold both pain and desire, each partner was better able to return to their own self, and hence to close intersubjective interaction, without feeling broken or split up as individuals.

Let us return to Isaac and Lee. Following a number of sessions in which both spent a great deal of effort testing each other's ability to sustain anxiety, I wondered if there was a way to help them both become more in-touch with their body and mind. I felt that helping them find a place in which they were each more closely attuned to themselves rather than being vigilant regarding the other could relieve part of the terrifying mirror fixation. Words seemed comprehensible yet were void of affect. I reasoned that without a sense of safety and containment there would be slow progress.

I first suggested the use of EMDR to find out to what degree Isaac could connect to his emotions. I knew that, as a child and to some degree into his adulthood, he has felt cornered and ridiculed for his shortcomings, however slight. His stepfather's criticizing him for minor and major mistakes as well as any choices that his stepfather felt were unacceptable, had made Isaac try to control his environment meticulously. To some extent his stepfather's spirit had entered the marriage through his hyper-criticism of Lee. In turn, wishing to be the good girl, who now becomes the good daughter-in-law—like the daughter she had been accustomed to being in her own childhood—she had taken on her husband's anger to be her fault and so had become the imperfect child Isaac had felt he was in his family of origin. That behavior had then allowed Isaac to observe himself in Lee. This in turn had given him the power he wished to have but does not have with his own stepfather and older sister.

Words were helpful to a certain degree. There was some understanding of how they have created tension and disappointment in each other. Yet their most intense moments, although highly articulated in their weekly retelling, do not carry the affect they sustain when dealing with each other outside of my office. Lee is able to describe the anxiety that precedes Isaac's return home without being able to predict his behavior toward her, yet she continues to feel reserved and vacant when Isaac attempts to get closer.

Modified BLS in tandem

When I first met Isaac and Lee, their daily connection consisted of living in the same house, with primarily solitary activities. A complaint by Isaac about the level of salt in a dinner dish would send Lee into a sulking retreat, perhaps by watching a movie quietly, or at other times demanding that Isaac pay the bills, something that on the surface seemed reasonable enough, yet the request would contain her pent-up disappointment in yet another promising evening that went awry.

Tripping each other up in the task of intimacy had been frustrating to both, but they had no idea what triggered these stalemates or how to change the path they were on. Because both were "doers," I suggested that they take ten minutes out of their day to talk to each other, before engaging in any other way. A bit of education about active, more compassionate listening worked well after a few tries. Both felt satisfied at listening and telling something meaningful about their day. They were happy to discover the other in their words and affect when there was no pressure to get air time. Each partner received a chance at a butterfly hug. (This is a self-soothing EMDR BLS technique performed on the self by crossing the body midline with one's arms to tap on the opposite shoulder with each hand. This technique is not introduced before a patient has some experience at self-soothing and is stable with the use of EMDR. It is not to be used by persons who may go into spontaneous abreaction without the presence of a trained therapist.) I suggested they try this while listening, allowing the listener to take care of his or her needs without feeling dropped by the speaking partner. Introduction of the butterfly hug technique and its adoption present reassurance that the time would come for being heard and receiving care. It also reduces anxiety when a challenging expression manifests itself in the other's words or gestures, and introduces the idea of holding one's self in lieu of expecting the other to care for all of their own day's frustrated needs. In relational terms, the use of EMDR's couples listening process, while the listener is using BLS, introduced the idea of interdependence as potentially replacing the shame of dependency.

Another BLS-like activity that I offered the couple was going for walks together, again taking turns talking while walking. In this technique, several elements of therapy were combined. Using the bilateral action of the body to create the BLS principle, cerebral rationality was reduced enough to allow some emotionally informed material to surface. Brisk walking contributes to the reduction of depressive and anxious moods, and can contribute to a sense of bonding in performing a physical activity together. Lee and Isaac found that in the context of walking together they felt less threatened and were able to collaborate with each other over time. Another suggestion came to mind while listening to Lee describe the stress of preparing dinner by herself and expecting Isaac's criticism. It involved a BLS-like action in which they could find pleasure preparing dinner together, occupying their hands in one task while telling each other parts of their day that they needed to process, so that when they arrived at dinner they were much more relaxed and able to enjoy their meal together.

In relational terms, it was important to recognize the timelessness of their emotional existence, along with each partner's own feeling of not being held by the other, which fostered a sense of interminable internal chaos. Creating some structure in which Lee and Isaac could express anxiety without feeling that it was a cavernous void, known from their past and carrying into the present without a respite in sight, was an essential step toward their imagining that possibilities for the relationship could emerge.

EMDR focus for Isaac

Isaac's sense of lacking control at his law firm makes him feel unsettled. Although he was offered a full partnership at the firm he deferred to a colleague, another junior partner who made a case for needing the position more urgently. However devastating this decision proved to be, Isaac secretly wishes he could pursue a different career path. His passing on the opportunity was a way to keep his independence. His course of study and line of work had been chosen by his stepfather, who narcissistically put his wishes ahead of his stepson's. Isaac does not know what else he would do, and feels no motivation to get himself into an additional commitment on a path he cannot see himself doing for the rest of his life, yet he feels powerless to say *no* at any particular point.

Lee cannot understand Isaac's motivations, in part because he has a hard time articulating his wishes to himself. After all, he is bringing money home, why would he overlook an opportunity to be more comfortable? She feels Isaac is selling out his and indeed both their futures because he is insecure and in effect had bowed down to his colleague.

What is unarticulated for Isaac is precisely the wish to be free to imagine his future with no restrictions on his fantasy life. We all need time to dream away. Winnicott (1971) suggested that creativity in searching for the self as it is between the internal and the external worlds requires desultory, formless functioning—or in other words rudimentary playing (pp. 63–64). Isaac's lack of this quality of private time, I assumed, contributes to his agitation. I suggested an EMDR session.

Working with individuals who are new to therapy requires some pedagogic attention. In addition, introducing EMDR to new patients who are settling into talk therapy can be intimidating. Hence, I began by explaining the reasons I wanted to employ this method with him at this time, and offered an opportunity for him to try the tapping device first to see how it feels. I then explained that I will only use EMDR to teach relaxation techniques he will be able to replicate without a BLS device, and by only following his breathing to relax when he recognizes a change in his anxiety level. Here I used the tree imagery guidance, inviting Isaac to imagine himself having a center from which roots and branches, leaves and fruit can stem. This preparatory low-risk method helps most patients relax, regulate their breathing, and feel grounded while simultaneously introducing EMDR elements to the patient, without overwhelming them. Many other metaphors can be used for this purpose. Resource tapping, including an introduction to some relaxation techniques, is essential when introducing EMDR to a patient who is new to psychotherapy or EMDR. Later on, in going deeper into trauma material, the therapist can alternate between dealing with disturbing material and developing self-regulation by demonstrating to the patient that he can go back to his well-regulated state, even after working through a most devastating affective field.

Isaac's response to the tree relaxation technique was no exception. At the beginning of the session, he opened his eyes frequently to check his environment. With permission to keep his eyes open, and with frequent interruptions to the BLS sequence (12 to 15 versus the standard minimum of 24 BLS iterations), Isaac grows accustomed to the sensation of the tappers in his palms, the quiet room, and my occasional response to minimal cues of his affective state. With every respite, Isaac shows signs of slight embarrassment. BLS breaks are designed to leave a space for the therapist to ask the patient what is going on, while avoiding specific directives. Here Isaac responds, "It is so quiet here." Dynamically, he is juxtaposing this calm with his constant inner noise. I then comment on the calm of his body and mind, as well as his constant inner noise, which helps him manage the discrepancy between what he wants and what others want of him. He says, "I am not used to it."

In the next round of BLS, I ask Isaac to look inside himself for a place that feels relatively protected, where he can plant his tree for a moment. He finds a place on an island, but feels restless. He mentions that he feels his stepfather's critical gaze on him. "Why are you resting, you lazy you? Go back to work!" Imagining his stepfather's gaze suggests to him that he is not worthy of rest. Were he an experienced EMDR patient,

I would have suggested going after the stepfather's criticism and finding its roots, not only in the stepfather's imagined words but also in the representation of his stepfather's actions as mirrored in Isaac's discourse. However, my goal here was to help Isaac find new linguistic capabilities with which to recognize and navigate his self-talk and feelings. This stage is similar to the process at the beginning of psychoanalysis during which we take note of the transferential material yet delve into it only after establishing sufficient rapport.

EMDR focus for Lee

Lee's sense of belonging to a caretaker is at the forefront of her concerns. Insecure attachment marks all her relationships, including the marital bond. Ever since she can remember, she does not know for sure if she belongs to her deceased mother, and whether she is her father's daughter. I do not mean this in a literal way, but psychologically Lee is never sure that if she gets lost someone will come after her and find her. More than once, she recalls that her grandfather neglected to pick her up following an after-school activity. She remembers waiting for hours, until someone, typically her father, showed up to collect her. In turn, she can never rely on being her father's or grandparents' child for the most rudimentary of needs. As a little girl she was never sure if her grandparents would still keep her as a family member if she somehow frustrated their demands. There were others who looked after her, but even then there was a price to pay for that care. Throughout her adolescence, her choir conductor took her under her wing, while also discouraging Lee from developing other areas of her musical interests, creating a pattern that up to that point in therapy hindered Lee from uttering her own wishes.

In her interaction with Isaac, I saw it take several attempts to tease out Lee's childhood wish to advance through music beyond singing. Her father and grandparents took no interest in her studies, and shrugged when she told them about her decision to become an attorney. What was deceiving at first was Lee's almost perfect presentation. Her rational, measured speech seems mature, capable of compassion, and reflective as she speaks of her own contribution to the difficulty in her marital life. What gives her away is a hint of brittleness that shows up in the most subtle of ways. A slight raise of a side of her mouth when Isaac is disapproving of her wishes or opinions makes me see how vulnerable she is to any discrepancy that may appear in the agreeable bond that is now so disturbed. When I ask about the shift in her bodily response, she backs up and dismisses her own words, playing down the immensity of her desire to calm the terror of hurting Isaac enough so that he might leave her. It is a dance that is painful to watch. I realize that with Lee words will only evoke her urgent need to defend her sense of temporality in order to protect her from the imagined ruinous result of being separated from a rather permanent if imperfect object. Because Lee is a woman who in her profession makes her words her sword, I know this will be a battle in which her rationalizations will easily win in any context over her need to find an internal relationality that feels sustainable.

When I suggest EMDR, at first to help Lee regulate her emotions at times of stress through relaxation techniques, and later on as a tool to help her recognize her wishes and needs without the constant threat to her ego, Lee is concerned. She does not want to "go under." She is afraid that something will be done to alter her current being as she knows it. In a way, Lee wants to protect the only object she knows to be hers. She cannot rely on an external object to be stable or reliable enough to surrender to. Hesitation about being treated with hand movements to access internal processes is not unusual, yet the quality of the anxiety is different in this case. It resembles a fear of being taken apart rather than that of fear of losing control.

Recognizing such basic needs in a patient is a crucial step in deciding the pace to take when using EMDR. Building a sense of full control of the body and mind can be achieved by performing a number of small, targeted segments until a level of comfort is reached. When primary process is close to the surface most of the time, it is important to use relaxation before every EMDR session to help the patient regain a sense of control. With Lee, who had no previous experience with therapy of any kind, introducing every component of the process seemed helpful. I thus first taught her the tree imagery guidance without any EMDR device, followed by having her hold the tappers for a few seconds at a time while I watched for a response, stopping to ask for her experience, and then repeated the technique with tappers on the lowest setting, if that was tolerated, and that seemed to work best with her. She liked the tree relaxation technique, was able to elaborate on her noticing her tight shoulders, and found the growing roots segment particularly helpful.

However, when she tries the tappers for the first time she reacts with a start. I then remind her of her roots and relaxed muscles. She spontaneously closes her eyes a few seconds after she holds the active tappers, while I guide her through the tree imagery guidance process. That is certainly enough for one session. For the first time, when I collect the BLS device, Lee lets herself fall back and sink into the couch. Up to this point she has been sitting up, very stiff and alert. She says, "I don't remember ever being so relaxed." She reflects on what prevents this in her relationship with her father, grandparents, and brother. It is a sad thought, and Lee touches the back of her hand to her eye. She sighs, "You know, I never knew it was possible to be so quiet inside."

Integrating EMDR and relational psychoanalysis through witnessing

In the sessions to come, Lee, still tentative but ready to work, allows herself to say in the middle of a dynamic process, "I think it is time to go back to the tappers." In the beginning, I had scheduled an individual session each for Lee and Isaac. After processing the experience, I raised the question of them witnessing each other going through the process. There are several approaches to doing EMDR with couples. One is to separate the couple, especially when the relationship is in a volatile stage where trust is scant, and working together may feel threatening to a member of the couple. Another is to have both partners be in the room, following the same instructions, which is possible in the case of learning a relaxation technique, or having a meditative guided EMDR session. The couple can also take turns in a session with one going through the process while being witnessed by their partner.

With Isaac and Lee, I employed a mixed technique, in which two preparatory sessions were done together. Isaac's clear preference to have his EMDR session be an individual session determined that there be separate EMDR sessions for both. Once the individual sessions were completed each felt they could allow, and indeed benefit from, having their partner witness and participate in the processing. Some couples may not require separate sessions, yet much can be said about the importance of witnessing in developing compassion. Some of the beneficial relational aspects of holding in mind and engaging are found in the invaluable input from the partner-observer in the form of questions or observations. In addition, given their life together, a comment or a question that stems from this observation can clarify the partner's own process.

Guided imagery with both partners

Before introducing EMDR's full protocol, it is crucial to assess the patient's self-containment abilities, and to help him or her develop some basic skills to fall back upon in case of a strong reaction to internal anxiety, whether that takes place in the session or outside of treatment. Teaching self-regulation through breathing techniques and guided imagery works best. Many variations of these are available, and proficiency in several of them allows the therapist to choose among different appropriate techniques for patients with different needs.

Guiding Isaac and Lee in how to follow their body's sensations and emotional cues, and helping them to develop language for articulating those sensations were a key components in beginning EMDR training. I have found that acquainting patients with the different components of the procedure helps them to be less mystified by it. Some components I have introduced to Lee and Isaac include the creation of a safe place, a calm place. In addition, symbolically securing good traits in their representation of their parents is an essential step before the EMDR can begin. This step is necessary to help the patient preserve the helpful parts of the parent from the patient's harmful thoughts and fantasized actions. I found that Isaac needed to perceive his mother's nurturing traits intact, and therefore he would place them in an imagined safe place (enforced by BLS) in order to begin his EMDR work on how he felt unprotected by her as a child. Only then is it possible to bring negative thoughts to mind while scanning the body for sensation. The goal here is to trigger the process of mindfulness. When the conflict is too pressing, when the fear of erasing the holding and nurturing parent and being left with the neglectful one seems too large, it is important to have the positive memories be secure, because that releases the guilt associated with killing off the parts of the parents that were less than ideally attuned to the patient as a child, and indeed as an adult as well.

Relationally, sharing what feels safe in a couple's session and following the anxiety as it develops within the couple or in relation to the analyst can serve as an opening for starting an EMDR protocol. EMDR offers wings to fly over hurdles that words alone cannot reach while emotions are blocked. The bird of experience can safely land on a softer known ground in which anxiety is experienced and conquered, making the talking about these emotions easier for patients while they are still in connection with bodily sensation.

In the following sections, I present a more detailed account of the individual EMDR work with Isaac to provide a better sense of an EMDR sequence. I then describe the impact it had on the integrative couples work. Although not fully offered here, similar EMDR work was done with Lee to help her with her body–mind connection to in turn allow for the more psychodynamic aspects to be explored verbally.

EMDR in the presence of only one partner

We schedule a double session for Isaac's first EMDR experience to make sure we have sufficient time to prepare and process what might come up in the session. Another reason is that I suspect that Isaac might fend off emerging emotions if he felt the time was running out. The illusion of bounty in relation to time is thus crucial. This is also the first time Isaac and I have a session during which Lee is absent. I suspect that anxiety caused Isaac to miss that scheduled session and be late to the next. With couples, there is always the question of whether seeing each partner individually is more helpful or disruptive to the couple's work. When I raise the question, Isaac has a clear preference to come to the session alone. His (presumably projected) worry has to do with an anxiety that his concern for Lee will distract him from his work. It is plausible too that Isaac's hesitation has something to do with the idea that his sense of appearing to be weak in her presence will be disturbing to them both. Lee feels that this is the right choice for her as well.

Before we start going through the protocol, we explore Isaac's ambivalence toward expressing his feelings or even having them. As he describes it in the meetings that led to this session, he is dreading not only his emotions and their nature—"I will find out what a monster I am"—but also the notion that his emotions will get out of control and that he will never be able to be himself again. In his primary fantasy, he will be like a beloved (or despised) toy that after a fall is left to decompose without anybody helping him muster up a way to put him back together again. His experience of being shut out without understanding what causes him to feel cold is evidenced by the mask that clouds his face at times when he senses criticism from Lee, or when my interpretation is a bit crude when his phone rings in the middle of a session.

Asking Isaac directly if he knows what triggers his flat affect, or his visibly restrained angry affect, is inevitably met with a shrug. He simply does not know. He is in the thralls of shifting emotions. His family history reveals that he often felt criticized by his stepfather for not measuring up to his stepfather's unrealistic expectations, and he was often a witness to his stepfather's vicious attacks on his mother. I suspect that Isaac's way of protecting himself is to be carefully attuned to changes in the relational field in his environment and to react by shutting down. He wants to protect his mother and cannot; he wants to defend himself but cannot. Instead he has developed an identity that keeps him amicable toward his stepfather's ideas, while avoiding celebrations with his mother on special occasions and treating his wife to the residue of a workday at the law firm filled with frustration and the resulting rage or depressed expression. This in turn has left him as lonely as before. Yet his attitude toward Lee makes him feel that he is reproducing an element his stepfather can approve, that of the man who runs his household without consideration of others in the family. Unlike his mother, though, Lee is able to express her thoughts and wishes even when they differ. Isaac is baffled by the difference, and is particularly concerned at family gatherings that he will be criticized, even ridiculed for not controlling his wife. I suspect that unconsciously Isaac identifies with Lee's fearless independence, and envies her knowing what she wants, while he cannot guess what his authentic wishes might be. He is shut down emotionally. To know is too dangerous, and for many years was simply not practical.

Many young couples are faced with the need to recognize the shift between being a child or dependent on their parents through the gray zone of adolescence, and then eventually arrive at the ever-changing and gradual adult-to-adult interaction with the same parents. But here we have to be careful with the use of the term independence. It is a relative idea, and children who simply grow older forever remain tethered to the history of the family and other relationships and the way these impact their being, both consciously and unconsciously. However, with repeated traumatic experiences, any idea of an independence that is genuinely distinguished from being cut off is thwarted. Isaac assumed he would never gain such a position, and had not bothered to develop an independent perspective of his own. When he and Lee met, she reflected, and at times reacted to, the forceful family dynamic. Isaac began to see a plausible new perspective, but felt caught between his family of origin whose rules he recognized and his potential for forming a bond of his choice with Lee. However, the idea of independence came with a cost. He imagined no longer being part of the seemingly strong boys club of his family, of his stepfather, including somewhat paradoxically his older sister, and himself and in which he was the least appreciated member, yet knew he was still a member. He realized that being a member also implied that he was a subordinate and that his role was to be ridiculed for the benefit of the others' sense of worth.

Let us return to the individual EMDR session with Isaac. His positive target is sitting on a remote beach, in the surrounding calm, alone, without anybody to demand his service or lurk over his shoulder. Scanning his body first, Isaac says, "I can't feel anything." He is strongly disturbed by it at a level nine on a ten-point scale. This is a scary thought that serves as a negative cognition. He then finds that by holding the BLS device his breathing flows more evenly, but that the back of his neck is exposed and feels cold. His head hurt and his temples throbbed. His negative thought is, "I do not deserve to want." This cognition later changes to, "I do not deserve to live." Tears start streaming down his face. Isaac is startled. In the scenario taking place now, Isaac's stepfather is yelling at him that he is good for nothing. He sees his mother standing by, fearing her husband's wrath, and not reaching out to save Isaac. At the end of this set, Isaac is sad but alive. He wishes Lee was by him. He wants her to comfort him.

His positive cognition is, "I want to work elsewhere, in a different field." Isaac does not like the part of his job that includes sitting in the office, and attending court is highly stressful for him. However he enjoys engaging with his clients, helping them solve their legal conundrums. Following the thread of his anxiety and change of physical sensation, I comment on this shift. He says, "I never wanted to be a lawyer." Going back into the EMDR sequence, Isaac imagines not only being on a distant beach, but moving onto one. He says, "If I had to choose my career, I would be working in nature, educating others about the beauty of the outdoors." His positive cognition is now "I care about people." At the onset of the BLS sequence, Isaac believes in this assertion at a level of two on a seven-point scale. He adds, "But I am sure Lee will never agree to that kind of a life change." Highlighting his short-circuiting in knowing his wishes, Isaac stays with the feeling longer to just consider himself rather than others in recognizing his wishes. His level of belief at the end of this session is six on a seven-point scale. It includes a variation on the positive cognition in which he is included in his original statement—"I care about people"—which now includes caring for himself. Here I would like to comment that for a major EMDR session I allow at least one and a half hours of time instead of the regular forty-five to fifty-minute session. This gives a better opportunity for responding to what comes up, especially when trauma material is present (either small *t* or large *T* trauma), as there is room for both preparation and integration. Winnicott (1971) commented on the importance of extended time while working with unformed primary process material.

In the next session Isaac tells Lee about his revelation. Although she is concerned about the viability of such a life change, she is able to enjoy Isaac's more relaxed manner, knowing that there is an option, and that for Isaac staying but imagining may represent new choices he could not imagine prior to this EMDR session and its permission to seriously play. They both report that Isaac was less depressed and more intimately involved in the week following the EMDR session.

I would now like to describe here another way of modifying EMDR in the service of helping the couple play together to engage unconscious emotional wishes and also explore analytically the dynamic that emerges out of this play.

Playing side by side

Winnicott (1971) was very aware of the importance of play and playing, writing that "in playing, the child or adult is free to be creative" (p. 53). For Winnicott, the idea of playing was a development based on what he described as transitional phenomena. Perhaps with what we have learned about brain activity and how we assume bilateral stimulation works in EMDR, for example, we can understand that occupying the frontal cortex, as in play, releases the amygdala to process emotions.

We can think about the busy hands and moving eyes that happen when playing in a sand tray, or the leg movement in walking, as BLS activity, as creating a transitional space. In the case of Isaac and Lee, I suggested various activities as something nonthreatening in which the walking could serve as a transitional object, promoting a sense of security while a potentially dreadful situation was held at bay with the metronome-like pacing. I often suggest walking to individuals who experience a heightened level of anxiety as well, both for the BLS benefit I just mentioned and for other brain health benefits. These come as an addition to a more traditional EMDR BLS procedure. Most relevant to our discussion is Winnicott's (1971) assertion that "If the patient cannot play, then something needs to be done to enable the patient to become able to play, after which psychotherapy may begin" (p. 54). The idea here is that when patients are frozen they cannot play, either in the simple form or through having minds that are pliable enough to be fully engaged in the analytic process, and indeed in life itself.

In my work with Lee and Isaac, I suggest that they work side by side with the sand tray. From the outset, Isaac takes charge of the sandbox of his choice, to Lee's dismay. However, Lee swiftly brushes off her sense of not being considered as an issue of no matter to her. When I inquire, Isaac's reaction is one of despondency and guilt about a shameful moment in which the humiliation threatened his homeostasis. Lee says she is used to it, both from the family she grew up in and in her relationship with Isaac; she expects to be sacrificed for the other's need, although she wants to have her choice be heard even if not granted.

In one of our earlier sessions, Isaac raised a concern that Lee would be hurt by his family, who had been invited to Lee's grandparents' home to celebrate the Chinese New Year. His fear was that, in his unfavorable position in his own family, he would not be able to protect either of them from his stepfather's verbal attacks. He would rather control Lee, who would not keep silent, than confront his stepfather's bullying attacks on him. The couple remains with Isaac's choice of Lee curbing her reactions to his stepfather's provocative comments, which later in the session leads to a discussion about the couple's reflexive control and surrender along gender lines, and the revelation that Lee is a take-charge person, while Isaac is a take-care person, someone who is vigilant about the well-being of the people in his family as well as at work. Isaac's family of origin demands that Isaac must be a real man and rein in his opinionated wife, while he is walking on a tightrope between his natural tendency to follow and his enjoyment of Lee's ideas, and his fear of being humiliated by his stepfather for not being a man.

Goldner (1991) commented on the impossibility of having an internally consistent gender identity. Her emphasis on gender identity as a cultural construct is clearly manifested in Lee's strong, stereotypically male traits, which she has had to disavow in her relationship with Isaac as they threaten not only his sense of being the providing, in-control husband, but also the persistent demand by his family of origin that he both "show and tell" and display manlike behavior. These tendencies were developed in Lee's family of origin too, and in her interaction with the world at large, yet when focusing on the couple it is essential to explore where these patterns are reinforced and redefined in their effort to find equilibrium in the face of internal confusion.

Working side by side reveals the great curiosity Isaac and Lee have about each other's sand-tray play. This is in contrast to the couple's surprising lack of interest when we have conversations during a session, or the lack of meaningful conversation when they meet at the end of the day. Here, seated on the carpet in my office, each with their own box of sand, with its various contents, they are permitted what their family cannot permit them: a sense of belonging to themselves and complex communication with their partner. Having their hands busied with the sand and the creatures in it allows them to begin and feel, and with my guidance listen to their internal process. It is safe to comment, and speak in unfinished sentences. It is the first time that I witness primary process in action in Isaac and Lee, and playful, spontaneous play. They both become acutely aware of the lack of play in their lives as individuals and as a couple.

Yet, as much as each partner deals creatively with their own sand tray, they also show a wish to play in the other's playground. Asking Lee and Isaac to reflect on how they feel about both playing in the same playground now, they agree to work in Lee's tray, but add elements from Isaac's box. At first they play side by side, Isaac seeking to interact by infringing on Lee's space, to her protest. She articulates her frustration and then invites him to do cooperative work in one box. To my surprise, once Lee's avoidance and Isaac's infringement abate, and using single words they proceed to create a more agreeable world and interact without losing their individual presence. It does not become her world or his, feminine or masculine, but their unique world. Lee's guarded body stance relaxes, and Isaac's color returns to his face. It is the end of our time, and as Isaac offers his hand to Lee, she does not shrug away.

In therapy work with couples who have suffered significant emotional and/or physical trauma in childhood, and especially when there is current lingering reinforcement of extended family influences, more than one method is needed to move beyond the surface. With Isaac and Lee, helping them soften their strong sense of shame and humiliation called for several approaches to help them forget and remember simultaneously. That is, they needed to forget the representational restrictions that had become second nature and enmeshed in rationality and familial structuring, and to remember who they were before it became too dangerous to be who they were. In particular, play was adding back the element of personal fluidity, in the realm of gender for example, while it also allowed them, both in the office and outside, to move into areas that had been forbidden earlier in terms of their interaction, but also in terms of their goals.

The couple found, for example, that when they cooked together (previously Lee's sole responsibility) they could talk and enjoy each other's presence, rather than remain separate under the earlier strict expectation that dinner would be ready. This collaborative effort reduced Lee's anxiety significantly. Isaac found a playground he really enjoyed as well as pleasure in sharing play with Lee, something that neither of them had experienced in their own families. The BLS provided by their busy hands released their thinking brain to allow for some emotional connection to emerge. Similarly, they found that taking a walk together (BLS by the act of walking) after dinner allowed them to talk without getting upset, as more reflective time was available to each of them. Their increased listening skills were trusted because they were emotionally and bodily relevant, and not imposed from the outside. It is hard to overemphasize the idea that no voice from the outside, when it has historically been detrimental to the sense of self, can easily be trusted.

Couples invariably are appreciative for the gift of release from that sense of false self they had to hold onto for survival. Reacquainting the self with its more complete range of possibility is freeing, and comes with the additional benefit of changes made in the real world. Having couples observe each other do their individual EMDR work has the benefit of letting each partner appreciate what the other is going through emotionally, and helping them to develop empathy that in turn reduces the friction when a manifestation of the internal struggle may reappear in the intersubjective realm.

That said, at times, as in the case of Lee and Isaac, there is a need to begin EMDR exploration individually before the side-by-side work, as holding secrets is detrimental to the sense of sanity. For example, Isaac's fear of being seen as losing control was overwhelming, and needed to be explored without Lee being present as a witness. However, his relief in exploring such worries about the self, recognizing that he does have feelings, and does have desire, only that they were stifled, was exciting to him, and from that point on Isaac explicitly wished for Lee to be present. Isaac benefited from her support of his change of career, albeit with some trepidation about sustainability. It took Isaac some more sessions, both EMDR and relational, to work through his fears about Lee's greater independence and wish to do things on her own to benefit herself, at points where he could not see the direct benefit to the family. It took Lee additional time to believe that her wishes, and indeed that she herself, had validation in this world. The opening of Isaac's secret aspiration allowed Lee to trust in her own changes within the relationship, and allowed them both to worry less about external threats to their relationship.

Summary

In this chapter, I described my work with a couple, Lee and Isaac, and the unique consideration given to working with both relational psychotherapy and EMDR methods. I described modifications that were needed for the case of this couple, and explored the usefulness of individual EMDR sessions versus the value of working with EMDR with the patients witnessing each other. I showed how a relational approach, along with sensitivity to gender studies, enhanced my work with this couple, and stressed that gender and other environmental and relational influences on the development of the self in interaction should be kept in mind in the treatment plan and as the work unfolds.

References

Dimen, M. (2003). *Sexuality, Intimacy, Power*. Hillsdale, NJ: The Analytic Press.

Eigen, M. (1993). *The Electrified Tightrope*. Northvale, NJ: Jason Aronson.

Goldner, V. (1991). Toward a critical relational theory of gender. *Psychoanalytic Dialogues* 1(3): 249–272.

Goldner, V. (2014). Romantic bonds, binds, and ruptures: Couples on the brink. *Psychoanalytic Dialogues* 24(4): 402–418.

Kaslow, F., R. Nurse, and P. Thompson. (2002). EMDR in conjunction with family systems therapy. In F. Shapiro, editor, *EMDR as an Integrative Psychotherapy Approach: Experts of Diverse Orientations Explore the Paradigm Prism*, 289–318. Washington, DC: American Psychological Association.

Kulish, N. (2002). Female sexuality: The pleasure of secrets and the secret of pleasure. *Psychoanalytic Study of the Child* 57: 151–176.

Nebbiosi, G., and S. Federici-Nebbiosi. (2008). "We" got rhythm: Miming and the poliphony of identity in psychoanalysis. In F. S. Anderson, editor, *Bodies in Treatment: The Unspoken Dimension*, 213–233. New York: The Analytic Press.

Pavić, M. (1990). *Landscape Painted with Tea*. New York: Vintage Books.

Ringstrom, P. A. (1994). An intersubjective approach to conjoint therapy. In A. Goldberg, editor, *Progress in Self Psychology*, 159–182. Hillsdale, NJ: The Analytic Press.

Solms, M., and O. Turnbull. (2002). *The Brain and the Inner World*. New York: Other Press.

Stein, A. (2007). Tricycles, bicycles, life cycles: Psychoanalytic perspectives on childhood loss and transgenerational parenting in Sylvain Chômet's *Belleville Rendez-vous*. In A. Sabbadini, editor, *Projected Shadows: Psychoanalytic Reflections on the Representation of Loss in European Cinema*, 131–143. New York: Routledge.

Winnicott, D. W. (1971). *Playing and Reality*. London: Tavistock.

Chapter 7

I-dentity

Is trusted love ever an option?

רק אשר אבד לי, קנייני לעד
— רחל המשוררת
Only that, which I had lost, is forever mine
— Rachel Bluwstein

This chapter illustrates my work with a woman who came in after experiencing frightening events in which she felt out of control with rage, anxiety, and the underlying depression. I discuss the use of EMDR to access these current events alongside her early experiences and explicit memories from various developmental points in her life, as well as preverbal, visceral, and deeply embedded experiences that had been haunting her for much of her life, relationally depleting her to the extent that she had had only minimal personal and meaningful relationships. In addition, I discuss some modifications I made to the use of bilateral stimulation (BLS) while keeping the psychoanalytic approach in mind, for the sake of blending the two methods without diminishing the benefits of either approach. I show how the use of EMDR in accessing and clearing embodied relational trauma helps initiate the beginning of a mobilized mourning process, while revealing attachment to that which is lost, as a form of what I call *I-dentity*, in the presence of limited actual relationships. I discuss how difficult it is for people who must launch their lives in the wake of their identification with the hollowness of real and meaningful human connection when that is all there is. Finally, through the use of EMDR and the development of the strong transferential-countertransferential bond that forms in this treatment, I describe the way some mental representations of loved objects as subjects form, so that gradually a transient intersubjectivity begins to emerge.

Anxiety as an emotional skin

The shaking stops. Not only now, not only here. Everywhere, all the time. It is an eerie silence she notices for the first time, for as long as she can remember. Now that the constant buzz is gone, some relief can be felt. She no longer fears entering a room, any room. "You know," she says, "I did not feel anxious coming in today. I think it is gone." But with it a renewed sense of loneliness slips in. Lynn was feeling a longing for a connection that might take the place of the now lost buzz.

Before we parted following our previous analytic hour, Lynn said, "This was important." She was referring to a discovery she had made. This discovery cut through decades of repulsion toward her mother and Lynn's own obsession with hidden love and a more recognizable anger toward her mother, who was emotionally lost to her early in life. I am saying lost as opposed to the more common "unavailable" to highlight the depressive melancholia that resides within her. What Lynn has stored in memory are the moments of anger and rejection she had felt as a preteen, and even a vague memory as a toddler. She remembers crying for a mother that never showed up. She remembers calling, terrified, to a mother who stepped in to scold her for wanting. She also remembers feeling brokenhearted by a girlfriend who bullied her in middle school and approaching her mother with a rare request for a hug of comfort only to be pushed away coldly. But with all of these memories she never remembers *this* that she has discovered in the session. "Astonishing," she thinks. It is astonishing that she doubts her own memory of things. Her feelings are of the magnitude of that earlier kind of a memory. But now, for the first time, there is a match.

She wonders why she feels so anxious. Rational understanding does not explain her lifelong companion of angst in every human interaction. She carries the sense that she cannot relax into a conversation, cannot be around others without a worry, and cannot feel comfortable with an intimate partner. "Yes," she says, she knows it has something to do with her mother, but why can't she shake it off, after all these years?

Of course I do not know the answer to this question. Something is folded up tightly in this Rubenesque body, in her coy smile, her discomfort in lying on the couch. Her moods shift, passing through with only the slightest change of expression or word. One moment she is soft, present, and wise, yet in another she is coiled and tensed up, unable to find a comfortable position, her lips twitching, saying that she feels stupid. Every change gives her hidden desires and fears away, but with no specificity.

Lynn, a woman in her early fifties, who grew up in the south, is a professional musician who works with students studying at a conservatory. She is not only a talented musician herself, but also an admired teacher for scores of young musicians who have taken the main stage nationally. She was referred to me by her physician, who had concerns for her emotional well-being, particularly the depression that has hindered her ability to perform and teach. Lynn has not been able to play her instrument recently, and—worse—feels that she is about to fall apart. She finds herself angry at the conservatory director in ways that surprise her, and she is afraid that she will further harm this important working relationship. In short, Lynn feels that she is out of control in a way that is destructive to her personal and professional sense of integrity. She cannot imagine not voicing her difference, but it never comes out quite right. She feels humiliated and embarrassed by her behavior, yet she cannot stop. She thinks about unpleasant events incessantly and feels a compulsion to act even as she sees the effect of the potential destruction. It is that perplexity that has brought her into my office. Lynn talks often about what she sees as her mother's abuse of her older sister, turning her into a boy and a "homosexual."

In the preceding weeks in therapy, Lynn has struggled through a series of exposures that are emotionally exhausting. In her twenties, she started a decade-long therapy that gave her a virtual home, although not much of a sense of belonging. This affiliation took away the remainder of her trust in knowing who she was, and the awareness of her deep wishes. She talks about a failed marriage in which she could not reconcile her wish for closeness with a conviction that she does not deserve to have closeness, especially as she fears sexual intimacy. There is no known incident of molestation in her history, though she felt overstimulated by both parents' enactments as a child. As we explore her fantasies about both men and women, in which only women have contact with her, she is both ashamed about and helpless to stop the power of her sin. She is also confused. Now, Lynn reports that she feels angry at me, saying that she fears I want to make her be a lesbian (in a later session, she says her real fear is that I will make her find out that she is a lesbian). In my being a midwife who is allowing her to utter her fantasies, she can hear another voice announcing how this shows her failure to be a decent citizen of this world. Through the exploration of her fantasy of what my motivation might be, she recognizes her own fear of not really knowing who she is, and that fluidity scares her (Harris, 1991). As Laplanche (1999) stated,

> It is the adult who brings the breast, and not the milk, into the foreground—and does so due to her own desire, conscious and above all unconscious. For the breast is not only an organ for feeding children but a sexual organ, something which is *utterly overlooked by Freud and has been since Freud.* Not a single text, not even a single remark of Freud's takes account of the fact that the female breast is excitable, not only in feeding, but simply in the woman's sexual life. (p. 78; italics in original)

The normalization of the power of fantasy and exploration, which expands the range of what these options might mean to her rather than simply determining her sexual orientation, helps reduce the level of torment. Gradually opening the door for a discussion of her preconceived notions of sexual orientation as badness helps create a potential space in which ideas can be examined without becoming concrete. This is the first time that Lynn describes a wish to be contained, which she begins by recognizing that maintaining what she feels are our separate perspectives on who she is feels burdensome. She needs for me to stay in an *as-if* position, in which we are both on the same illusionary page. I am reminded of a patient who said, with disappointment in his voice, that he felt completely understood by me until I started talking, at which point he had to see that our subjectivities were separate, and he did not welcome that. As Slochower (2005) suggested, holding may be attained by way of not necessarily having to interpret. She wrote, "It seems clear that the holding process requires that both patient and analyst bracket their awareness of the illusory nature of absolute analytic attunement for a time" (p. 38).

The hardware and software of co-(l)laboration

In this afternoon session, however, Lynn feels that she would like to work on why she is so anxious in most situations. She becomes teary, and when I acknowledge her distress she says that no one has ever taken care of her.

Suddenly she stops crying and says that perhaps her mother could see that she did not want her to come near her. "But why am I afraid of her? She is frail and can no longer hurt me, but I am afraid of her." As she ponders this she says, "I have a feeling that something happened when I was young, but I do not have any memory of it. I just know." Although I hear this distress as also pertaining to the transference, so that she is now afraid that she will not open up with me and will miss opportunities for closeness and change, I suggest we try an EMDR set, sensing that she needs to express something possibly preverbal that resides in her body and to which she has no access in her thinking as such.

I can tell when she begins lifting her shoulder toward her ear, her head turning away and her mouth twitching, that she is "there," dissociated and haunted by the "it" that has no name. In this case, when she uses the tappers and sinks into her fear, the image changes. She is agitated and cannot find a comfortable position. She says that she is alone, playing in her crib, when she hears her mother come into the room. She feels her entire body tense up. She looks up and can hear the door. Her mother is entering. She is mortified. As we stop for a short debrief, Lynn says she does not know why, but she is certain her mother hurt her. She is not sure how exactly she was hurt, maybe in changing the diapers, perhaps sexually. She does not know why she feels this way, as she has no memory of anything like that occurring. We process the fear with that scene in mind. Her thought is of her mother finding her to be unworthy.

With a few sets of BLS, Lynn feels the anxiety begin to release. The next break we take as we check back in, Lynn is flabbergasted, but feels that something like that must have happened. I comment that the anxiety is an accumulation of her excitement about her mother's entrance into the room and a deep dread of what her mother would bring, together with her presence that itself is terrifying to her.

Lynn takes a deep breath, her eyes wide open and says, "That sounds possible." She stops breathing and then continues, saying that that explains so much about her relationships to others. Although she seems rattled, the color returns to her face. She feels guilty for her thoughts about her mother and we process some of these feelings, putting them in context. Following the conversation, I offer that her longing and shame for having a woman's body might be triggered by being both over- and understimulated. She says, "Now I can see why I feel that I was abused.

That explains so much." We part, each of us feeling the weight of what we have witnessed, a weight she has carried all along without sharing it until that moment.

With the example of Lynn's experience of the integrated treatment modality we can begin to grasp what EMDR does for the benefit of the relational psychoanalytic inquiry. It is activating, through a subdued rattle to the body, and with the holding direction of the therapist, the hardwired strata of the patient's anxiety, which is fixated in motion on pathways that were born in trauma, yet is also now inviting the possibility of gaining access to the yet unthinkable. We can liken the EMDR protocol to an intervention at the hardware level, allowing the mind to create new pathways in part by making possible access to the thus far unused software. In this example, following several sessions of EMDR, which are always combined with a more relationally oriented analytical process, Lynn begins to access feelings she did not know existed, and finds new layers of her psyche of which she could not be aware earlier. From this place of awareness, Lynn starts on a gentler path outside of therapy. She is able to see her attachment to old ways, begin to stand on the side of her own internal interests, and subtly change her attitude toward her right to consider her needs and wishes first. Some of these changes are unpleasant. She finds that instead of general fear of her mother, she can now feel anger at lost opportunities. Her anger is more focused and the fear does not disappear, but she feels that she has a beginning of clarity about the feelings that are triggered in her in certain situations. That clarity she can feel in her body. She knows it to be right and therefore trusts it more in real-life situations.

EMDR's contribution to potentiating the analytic work

Describing the depth and breadth of the permutations of EMDR and of relational psychoanalysis is beyond the scope of this chapter. However, EMDR opens access to a fountain of memories and emotions through which analysis can take place, and that are a far cry from the insidious grasp of depression. Now we had a mess, but it was one that we could see and work with. Lynn is able to recognize losses and can begin to mourn. Through EMDR and the analytic process she has come to recognize that the losses she has known are not ephemeral occurrences, but experiences that have dictated the cadence of every choice she has ever made. You might expect an even greater depression, but in Lynn these now recognizable losses invite hope that things can be different. Walking home happy after a session in which she reveals her fear of the power of her fantasy Lynn finds herself feeling hopeful that perhaps one day she can be that open with others in her life. Now she is back on the path.

EMDR has offered access to an exploration of fundamental aspects of Lynn's self-perception, and has provided a glimpse into her interactions in both internal and external relationality. This has allowed a core internal structure to evolve in which the anxiety about new and renewed interactions feels both exciting and intrusive.

We must consider that wishing that no door would open is a form of protection against intrusion. Intimacy is hard to come by without the trial and error of intrusion. Lynn had chosen to shut the door completely lest a potential intimate partner in the form of a friend, family, or a lover might intrude and find her defenseless. Part of the difficulty is that Lynn is yearning for real human connection. Intelligent and warm, Lynn is a sensitive person who wishes to take care of others. Unlike some, whose narcissistic wounds leave them with little to no interest in connecting with others except for gratification, Lynn thrives on authentic interaction with others. Her fear has kept her away from potential intimate friendships and now she is beginning to have a glimpse into the complexity of the person she has been.

A poem by Mary Oliver comes to mind here, as she highlights the inevitability of interaction on the path to intimacy as well as the risk involved, both imagined and real:

Meeting Wolf

There are no words
inside his mouth,
inside his golden eyes.

So we stand, silent,
both of us tense
under the speechless but faithful trees.

And this is what I think:
I have given him
intrusion.

He has given me
a glimpse into a better but now broken world.
Not his doing, but ours. (2009, p. 59)

Up to this point Lynn has believed that there is something repulsive about her. She has believed that she is not attractive, and that no person would dare to get near her. She remembers high school and college experiences in which she had felt passed over or was invited only as a last resort. This conviction, which appears in many interactions she has had throughout her adult life, is a mechanism she has used as a way of finding the locus of any of her difficulties outside of herself. This situation has been made more complex through her notion that her outside is a separate internal entity. Lynn believes that her perceived lack of attraction causes others to be appalled by her appearance. She thus tended to find an external cause on which to hang her anxiety. However, in our work we have been able to articulate how internalizing the bad mother she in fact did have was then repeatedly funneled into translating all other experiences to mean that she is a person that terrible things can be done to. Yes, her mother seemed appalling to her, but she, by a double association of having the dangerous mother and being the person her mother damaged, is not only guilty but also appalling.

Following a later EMDR session, Lynn reports that for the first time she is unafraid as she is sitting in the waiting room. She is less angry about her mother's abuse of her sister and more focused and clear about what has happened to her. She is no longer afraid of doors opening and the sound of footsteps in the hallway.

What kind of change does she hope for? At this time, all she wants is to not forget what she has learned with clarity. She also wishes to understand how much of the past is still penetrating her relationships now. I reflect on the unforgettable nature of what is etched in our minds early on, and the power of having a recall not of the original memory but the accompanying anxiety at a point when the body can imagine something else that is more adaptive than the original cocktail of fear and self-doubt so common with trauma dissociation and its aftermath.

I find myself drifting, thinking of the conundrum of women who may be masters in their professional life, where they exude confidence, knowledge, and personal charm, yet who in their personal life may feel privately depleted, believing they do not deserve to be considered for a space they wish to call their own. I am thinking about Lynn and her lost opportunities as I watch her cry over spending a life without an intimate partner, without an offspring she wishes she had, having sat on the train of trauma's ramifications until it is too late for certain changes. Now she is ready to disembark and look at what she can still want, and what it is not too late to ask for.

Lynn is kind enough to allow us to explore the span of her beliefs. We begin by using EMDR to define her preferred modus operandi of seeing herself as less than a full member of this world, somehow deserving little in the way of participation. She can imagine herself being a proxy. To give a few examples, she can embrace being a surrogate mother to her sister's sons, she can be a music teacher to stars in the making, or a good friend to the men she once loved but has been too afraid to approach openly. Taking something fully for herself, without feeling that she is stealing is too hard to imagine. When Lynn talks about the succession of men who she externally overlooked while feeling tormented by her longing for love, she breaks up as she counts the families that have been created in the wake of her lonely, fearful boat that has never anchored.

Creation of I-dentity versus loyalty to a narcissistic love object

The day after this particular EMDR session, Lynn reports that a question lingered in her mind when she had left my office. She asked, Why was she so loyal? We spent the next moments trying to understand the demand made by her needy mother that Lynn would be loyal to her alone. And that perhaps being close, first to her beloved father and then to young men of her age, was a threat to the emotionally fragile mother. The question we ponder is how to create an identity that puts Lynn at the center of her interest, developing an *I-dentity* through a relationship, allowing Lynn to keep her curiosity, and have her fantasies accepted as part of her internal private life, rather than seeing herself as a sinful object that should be rejected. I comment that this challenge is here between us as well. In order to separate and find her own I-dentity, she is bound to relate to me, a risk as great as the door that opens and closes with all its excitement and dread.

Since this metaphor has become a stronghold, Lynn finds herself eager to try to open emotional doors. They sometimes slam, and often gingerly open.

Lynn is no longer afraid to convey her wishes and fears for our work. She reports feeling happy at the end of a session when she conveys a burdensome transferential secret and no longer has to carry it alone. She is free to roam her world, purposeful and calm. And as for the countertransference, you may be asking? Well that is another story of importance.

Relational psychoanalysis: Keeping in touch, without

An element of relational psychoanalysis is keeping in touch, without touching. EMDR inadvertently challenges the notion of complete distance by allowing the practitioner to tap, for example, on the patient's knees as part of the protocol. I have found that working with analytic patients, either in formal psychoanalysis or in psychoanalytically informed psychotherapy, does not go hand in hand with actual tapping of that kind. Experimenting with several devices, such as eye movement, tapping, and following a light or sound, I have found that electronic tappers work best in providing the necessary brain stimulation without an actual or proxy of touch.

However, I have noticed, with Lynn and other patients, that using the tappers can be a subject of transferential cathexis. The therapist's holding of the control box provides a proxy of touch by having the cord between the box and the tappers sway with the patient's or the therapist's slightest movement. I have come to think of it as a symbolic umbilical cord, the closest to the principle of keeping in touch, without touch. It represents a physical parallel to the psychological holding in psychoanalysis. There is also the aspect of transaction, similar to other transactions in therapy in which there is a close proximity, such as in handing a check, or holding the door at the beginning and ending of a session. This intimate encounter is more frequent with the use of EMDR, and—in a way that is similar to remarking on the ending of the hour (Winnicott, 1949, p. 71)—represents power, sometimes alongside aggression or hate, or regret at having to abide by the law of limitation.

Another patient said to me, as she elaborated on a disturbing image at the beginning of an EMDR session, "You know this [the tappers] is not on," as if the power of turning on a mechanical device indeed ignited an internal process, a pulse that could not be otherwise attained. Perhaps this example may serve as a symbolic starter to an analytic process via the use of EMDR above and beyond EMDR's multiple benefits through bilateral engagement of the brain.

To carry the idea of an umbilical cord further, the other side of the power of this process can be seen in the important temporary illusion that the combined apparatus of the EMDR protocol and psychoanalytic exploration of meaning provide a safe base for the movement toward healing of severed early attachment in a way that illuminates and encompasses all aspects of mental life. For Lynn, experiencing a significant improvement in the sense of self in her professional world, regaining her professional self, helps her trust our work with its mixed modality. Holding on to the tappers, scanning her body sensation for tension, having an image with negative self-perception and inviting plausible and desired positive views on that same image, followed by BLS sets, feeling a shoulder relax or finding a renewed regular breathing pattern, is encouraging enough for Lynn. These experiences increase her willingness to consider change in her state of mind as a possibility. And, in association, she is willing to suspend disbelief in the existence of a span of possible meanings specific to her.

After spending a major part of her life believing in one story of her being undesirable without ever considering there could be another version of that story, Lynn could see no outlet from her misery. When her professional self was threatening to follow that script, there was no outlet for Lynn's sensitive and caring self and her own need to love. If not in her personal life, at least she can imagine possibilities in her work. There is an element of humiliation for a highly intelligent woman in recognizing that she cannot figure herself out fully before entering therapy. Of course there is the consolation of improvement, yet for the patient, staying with her sense of having lived a life with unintentional self-deception can be quite daunting. It is here that I feel that the holding of *what is*, directly in the moment, could help ease the self-deprecation that is felt in accepting her survival blindness.

Another outcome of our work is the activation of her sense of badness. How could she burden me with her love? She is not worthy—not only of being considered, but also for wanting.

In one session in particular, there is a lull. Lynn says she feels uncomfortable. I am listening for her words, looking at her posture. Her head down, she says that she is afraid that in this silence she will let herself know that she might be falling in love. She is mortified to think that if the silence grows, her mind will wander into sexual thoughts about me, and that she will get out of control and try to act on these feelings. She is fearful and gutsy. In the next weeks, we deconstruct the meaning of all the funneling of her grateful feelings for change in her life—her loneliness, her wish to show loyalty by attaching herself to the person she perceives to be in power—into our work. That is the last session of the week.

When she returns the following Monday, Lynn says that she felt very happy after leaving that hour last week. She does not know why, but she has not felt that way in a long time. She had found that she was invested in her environment with a calm and energy that was new. I wonder with her if leaving the secret with me, and of not having to carry her fear of her bad behavior alone, had released her to enjoy her activities without feeling burdened. Lynn thinks that that is possible and adds that her angst about keeping her "bad" thoughts with us had taken away the fear that she is stealing something from me that she wants and that I can never be interested in sharing with her. At least now she is honest, and the burden to somehow punish her for her fantasy is mine, no longer hers. I am struck by her sense that she cannot wish herself on anyone, that somehow I will be appalled by her presence or her fantasized wishes. When I say she is gutsy, I think I mean to say that, given her view of herself, she is prepared to lose everything in our working relationship—my respect, my care, my investment in her well-being. She had expected to be rejected by me for merely having a fantasy. She had not felt equal. Yet Lynn had taken a serious psychological risk and reaped the fruit of her effort. She had immediately felt relieved.

Timing interventions when integrating EMDR with relational psychoanalysis

In using EMDR along with relational psychoanalysis, questions of timing change the frame. We often wonder if we should convey a thought or hold back, letting the process evolve and considering the reasons involved in making the choice. Using EMDR adds another element we must consider. The value of intrusion at a moment that can otherwise be used to hold a primary process and its exploration needs to be weighed against the possibility of focusing, in more concrete terms, on the image and thinking about it, before entering the primary process through sets of BLS. I find that both are rewarding to the analytic work, and I rarely regret either staying with the analytic process or starting with EMDR, as inevitably they each lead to greater emotionality, instead decreasing anxiety while leaving a greater virtual playground for the patient and therapist's exploration.

Summary

In this chapter, I explored, through the example of my work with Lynn, how the weaving in of EMDR can benefit the relational psychoanalytic process. I highlighted my work with the transference and countertransference, and showed how at times EMDR can help bring to the surface aspects of the transference that are otherwise buried. I also elaborated on the use of preverbal trauma, using the as-if of potential space to create a more coherent narrative, specifically in relation to embodied experience, while at the same time increasing the patient's capacity to tolerate the unknowable, paradoxical, and ambivalent.

Note

The line of poetry in the epigraph is from "Metai/My dead," a poem written by Rachel Bluwstein in 1931.

References

Harris, A. (1991). Gender as contradiction. *Psychoanalytic Dialogues* 1: 197–224.
Laplanche, J. (1999). The unfinished Copernican Revolution, L. Thurston, translator. In *Essays on Otherness*, 52–83. New York: Routledge.
Oliver, M. (2009). *Evidence: Poems*. Boston, MA: Beacon Press.
Slochower, J. (2005). Holding: Something old and something new. In L. Aron and A. Harris, editors, *Relational Psychoanalysis: Innovation and Expansion*. Vol. 2, pp. 29–49. Hillsdale, NJ: The Analytic Press.
Winnicott, D. W. (1949). Hate in the counter-transference. *International Journal of Psychoanalysis* 30: 69–74. Reprinted in *Through Paediatrics to Psycho-Analysis*, 194–203. New York: Basic Books, 1975.

Chapter 8

EMDR in absentia—The power of "No"

> "For your Sake!" It was impossible to describe the contempt bundled into those words. "I'm pulling out weeds because it helps me think, and because I happen to enjoy it."
>
> — Hans Fallada

This chapter raises the question of how extensively EMDR can be modified and still be considered a modification rather than a new technique. Through clinical illustration, I explore the use of specific tools that the patient and the analyst co-conceive during the patient's tenuous relationship with her efforts to conceive a baby and see them through to fruition. While the patient was reluctant to use formal EMDR technique, following our conversations about incorporating this option into the psychodynamic work she reported that she found herself in a state of reverie when she spontaneously engaged in completing a puzzle. This process allowed her to see the value of unwittingly occupying the thinking brain as a way of assisting the emergence of affective content that is similar to the process stimulated by EMDR's bilateral stimulation (BLS). That finding then led to a conversation about other forms of bilateral stimulation she could use in the session and feel safe for the purpose of supporting affect emergence and the process itself, both through the EMDR protocol and relational exploration of emotional material that was otherwise bracketed.

At times, the use of the full EMDR protocol is limited or even impossible. That may be the case, for example, when a person with severe dissociative states is unable to stay with the process because getting into a deeper search for anxiety can cause further splitting to protect the self from painful experiences. At other times, a patient may be reluctant to try EMDR for fear of losing control over his or her emotions and the examined situation, or from sheer anxiety about experiencing the dreaded emotion.

The following discussion presents a case in which a patient opted out of using EMDR as part of the treatment, yet did use some of its qualities in a creative form in order to benefit from some aspects of it. Analytically speaking, the modification I describe here, made unconsciously by the patient, is an embodiment of the complex difficulty that she is presenting. Here, it is a combination of reality and fantasy that caused her to resist the use of EMDR. However, the idea of EMDR's potential benefit sinks in unconsciously and lives on in an unexpected way. This is possible, in part, because I follow the patient's anxiety, at first, with the belief that using EMDR's full protocol in her situation may not be indicated. A pertinent point is addressed in Tom Cloyd's (1999) article, in which he reminds us that although, in formal EMDR trainings, one is cautioned against doing EMDR trauma therapy with pregnant women, the postponement of therapy may sometimes be more problematic and complex than one might expect.

Laura is a 38-year-old physician, born and raised in the Midwest. She is poised and savvy. She is outgoing, with a huge smile that appears when I greet her in the morning. Her smile appears when she is amused, when she is embarrassed, and when she is deeply sad. Like a puzzle solver, I am left to decipher the emotion underlying it before I can look for its context, and before its content is revealed.

Laura is yearning to have a child. Treatment so far has produced only disappointment, and she is now counting the time passing by in years. Laura wonders whether she is fit to be a mother. Not only whether her body will produce an offspring, but whether her body is defying her wishes for a reason. She fears that she is not equipped to function as a mother. Thoughts of having a child, and of *not* having a child are agonizing. She finds it difficult to be around mothers and even harder to be around expectant mothers. This worry of not knowing if she will ever conceive also gets in the way of her relationship with her husband. Although he is very supportive, encouraging, and helplessly optimistic, tension has arisen between them around times of fertility treatment and the nerve-wracking waiting for the results.

Laura is torn between focusing on renewed hope that this time a baby is on its way and suspicion, garnered from experience, that the failures will repeat. She says, "I am not sure that I can continue with more invasive treatments. Perhaps I should get used to the idea that we will be a couple with no children and focus on what kind of a relationship we can build together."

When Laura is referred to psychotherapy she finds it hard to carry on her professional work. The long days at the hospital, especially after a fertility treatment, are exhausting. All she wants to do is to lie in bed and read a magazine, forget it all, and wait for an answer. This bright woman with a wide range of interests in her profession and beyond now finds any past pleasure unessential. The fear of being abandoned by her husband comes in and out of her consciousness. She feels judged by her peers; she feels that she is an outsider, and that if she does not produce a child she will be considered less than a full member of her family and her social world.

"Perhaps it is right that I should have no children," she says one day. Her thought, which we later understood, stems from her fear that she will be an envious mother who demands a lot and gives very little. Perhaps she too, like her mother with her, will be competitive with her child. The thought is devastating. It is perhaps a recognition that her mother has helped embed in her, through the process of representation, some of her mother's most rejected traits, including those that cause Laura to evade any association with or mention of her mother.

When Laura was a child, her mother relied on her for support amid a crumbling marriage. Laura was forced to take sides and to put her mother's needs ahead of her own. Now, fearing that her marriage will not withstand the pressures of fertility treatments, or even worse the possibility of their failure, she meets these with a dual response. In the first response, she is confident that the marriage will last, however difficult the situation may end up being. In the other, more insidious response, she fears that perhaps her husband will see no value in a relationship without children.

Stress is contraindicated when a woman is hoping to conceive. Laura has a sense of that. However, since childhood, she has been swimming against many competing currents—the current of wishing to be a dutiful daughter, and the current of knowing that academic and then professional successes are a key to leaving behind an oppressive family situation. She also feels the need to create a distance between a depressed mother and herself, yet still fulfill what her mother never could, by allying herself with her successful, if problematic, father.

Laura does not want to feel sad, does not want to cry. Some weeks she holds up well. Other times the well is overflowing. In her sessions, she talks about her secret about the fertility treatments that she keeps from others: the shame of telling that something is not quite right when she is around rounded bellies and newborns. The pity she reads in their eyes and the associated pep talk she imagines hearing from those who believe they have gone through what she is going through are cutting. The term infertility is injurious. It reminds her that she cannot respond. Not the way she wants it, perhaps not at all. All her life, until this point, she could. For someone who prides herself on always succeeding in the most difficult places, as in choosing a challenging specialty and adding a doctorate degree to her medical studies, to mention only a couple of examples, the sense of this repeated lack of success is perplexing. It reminds her of her mother, who is exceedingly intelligent but who has never found a fulfilling path for her varying talents. Now the criticism Laura feels toward her mother's depressed position seems to turn around and haunt her in herself. "I have everything I need to succeed, but then again, I can't get what I want most," she says. A focusing question formulates in my mind, "How do you learn to have less stress when you are on the run from stressful demons, current, past, and future?"

Shortly after she asks to increase the frequency of our appointments, Laura recants, saying she hates coming multiple times a week. "I liked it when I could come in less often and then had a sense of relief afterward, as if I solved a riddle." I wonder aloud if she is so used to living under stress that she feels banal without it. I wonder if she feels as if she has lost a companion. I think that the building up of anxiety through the week and then having a chance to work on it head-on is familiar. She laughs and says that somehow that rings true. Additional causes may have been her sense of having no control over her body's responsiveness to treatment, her pressure at work and in the academic environment, and her endless appointments, all leaving her without much time to call her own or the ability to have a say over what should happen to her and when. At least in therapy she can say "no."

She avoids meeting friends in the face of her fierce envy. She has lost interest in going to work, although she feels blessed while engrossed in her clinical work. Teaching proves to be challenging, as it requires preparation and a level of engagement that she sometimes feels reticent about providing. Laura feels irritable. She often thinks that perhaps her husband will be better off without her. She feels that, at this time, the mountain of busywork that has kept her upright and climbing all these years since childhood is eroding and crumbling away in front of her eyes.

I decide to bring the idea of using EMDR to the table as part of an approach to help reduce Laura's stress. We talk about elements of the protocol that might be helpful, without touching directly on past trauma that might increase stress before it tones it down (Cloyd, 1999). Laura finds the rhythmic motion in her palms relaxing. It feels as if she is being rocked in someone's arms. "Not my mother's," she laughs, "but someone who cares, perhaps my husband." She hands the tappers back to me and shakes her head. "I do not want to risk it," she says. "What if it caused some harm to the baby I may have inside me?" and "What if it sends electric waves into my brain that can interfere with my getting pregnant?" We both want to avoid iatrogenic effects, although the literature only cautions against using EMDR in pregnancy with PTSD cases, as then the stress can be counterproductive. It is suggested however, that at times when the stress is very high, EMDR can be used to reduce stress even during pregnancy and possibly without increasing trauma-related stress (Cloyd, 1999).

Yet I feel that following Laura's lead is right, even as a measure of having some control over her body and treatment that she lacks in other areas of her care. I also feel that not having access to EMDR work is a loss. As a part of the treatment that could reduce Laura's anxiety, it could be a tremendous tool in her journey toward accepting herself as a deserving mother of a child, indeed as a deserving partner and caretaker of her own patients.

I resort to singing the praises of the method as one that allows for the emotions to be brought to a tolerable level. Laura is curious, but prefers to refrain. We leave it at that although, at times, I wish we had it at our disposal as a tool when her misery is mounting, her voice changing to a young version of herself defying the need to participate in any activity in her life. Joining Laura at her helpless place, a place in which she does not want to wish for anything again, helps me feel with her the pain of being left to fend for herself with no tools. Here, words will not do. She is parentless, and I am a neglectful parent who lacks the ability to take away her misery. She second-guesses the benefit versus the potential harm. She has to be the parent and the child combined, but not integrated. In this primary process, Laura succumbs not only to tears and sadness about what is not, but to helplessness itself. Still, it is an improvement on her constant effort to pull herself up by her bootstraps since childhood. I witness her in her pain, despair, and resignation, feeling that my hands are tied, just like she feels, capable, but not. That in turn helps Laura create an environment in which the witnessing eye turns inward. She can slip into despair and a downward spiral of *not*, but she leaves a lifeline to return to function, albeit with a deep sigh.

Alternative BLS: Puzzles

In the next session, Laura describes how her misery continues. She wants to talk to nobody and certainly not see anybody. Instead she says she has started an infinitely large puzzle. She finds that that relaxes her, helps her console herself, releases some of the pain, letting her thoughts and feelings flow while suspending her self-criticism. I mention that she has invented an EMDR tool for herself, one that feels safe. In it, she stimulates her brain bilaterally with her hands, searching for the right piece in the puzzle that fits her current life. And although nothing is predictable, and she can no longer force solutions through with her brain power, working in the dark with very few clues has a calming effect. She finds solace in watching herself in the process of completing a project, even when she does not know where the next piece will be found. She knows the pieces are all there, as they are in herself, and in her wish to parent. We come to think of it in the context of her seeing some choice in the search of becoming a mother. Perhaps it will not be exactly as she has envisioned it, but if she wants to experience being a mother she will find a way, biologically or otherwise.

Meryl Dorf (2011) expanded on the importance of recognizing options to having a biological child when fertility treatment begins and when there are signs that treatments might not work or that the emotional toll is too steep for the woman. Susan Kraemer and Zina Steinberg (2012) and Dorf (2011) discussed their clinical experience with women who employ dissociation amidst the trauma of repeated treatments and the deep fears about one's physical and emotional integrity, as well as the fear of abandonment and rejection. Both the fantasy and the pressure to conceive and keep a child are so great that while going through treatments the dissociation has psychologically protective aspects that defy the pain and worry of the repeated cycles of hope and disappointment. To that, the authors added consideration of the embedded loneliness, particularly at times when articulation of the fear is withheld from others, notably the partner, which increases the isolation and the traumatic effect on the woman.

Laura can now see that there are more ways she can feel peace of mind than rushing to achieve external recognition. She begins to find more EMDR-like activities that bring her to a place of feeling and contemplation and eventual calming of the mind. She can now return to the grind of treatments, finding a way to a separate space between the often painful fertility treatments and the hormonal rollercoaster, and redefining who she is as a whole human being. She still sees herself as separated from others by her experience, but perhaps with less shame. Her self-loathing is slowly replaced by an observing object, not loving yet, but not hating either.

The power of "No" and a new way into emotionality

In another session, Laura declares, "I did not want to come today. I do not want to deal. I do not want to have the need that brought me in here. I simply do not want to talk."

We sit quietly for a while. I was thinking of her being younger, bombarded by life events and a family that could not offer warmth as life got to be too overwhelming for them all, and how she wanted to stop the train and get off and couldn't. Her solution then was to become intellectual and deny the tumult. In this session, I think I meet the previously unexpressed representation of Laura at a young age in which she needed someone to understand what she was going through, and to remind her that she is the right person in the wrong time and place to change the schema she is led to believe was her calling. I ask, "Do you want to play?" Laura, who until this moment is curled up in a ball on her chair, her head tucked, holding onto her knees, as if she has bundled herself lest she fall apart, looks up. Her face lights with curiosity. "To play?" she asks with an astonishment. I confirm. "Play what?" she asks. "Where?" she adds, looking around the room, fishing for clues of a jungle gym she may have missed by being self-absorbed and gripped by her pain. "The sand tray," I suggest. Laura looks around searching for clues. Still she can find nothing. She chuckles as if I am telling a joke she cannot fathom. I stand up and fetch the two containers that I use in my office to help patients express what is beyond words.

Over the years, first in working with children and then with adults, I have found the use of a sand tray helpful at times when a patient is highly distraught or unable and unwilling to talk. Now I see this as an expansion of EMDR, as patients often use both hands to operate the objects, with or without talking. I notice ultimately that occupying the hands with objects in the sand encourages a process that is otherwise avoided, especially in younger or primitive self-states. Almost invariably, that process results in the reduction of anxiety and the return to self-regulation. Stories, memories, and emotions emerge if enough dreaming time is allowed at the tray. Here too, self-regulation is achieved through witnessing (Arad, 2002b). The patient is both lost and found in this particular sparsely verbal holding environment.

I pull out a glass box with white sand, followed by another glass box with black sand. Inviting Laura to choose a spot to sit, she opts for the carpet by the couch. I am aware of the conundrum. She said she did not want to participate in the session. She declared she did not want to be here today. She also shows me that she does not want to talk. Here, I give her a choice for something she does not want. On the one hand, in doing so, I agree to play by her rules. Not talking, yet by asking her to choose where she wants to sit I also avoid hearing what she asked for. This quality of hearing the verbal and nonverbal communication, yet listening to potentially deeper, more primitive processes, for example one of wishing to be held in ways that can't be openly expressed, allows for a witnessing process that is deeper.

I can hear that the fresh air of unexpected opportunity is part of what can be potentially helpful, while rehashing the agony and its cyclical exploration resembles too much of her current reality. Anything that can lead off that track is welcome.

Laura sits by the glass sand trays. She says she does not know what she is supposed to do. I free her to explore, thinking that I am letting go of the analytic opportunity to explore her reluctance to "know" what she is supposed to do. It feels more congruent with the moment to stay with where she is emotionally, and to accept that with her mother she did not know what was next or even what was now. In her youth, there was no goose to follow and imprint on. I feel that I need to be the goose at these moments. She touches a mini rake and starts raking the white sand gingerly. She says, "I hate sand." She looks at the black sand in the box and says, "This is more like me today. I feel black." She moves some brushes around to create room to move objects around. The black glass beads do not stick to her fingers and she is a little more settled. Her breathing shifts. It is quiet in the room. She points to green and orange objects "They are—ugly!" she sneers. "I think I need to bury them. They are not to be seen." She starts digging with a rake. She lifts a slant-topped opaque glass structure and says, "It looks like a tombstone." She giggles and says, "Everything is death to me today." I am thinking of her emotionally deadened mother, her chemical pregnancy, both almost but not quite what she yearns for. I say nothing. She arranges the rest of the house-like glass objects on the black sand in a semicircle.

"There!" she exclaims. "I have a whole cemetery." Just then she notices a stray tombstone. "Oh," she says. "I didn't plant this one." She pauses, holding it in her hand, and then says, "No. It does not belong." She sets it outside of the glass box, on the carpet. "I don't know why. But it feels complete without it." I ask, "How many treatment cycles did you go through?" She counts and says, "Six. Now I am on my seventh." In the black sand, neither of us need to count, are six tombstones. The jury is still out for the seventh trial seated by her side on the carpet. We sit quietly with the heavy feeling of her losses, of so much effort and all in vain for now. She says, "The unconscious is powerful."

Though we witness her burial of potential babies that are not, both seeing how finite each trial is, Laura is now much more alive and relaxed. She looks up, hanging her big eyes on mine, pointing to the house on the carpet. She says, "I still have this one, right?" I notice that the doubt in her voice is no longer complete. She can imagine a possibility of success. No matter how many losses she has experienced in her life with failed attempts to be mothered, she still is willing to find it when it offers itself. Now she wonders if she can find the green and orange "Uglies." She pulls a green one out of the black sand and says, "Maybe it's not that ugly. Someone can love it. It is okay that it will see daylight. Be loved." She gently puts it on top of the black glass beads.

As she is readying herself to leave the room, she says, "Thank you for inviting me to play in the sand." There is no shame for playing, there is no self-hatred, there is the calm as one is witnessed.

Reflection

The progression of this session is perhaps the narrative of a screen memory, in which many of the current losses of potential pregnancies represent the repeated loss of being mothered well enough throughout Laura's childhood. The way we are together also includes my affinity to witnessing, as a core element in dealing with segments of psychic trauma. Often we repeat an action compulsively until interrupted by sufficient witnessing and understanding (Arad, 2002a).

This modified EMDR session attains the anxiety reduction of an unnamed trauma, the trauma of repeated loss and lack of witnessing. For Laura, each loss not only represents a failure of the body to conceive and hold a fetus, but also proof that the one who is not mothered properly will not be allowed to mother another. As if her failure to make her mother into a good mother for her makes her into a person that does not deserve to be a mother of a child either.

The repeated attempts with her mother are paralleled by the repeated attempts to conceive. Simply put, she has failed to create a m(o)ther out of her internalized maternal figure. Part of her rejection of therapy is the wish to do it on her own. To find a modification to EMDR by herself is to do it independently. It works for her because it offers a different vocabulary for her experience. When she says she does not want to come multiple times a week after requesting it, it is as if she says, "I can do it all by myself." That fantasy of "I must be self-sufficient" is being turned on its head with the experience of fertility treatment. Now she has found a way that she can do it herself, articulate with her sand-tray play, that she knows about her trauma, and only needs a safe place to express it in its full magnitude. She needs to be witnessed as the horror is exposed. Not incrementally, but in full, and in daylight.

Summary

EMDR is a complete protocol, quite distant from the process of psychodynamic clinicians, and it often seems inaccessible to most of those working in that area.

In this chapter, I described how aspects of EMDR can be distilled in a more subtle form that may hopefully be more accessible for many clinicians, while still achieving the core benefit of allowing the patient to reduce the continuing internal tsunami to a level that allows it to be witnessed and processed.

The case presented here examined modifications of the EMDR protocol, as when a patient or therapist believes that using a BLS device would be ill advised. I explored the way in which a childlike self-state nevertheless introduced the possibility of play as an alternative to formal EMDR, a merging that was able to marry the relational engagement and the dreamy quality of both psychoanalysis and EMDR in this play form, and was able to serve as a child like therapy replacement when the unspeakable needed an outlet that could be witnessed.

Note

The conversation in the epigraph is drawn from Hans Fallada's *Every Man Dies Alone* (Brooklyn, NY: Melville House Publishing, 2009), 342.

References

Arad, H. (2002a). Dialogue continues . . . (violence, terror, compassion, and forgiveness). *The Alliance Forum: The Newsletter of the Northwest Alliance for Psychoanalytic Study*: 9–12. Seattle, WA.

Arad, H. (2002b). Focus on Violence. *Plenary Session: Focus on Violence.* Presentation at Forum 2002: On Violence. The Northwest Alliance for Psychoanalytic Study and Seattle Psychoanalytic Society and Institute Forum, April 27. Bellevue, WA.

Cloyd, T. (1999). Pregnancy and EMDR: Is any form of EMDR safe in the context of pregnancy? *Mental Health Co-Op.* Retrieved from Mental Health Co-Op website, http://mhpc.wetpaint.com/page/Pregnancy+and+EMDR+-+is+ANY+form+of+EMDR+safe+in+the+context+of+pregnancy%3F (accessed on 7-20-2012).

Dorf, M. W. (2011). Rewriting Cinderella: From infertility to adoption. *Psychology Today*. Retrieved from *Psychology Today* website: www.psychologytoday.com/blog/psychoanalysis-30/201108/rewriting-cinderella-infertility-adoption (accessed on 7-20-2012).

Kraemer, S., and Z. Steinberg. (2012). The dark side of fertility treatments: Lessons from a neonatal intensive care unit. *Psychology Today* website, www.psychologytoday.com/blog/psychoanalysis-30/201207/the-dark-side-fertility-treatments-lessons-neonatal-intensive-care-uni (accessed on 7-20-2012).

Chapter 9

Conclusions

Reintegrating the music with the lyrics

> "hands learn from the soil and broken glass,
> you cannot *think* a poem," he says,
> "watch the light hardening into words."
> — Ilya Kaminsky

Grief and Livingston (2013) quoted Bromberg as saying:

> The ability of the mind to function creatively is dependent on the brain's neuroplasticity—the brain's adaptive ability to *modify* its synaptic writing by learning new information that makes its neurons fire in new patterns and combinations. Insight, the centerpiece of Freud's clinical contribution, has been shown to require that the brain's synaptic networks, especially those of the right hemisphere, be transformed by accidental, serendipitous connections. Current work in the neurobiology of interpersonal experience demonstrates that such serendipitous connections are facilitated by *conscious and nonconscious interactions with other minds in new ways*—such as in an analytic relationship—whereby new combinations of neurons increasingly wire together, allowing self-state evolution to modulate the rigidity of self-state truth.
>
> Increasing the fluidity of state-sharing therapeutically increases affect tolerance and lowers the fear of dysregulation. (p. 347, italics in original)

Bromberg makes the observation that restoring coherence across self-states requires that both partners' self-states be capable of easing-up on their deep convictions and recognizing "otherness as more than 'not-me'"

(p. 347). He adds that the *relational unconscious* can be mitigated through this state-sharing, to facilitate the improved mental functioning that was thwarted early in development.

I wrote this book to share with other clinicians the potentially fruitful integration of EMDR into and with relational psychoanalysis and psychodynamic psychotherapy that I stumbled upon by chance. I have found that this integration opens the door to modifying both methods just enough to allow the clinician to transform cases that otherwise may be difficult to reach, or where the work is held back or limited because of finite verbal access to the richness of material that is associated with affective neural pathways that are expressed in the self and that impact intersubjective exchange.

My hope in presenting this material is to help clinicians who see relational psychoanalytic ideas as their base, and who are open to integrating EMDR into their practice, to achieve benefits similar to those I have seen in my own practice. Additionally, I wish to invite EMDR practitioners to consider relational ideas and practice as worth pursuing for the benefit of their patients' lasting relief of debilitating anxiety, stemming from big *T* and small *t* trauma, through engagement with the therapist in the process of re-creating relational scenarios to help release some of their traumatic power. What may need to be reconsidered by the EMDR practitioner is the recognition that the transferential-countertransferential relationship that the patient and therapist share can both enhance and make the patient's experience more believable. It is then the hope that this relational context will help the patient—through the transferentially borne metabolized experience—to employ the same sensibilities in her real environment. Both methods believe that the embodied experience, arising from EMDR desensitization and reprocessing, and the embodied transferential-countertransferential encounter and processing in the relational interchange, can lead to the creation of new neural pathways that allow the patient to change relationships with herself and others. I have argued here that the integration of both methods helps the patient to reach forbidden areas of the self originally created by relational trauma, hastens the arrival of an affective state that makes it possible for the relational psychoanalytic engagement and exploration to begin, and, through the transferential bond, helps the patient to lead a life with greater potential and with closer examination. Throughout this book, I have shown through clinical examples the emotional ripple effect of the integrated methods on the patient's psychic and real life.

Summary of main ideas and applications

In this book, I began by introducing and covering the theoretical background and literature of EMDR and related brain research, as well as attachment and relational theories, to present a background for a deeper understanding of concepts that have served me in the integration of these methods. I then described a number of clinical cases to illuminate aspects of this combined approach.

I first described the situations and the types of clinical issues for which EMDR can be helpful. The protocol for the steps involved in applying EMDR in itself was described in Chapter 1. I then elaborated on how to integrate the treatment following EMDR sessions back into the relational work while still holding EMDR's sensibility in the background. In addition, I described special considerations regarding the various tools it is possible to use for BLS. Brief descriptions of the earlier chapters follow.

In Chapter 1, I described, the history, theoretical underpinning, and pragmatic aspects of EMDR, and made the case for considering that EMDR and psychodynamic psychotherapy are productively integratable. The material presented here is intended to expand the understanding of potential uses of EMDR's highly structured protocol, which was originally established to treat trauma cases. In addition, I described the origin of EMDR and some existing variations of the use of this therapeutic method. Together, the material here offers a wide range of relevant trends in current EMDR thought and practice, with an emphasis on views that appreciate psychodynamics as part of a whole approach to treatment.

In addition to describing the underlying brain functions related to EMDR, as well as its usefulness when used to intervene in the service of engaging blocked emotions, I presented some of my own views and ideas about the reasons EMDR can or may be effective in areas beyond those we already know from research. With infant and adult attachment research in mind, I suggest that EMDR might provide interactions analogous to and essential in basic mother–infant interactions, as well as those between intimate partners or partners in therapy, in establishing patterns of interrelatedness, presenting some patterns that are anxiety provoking and others that are more organizing. My belief is that EMDR may offer the missing link between the semblances of bodily connection and the organizing but desire-restricting speech.

To help guide the reader, this chapter also introduced EMDR concepts and terms that are used throughout the book, along with references to EMDR's conceptual and technical terms. Additionally, I described some modifications I made to the protocol to better suit relational psychoanalytic work. To conclude the chapter, I presented an EMDR protocol chart. Here I combined a more traditional EMDR process with modifications that I have found allow for a better integration with a relational psychoanalytic approach within a given session, and across the course of treatment.

In Chapter 2, I have provided a literature review of current brain research, in order to offer a basis for understanding the strong impact that trauma and development in general have on memory and on the ability to express a sense of the self affectively, both within the self and among its representations, and in the intersubjective field. In my work I have found that EMDR seems to have an effect on memory, and especially on trauma memories, that surpasses that achieved by other therapeutic methods. From this perspective, EMDR may be especially useful in supporting psychodynamic work with patients whose symptoms seem resistant to treatment. In my experience in treating patients' relational trauma, the use of EMDR has opened the door for relational psychoanalytic treatment that was blocked or limited prior to the use of EMDR. That said, and although many studies have been done to directly assess the effects of EMDR and its outcome, as well as those approached indirectly through current neuroscience research, we must still assume that our theoretical formulations of how EMDR works are speculations. However, the use of EMDR in treatment should be considered while further studies are amassed, as clinical experience is showing us that important pathways can be opened to rich relational analytic work that otherwise would be considered unattainable for some patients, owing to their high level of uncontrolled anxiety with exposure to in-depth clinical material.

In Chapter 3, I reviewed relational literature that has dealt with the role of the body in psychoanalysis, and on the self-reflexive mind and its importance in each patient's capacity to experience, observe, and reflect on the self as both object and subject. In EMDR, both the process and the body's response are integral to the protocol. Here, the therapist is shifting attention to the patient's bodily responses as a thought or a feeling is generated, because, as we see in Stolorow's (2012) clinical vignette, this attention to the body is part and parcel of the observation and opening needed for self-reflection. Developing mindfulness, first in enactment and then in real life, is an integral element of relational analysis as well. With the benefit we know both approaches offer in expanding the function of embodied experiences, it seems clear that their integration would increase their effectiveness.

In this chapter, I also discussed the role of enactment. My intention, in presenting these concepts here, was to help therapists keep in mind the qualities of embodied experience, enactment, and the capacity to dissociate, and also to understand the patient's need to lodge disavowed parts of the self in the analyst's countertransference, as manifested in her reaction to the patient. It is important to recognize enactments as they unfold in any particular analytic pair, as well as in recognizing these self-states not only in the patient but also in the psychoanalyst.

Enactment is bound to happen in any relationship, and the analytic relationship is no different. It is mutually constructed, and therefore can be understood in tandem. Moreover, since it is first and foremost an embodied experience, it remains malleable to resurrection, with EMDR opening a personal path leading to relational exploration. In this way, EMDR can be considered a form of restorative enactment through which, in enacting internal representations, the patient is brought to consider that a wider variety of options to increase mentalization and reflection may be open when viewing herself and the dynamic of the enacted.

In Chapter 4, the discussion turns to the importance of early attachment between infants and their caregivers at the dawn of life, and the implications this relation has for all other relationships, including the therapeutic relationship. We understand that both well-being and trouble develop in the context of the to-and-fro negotiation of early needs and wishes, and that participation of both partners in an interaction is essential and influential, just as infants from the very first hours of their birth, and perhaps even before birth, contribute significantly to their relationship with their mothers and others in their lives. These interactions are nuanced, yet profound, and span the range of bodily expression from the gesture to stages of meaningful sound-making to verbal communication. When this process goes awry in interactions that are repeatedly disrupted, as happens in trauma situations, we saw how traumas carry their intricate implications into therapy. There, they may be reenacted and hopefully, over time, it may be possible to create new language, a believable relational discourse that is both verbal and nonverbal, and one that can allow space for uncharted paths to be explored in the therapeutic and extra-therapeutic realms. Diagnostically, knowledge about the development of attachment can inform therapists and help them use their countertransferential responses and reactions to the patient as a guide to what has happened. Modifications to the EMDR protocol that include attachment-focused steps to enhance the safety patients need for therapeutic work may be necessary, especially in order to meet those who have suffered relational trauma as they begin to approach the path to repairing their attachment capabilities (Parnell, 2013, pp. 14, 27).

Let me describe the reasons for choosing the particular cases in Chapters 5 through 8. Initially, I thought I would explore the integration of EMDR and relational psychoanalysis with a particular presented problem in mind. For example, I believed that shining a light on issues of chronic illness and chronic pain in which EMDR helped specific patients, or focusing on suicidality, parenting, trauma, and somatization would help in isolating this modified EMDR approach to certain clinical challenges (R. Shapiro, 2005, 2009). This approach was intended more generally to show how I combine the two methods in one practice, rather than to illustrate a more integrative approach in which sharing the wisdom of both approaches can enhance the benefits of the other, or decrease the limitation of the other approach when dealing with complex clinical situations. Over time, I realized that contemporary EMDR literature commonly keeps this classification in mind (R. Shapiro, 2005, 2009). The more I worked with patients utilizing EMDR to accompany the relational analytic practice, the more integration was called for, rather than a simple side-by-side approach. Therefore, I opted to concentrate in this book on the relational conundrums presented in the work, in order to highlight the ways in which the overlay of the two methods might be integrated in cases that are rather atypical for EMDR writing with its focus on trauma, depression, anxiety, or pain, for example. This modified integrative approach facilitates an emphasis on the relational base for clinical work that is not void of attention to issues, yet focuses on the interweaving of EMDR into the complex relational matrix of the psychoanalytic work itself.

In Chapter 5, I described the situation that first brought me to think about EMDR as integratable with my relational analytic practice, as I noticed a patient spontaneously finding a natural BLS in an inanimate object in my office. That action, in turn, resulted in a genuine emotional response for the first time in our work together. I then related how time-sensitive considerations prompted me to relinquish a therapeutic approach that had generally kept EMDR and psychoanalysis segregated. I then brought in some details of the case and showed how I interwove EMDR into a relational psychoanalysis, including a discussion of the EMDR tapping tools I found most compatible. I also discussed the limitations that each approach imposes on the other. Here, I made the case for using EMDR as a process that can help make the depth of the relational psychoanalytic approach possible for the patient's clinical benefit.

In Chapter 6, I described my work with couples, and introduced some of the unique considerations needed when working with relational psychotherapy as well as EMDR methods. Here, I also described the specific modifications that were needed for each partner in a couple, and explored the usefulness of individual EMDR sessions versus the value of working with EMDR with the patients witnessing each other. The progress of the work allowed me to show how a relational approach, along with sensitivity to issues that gender studies have brought out, enhanced my work with couples. Especially in work with couples, I believe that it is important to pay particular attention to gender and other environmental and relational influences on the development of the self as these appear in their interactions, and that these elements should be kept in mind in the treatment plan and as the work unfolds.

In Chapter 7, through an example of my clinical work, my aim was to convey the feeling of what happens during the interweaving of EMDR practices to benefit the relational psychoanalytic process. I highlighted my work with the transference and countertransference, and showed how, at times, EMDR helped bring to the surface aspects of the transference that were otherwise buried. The progress of this individual therapy also allowed me to elaborate on the importance for therapists of understanding the effect of preverbal trauma. In response, as in this case, the work can then lead to the creation of a new, *as-if* potential space where a more coherent narrative can be tolerated, specifically in relation to embodied experience, while also increasing the patient's capacity to respond more freely in relation to spaces that are unknowable, paradoxical, and ambivalent.

In Chapter 8, I described how aspects of EMDR can be absorbed by the patient even when they are not used directly. These can then be distilled to create more subtle and hopefully more accessible forms that many clinicians may be able to recognize and access, while still achieving the core benefit of allowing the patient to find a way to reduce the internal tsunami to a level that allows space for the processing of actualities that had seemed impossible to approach.

More specifically, the presented case examined the modification of the EMDR protocol, following the patient's feeling (or a therapist's belief) that using a BLS device would be ill advised. I explored the way in which a childlike self-state introduced the possibility of play as an alternative to formal EMDR, in ways marrying the relational engagement and the dreamy quality of both psychoanalysis and EMDR in this play form, where it was able to serve as a child therapy replacement when the unspeakable needed a witnessed outlet.

Reflection and insights

I have found that EMDR helps open emotional doors that are otherwise closed to certain patients. When EMDR follows work grounded in a more psychodynamic approach, it helps the transferential-countertransferential relationship flourish and be explored in the hour. For example, EMDR can unintentionally have an almost magical effect, not unlike some of the realizations described in the historical classical psychoanalytic approach. The practitioner, without many words, instructs the client to follow certain relatively simple and prescriptive steps and processes alone, while at the same time the EMDR practitioner stays out of the picture by not getting involved. A patient may wonder, given her heightened emotional intensity during an EMDR sequence, if I feel the same level of intensity in my own mind and body. In reflection, and although I can and do empathically respond to various emotional cues in the patient's process during EMDR, the feeling is a different one. While engrossed in the transferential-countertransferential flow in which both participants are emotionally entangled in a co-created situation, as their subjectivities are engaged, including relevant personal histories, two different individuals are still involved. This clarifying question highlights an important difference, simultaneously showing the interconnectedness between the EMDR reprocessing and the irreducible matter of transferential engagement on the one hand, and on the other the patient's need to know that she is witnessed by and somehow together with the person who represents an important container for her: her psychoanalyst.

The "softening" of EMDR through its being embedded in a psychoanalytic envelope makes it possible to use EMDR for a broader spectrum of patients. These include those who employ various levels of dissociation, but also patients who are working with the ramifications of relational development that have precluded a relatively safe and affective engagement with self and others. The soft relational envelope allows for the gentle to and fro of various kinds of intensity. Because relational work is engaging, yet not an instructive kind of intervention, EMDR can be engaged in, off and on, throughout a session or between sessions. For example, BLS can be used to induce access to feelings when an area of dissociated material that is potentially intense emerges through shifting self-states, as it can allow for a longer emotional engagement, or one that can be tapered down when needed. On other occasions, when the patient feels emotionally aroused but then shuts off any emotionality, the shift to using words may take him or her away from the embodied experience. Yet in other instances, words are introduced to help contain overwhelming feelings in the holding dyadic environment, and to help reconstruct both the experience and the meaning of the unspeakable. All of this often takes place in a single session in which difficult material can be processed and cleared, while also bringing the processed material back to the current contextual relational interaction. In a way, these alterations of intensity help increase the patient's tolerance of emotional material that was once unbearable.

I suggest that EMDR creates a situation in which the patient engages in mimetic experience with existing parts of herself, whereas the therapist primarily serves as an important holding shell and a relational container. This allows the patient to find, within herself, a minor positive voice that may then be amplified through the desensitization and reprocessing of negative cognition that originated in trauma, while also integrating positive cognitions as a reference point, matched by bodily position, while integrating a less anxiety-provoking parental figure. This assumes that each surviving patient has a positive mimetic experience within her, however faint or seemingly lost due to excessive trauma.

EMDR assists patients in gradually disengaging from pain as their identity, while at the same time they find another psychic envelope to hold their individuality with less pain and greater connectedness. It's important to note that this is different from disavowing the patient's awareness of the trauma. Instead, the patient is invited to enter a new, enveloping dyadic relatedness with the self, and with the therapist.

Some important areas in EMDR overlap with analytic work, especially with regard to the association process. The actual travel into thought, feeling, and/or pain during EMDR sets is dynamic in nature and resembles a deep primary process in analysis. The structure of the procedure on its various levels is somewhat different, however. It is directive and deliberate, and contains interruption of the associative process and redirection of the stream of consciousness. EMDR practitioners (Parnell, 1997; F. Shapiro, 2001, 2002; and others), as analysts, do follow the patient's anxiety. EMDR abundantly uses cognitive reframing and guided imagery, along with intermittent occupation of the cerebral cortex through the use of BLS, in order to release arrested amygdala function, and to create bridges between emotions and memory.

EMDR is different from psychoanalysis in some other ways as well. In psychoanalysis, we strive to provide a potential space in which affect-rich associations and projections can thrive, where transference can be addressed, and where countertransference can be used as a diagnostic and analytic tool. With some limitation, there is time for exploration to occur. Sometimes inadvertently, or at least unconsciously, a less-careful interpretation can hasten or slow down the analytic process by the stirring up of the transference and countertransference dynamics. Yet, in psychoanalysis there is little attempt to rush the process to get to measurable therapeutic results, although they are valued as part of the patient's growth and development.

Not unlike relational psychoanalysis, but with greater concentration and focus, EMDR strives to help with trauma and its aftermath in an effort to remove resistance to affective engagement. It expressly negotiates a path by which trauma can be desensitized and reprocessed in a way that allows the creation of a personal and internal mastery of the potential to avoid repeated attacks on the psyche. It involves a directive approach, and focuses the therapist's attention expressly on the patient's process and not on the transference.

A large part of EMDR is nonverbal. The patient is instructed to limit the verbal description to a brief description of an anxiety-producing situation, the related negative cognition, a related desired positive cognition, and a goal, and has to report her emotional and physical position in between sets of BLS intervention. Patients are also asked to rate the level of their discomfort, and of their belief in both negative and positive cognitions. The goal of EMDR is therapeutic, rather than explorational, whereas psychoanalysis carries a constant tension between the analytic and the therapeutic.

Although a central goal of EMDR is for the patient to reach affect regulation, the work of reprocessing is crucial. Reprocessing resembles dynamic approaches in that it strives to engage emotions that are locked up or dissociated in the body, a state that inhibits psychological flexibility in the relationship to self and others. With certain patients with significant fragmentation, the use of EMDR can propel independent analytic association by training the body and mind to tolerate moderate affect.

Merging EMDR into the psychoanalytic framework nevertheless raises the question of touch. EMDR accepts certain touches like tapping as part of the work, where psychoanalysis does not. In the case of Sheila, in Chapter 5, I had to make a decision about using a tactile device, as I realized that using eye movement had some limitations. As a first attempt to integrate EMDR with relational psychoanalysis, I tried using knee tapping, which the patient responded to better than the eye movement bilateral stimulus. However, I found my hand tapping on the patient's knees was counter to the principle of being in touch without touching.

A unique and new phenomenon that I observed in looking back at my work for this book was that when I combined EMDR with relational psychoanalysis, I noticed that oftentimes the use of EMDR found its way into the analytic work, and even kept the cadence of the EMDR protocol, without the use of bilateral stimuli. For example, when an emotional cue is detected by the analyst, typically a point at which the use of BLS would be indicated, patients who have already experienced several EMDR sessions may follow the protocol without the use of the BLS device, as if they had integrated its sequence and can now follow it without an external direction from the therapist. This may be the result of a process, similar to the attachment process, specifically as it is related to the mimetic aspect of attachment during which the process was incorporated well enough so that a whole scenario could be elaborated upon with the first trigger, usually an image.

An example of such a shift can be found in Chapter 5 in my work with Sheila. Finding and sometimes losing this special cadence, going in and out of examination of the self, typically varies between patients, but more importantly can vary within each patient's self-states. For the analyst, the benefit of recognizing this process is understanding that patients can outgrow the need for BLS, and will be able to use their own attention to shifts in self-states outside of the consulting room with greater trust, not only in their ability to deal with a single scenario, but also with other similar and different situations, and in connection with certain emotional triggers. Future research will be helpful in determining if such a connection exists, how it arises, and if it can be made more approachable for a broader set of clinical cases.

Future research

During my work on this book, I was asked if I believed EMDR has a lasting effect. From my experience, EMDR embedded into psychoanalysis helps cement new learning. Longitudinal studies would be helpful in determining the effect of each method with respect to quality of life, both when followed separately and when the methods are combined. In my practice, I often see people who have spent years in treatment with some important improvement but who continue to have a persistent state of mind that still causes them much pain. This is frequently accompanied by a sense of doubt on the part of the referring clinician regarding his ability to help his patient. Some patients, often those who feel hopeless, benefit from the combined method I have described in this book, and it would be of much value to learn whether this is a systematic trend or anecdotal results that could be attributed to other factors such as the change of therapist, a willingness to be more open with the new clinician, or something about familiarity with exposing the underlying emotions and having them contained in the dyad through relational psychoanalysis.

It is possible that with further research a more complete theoretical framework for the complementary use of EMDR and psychoanalysis can be developed, and I have presented explicit and detailed cases that may help create a lexicon for use in future discussions. In the meantime, I hope that the clinical cases I have described here may offer an entry point for those who wish to widen the horizon of their work, and welcome the interest of other clinicians in exploring this fruitful integration.

Note

The lines by Ilya Kaminsky in the epigraph are from his poem "Praise" in his book *Musica Humana* (Montpelier, VT: Chapiteau Press), n.p.

References

Grief, D., and R. Livingston. (2013). An interview with Philip M. Bromberg. *Contemporary Psychoanalysis* 49(3): 323–355.

Parnell, L. (1997). *Transforming Trauma: EMDR*. New York: Norton.

Parnell, L. (2013). *Attachment-Focused EMDR: Healing Relational Trauma*. New York: Norton.

Shapiro, F. (2001). *Eye Movement Desensitization and Reprocessing: Basic Principles, Protocols, and Procedures*. 2nd ed. New York: Guilford.

Shapiro, F. (2002). EMDR treatment: Overview and integration. In F. Shapiro, editor, *EMDR as an Integrative Psychotherapy Approach: Experts of Diverse Orientations Explore the Paradigm Prism*, 27–56. Washington, DC: American Psychological Association.

Shapiro, R. (2005). *EMDR Solutions: Pathways to Healing*. R. Shapiro, editor. New York: Norton.

Shapiro, R. (2009). *EMDR Solutions II: For Depression, Eating Disorders, Performance, and More*. R. Shapiro, editor. New York: Norton.

Stolorow, R. (2012). The renewal of humanism in psychoanalytic therapy. *Psychotherapy* 49: 442–444.

Index